dedicated to all my brothers and sisters
struggling for acceptance, in all walks of life

I feel your pain...

I'm on my way
A Novel

Daray & Kaveio

Stay Strong,
Remember to Always
Be proud of who
you are o

2024

ISBN: 1-4107-8430-4 (e-book)
ISBN: 1-4107-8431-2 (Paperback)

Library of Congress Control Number: 2003095691

This book is printed on acid free paper.

Printed in the United States of America
Bloomington, IN

Cover Photography: **Greg Scaffidi** • Art Direction: **R. Croudy & A. Katz**
Author Photo: **JonJo Raysor** • Website Design: **Sakara Bey**

1stBooks - rev. 08/18/03

Acknowledgements

I never thought this day would come. A day that would see the words of a young man born in Brooklyn New York and raised in its heart, Bedford Stuyvesant, grace the minds of readers around the country and possibly, the world. And now, that this day has finally come to past I tell you first and foremost that I am honored, but more than honored, blessed to have been chosen to share my truths with you. And two, to warn you: this is only the beginning; for where there's a will, there is most definitely a way.

No one can do it alone. Absentee parents that think one is better than none are sorely mistaken, because the balance of night and day is but one force that holds our lives in order. We need each other, a songwriter once wrote, like water needs the rain. Without the following people believe me, I don't know where I'd be…

God. I know a lot times I piss you off, but you know what, sometimes you piss me off too. But, I'm glad we're working on our relationship. I love you. I need you. And I know one day you're going to make clear to me all that I still do not understand. I await the answers.

My Family. It's amazing how you can grow up with and around people and still not know shit about them. Honestly, I don't know all ya'll, and ya'll damn sure don't know me, but hey I'm just glad you guys love me, for me. And I'm glad too that you guys didn't ostracize me, as much as I ostracized myself. I didn't know any other way. I was young and naïve so it made sense to hide. But not anymore. I'm in the light now and you know what…it feels *damn* good.

My Friends. You guys are the people I turned to when I discovered I had nowhere else *to* turn. You held my hand, raised my head and whispered sincerely, *"Chris I'm here, and I ain't going nowhere…"* Honestly, you guys will never know how much that shit meant to me. Thank you sometimes doesn't seem enough. But, as you guys read these words I'm working on a better way. Just wait and see.

My Love. Patient, understanding, willing, able, dependable, loveable; these are but some of the requirements I jotted down while on my search to unmask true love. Never in my wildest dreams did I imagine I'd find someone who encompassed them all. I know sometimes dealing with me and my shit isn't always easy, but you somehow in someway always manage to make it seem painless. Our love has flourished even when I feared it wouldn't; even, when some of our closest peers rocked the boat. But like my girl *Shania* crooned, *"I'm so glad we made it. Look how far we've come my baby…"* Thank you, for being everything and more.

Special, Special Thanks Goes Out To: Greg, Bobby, Ron, Eric, JonJo, Steve, Jyri-el, Sakara, Jay, and T. Kearney. Wow! You guys are truly amazing. Without your patience, support and talent this shit just wouldn't be the same...believe that!

Last, but definitely not least, to those who came before me and carved a path that I might tread safely, I thank you so much for your inspiration and fortitude. Your journey has made my journey that much easier but no less necessary. **The literary world:** E. Lynn Harris. James Earl Hardy. Heather Neff. Neale Donald Walsch. Terry McMillian. Iyanla Vanzant. Walter Mosley. Ernest Hill. Toni Morrison. Terrance Dean. Langston Hughes. Ralph Ellison. Essex Hemphill. Keith Boykin. Og Mandino. Don Miguel Ruiz. Khalil Gibran. John Grisham. Michael-Christopher. Lisa C. Moore. **The musical world:** Dianne Reeves. Will Downing. Stevie Wonder. Cassandra Wilson. Nancy Wilson. Lalah Hathaway. Rachelle Ferrell. Chaka Khan. Barry White. Marvin Gaye. Michael Jackson. Prince. Seal. Sade. Maxwell. D'angelo. Syleena Johnson. Kelly Price. Faith Evans. Joe. Mary J. Blige. Jill Scott. Chante Moore. Kenny Lattimore. Ce Ce Winans. Be Be Winans. Yolanda Adams. Nas. The Notorious B.I.G. Dave Hollister. Aaliyah. Toni Braxton. *Early* Whitney Houston. Nina Simone. R. Kelly.

Man

I've done it
I've made it
For today I am a man
No I have no child, nor wife
All I have is myself
And a love others choose to ignore
For years I've lived in fear of who I am—because of you
Because of you I am a late bloomer
Because of you I didn't love sooner
But it was because of you I grew *stronger*
Because of you I stand *taller*
Proud as a man

BOOK ONE

bitter
-Meshell Ndegeocello

PROLOGUE

K now this. Everything is *not* what it seems. From the outside looking in I realize it is impossible for you to understand why I did what I did. Why I, Jared Covington, son, brother, friend, lover, would commit such an act? How, you wonder could I *stoop* so low, a handsome, professional, college educated brother?

I see the scrutiny in your eyes, the anger in your face. And yes, I feel the frustration in your heart. I see and I feel it all as you watch me, searching for a fraction of understanding.

Yet I tell you: there *was* no other way—*no* other choice...

I only hope one day, you'll understand...

ONE

J ANUARY NINETH WAS AN UNUSUALLY warm winter day for the concrete jungle known throughout the world as The City that Never Sleeps. Having just celebrated the birth of another New Year, I was out and about shopping with one of my closest and dearest friends in the life Kevin Stephon Smith, who as usual, was all in my business trying to get the low on my personal life.

I met Kevin a few years back while dating his then best friend Vince. They'd both moved from Los Angeles to New York City in hopes of making it big in the music industry. The first time I actually met Kevin was at a house warming party Vince and his roommate threw. Around twelve thirty, one o'clock he walked in smiling from ear to ear. I laughed to myself thinking, that's got to be the biggest smile I'd ever seen. Right away he set about cruising the crowd for any signs of New York's most notorious brother: *the ruff-neck*. Vince had warned him that more than enough cuties would be in attendance so he wore his best ensemble, (a pair of knee length *Guess?* shorts, a *New York Knicks* home jersey, a pair of white on white *Nike* uptowns, and his signature thug bandana hanging rather purposely from his back left pocket,) all in hopes of attracting that right niggah. Whenever the dee-jay happened upon a song he liked he practically cleared the floor doing what he termed dancing. At times it seemed almost synchronized, as if he'd practiced for hours before he'd gotten there *(one-two KICK, three-four DIP, five-six SPIN)*. He had way too much energy for one man. At one point having laughed my ass off I leaned over and asked Vince who was this guy. He sucked his teeth, "Oh that's just Kevin. He's a mess ain't he? You'd think he was at an open audition for Fame and shit..."

"Either that or Solid Gold!" His roommate scoffed. "Please whatever you do, don't let him drink anything else. Ain't no telling what he'll do next!"

"Drink?!" Vince laughed. "That bitch doesn't drink! That's one hundred percent pure adrenaline. Your best bet is to hope the dee-jay fucks up."

Later that night after most of the guest had gone home I learned that not only was Kevin an "accomplished" dancer he was also a closeted Diva. My mouth dropped as I watched him sit, cross his legs, and then with ease proceed to read everyone that had graced the party. At the time I had just started hanging out in the life so I really didn't know what to make of it. I mean to me he seemed masculine, almost straight. But when he switched it on me I was like, *"Ill he's a queen!"* But later, after learning the true definition of a Queen, I had to give him a more appropriate title: *Diva Extraordinaire!*

Over the years Kevin and I managed to form a very close friendship despite the demise of my relationship with Vince. At one point we became roommates. Back then Kevin couldn't keep a date. He claimed, and still claims to this day that it wasn't his fault, because most of the niggahs he fucked with weren't shit, but, from the outside looking in, I swear he ran half of those guys away screaming for their lives! His personality was *so* overbearing even I couldn't take him—and I was his best friend! Imagine what he put his dates through?

But right as Vince and I were breaking up, Kevin and Aaron were hooking up. Aaron was the total opposite of anyone I'd ever seen Kevin with: intelligent, independent and clean cut! I don't know what it was about him, but, whatever it was Kevin loved the shit out of it. They had been together for about two years, and were looking forward to their up coming anniversary.

I have to admit it was funny seeing Kevin in a stable relationship for so long. It was as if we had switched teams. He was playing doubles, and I singles. Now I couldn't keep a date.

"So bitch," he said in his usual playful manner. "Have you found a man yet? Cause, I know you want one. I can see it all in your eyes."

"No, I haven't! And why are you always in my business when, what you should be doing is worrying about yours and Aaron's. I'm sure you guys have some problem you haven't worked out yet."

"Don't try it bitch! Me and *my man* are quite happy!" He sneered pumping up Fifth Avenue. "I can't *take* these lonely bitches always trying to come for me and my man."

"Whatever…" I said laughing.

"No but for real Jared," He said sincerely, "I want to see you happy again. I still remember when you and Vince were together, how you guys used to always find someplace to go on Sunday mornings. I don't know where you guys went half the time, but I would find myself sitting in the house alone like damn: *one day Kevin, one day…*"

Instantly, I was transported to a time I had long tried to forget. That time in each of our lives, when love really *was* enough despite the shit you may have had to go through to get it. Because, at the end of the day you knew you had it, and that was all that mattered.

"Yeah," I said softly, "Vince and I were something else on our good days. As funny as it may seem, I haven't been able to love anybody since."

"Yeah, I've noticed." He replied in a tender whisper.

"Every once and a while," I continued, "I think about him, and I wonder how he's doing, or who he's dating, or if he's just as lost and lonely as I am. But, in my heart I know Vince and I were never meant to be so I usually, let the thought go. We were like fire and water you know; we just didn't mix."

"Tell me about it! You girls use to go at it! Do you remember that time you threw that speaker at that skinny bitch's head?"

"Oh shit Kev!" I laughed covering my face in embarrassment. "You still remember that!"

"Bitch, how could I forget it? You bitches fought from the third floor to the basement. I'm sure no one on South Oxford will ever forget that day!"

As we laughed a silence fell over the city, and all at once it seemed we both felt it. We each went back to that violent day in November. For me it was the day I walked away from the person I loved most in the world. For Kevin it was the day he and Aaron agreed that whatever they became, fighting would never be an issue. A passing taxi ruptured the silence…

"Kevin, there's nothing I want more in this world than the opportunity to meet someone special. I dream about it all the time. I know the way he looks, the way he smells—even, the way he laughs. It just seems we keep missing each other."

"Bitch," Kevin barked, "how are you gonna miss him—or *anybody* for that matter—sitting at home? You never want to go out, and then when you do, it's like you avoid everyone checking you out!"

"That's just it Kevin, I don't want to meet him in a club! I didn't meet Mark or—"

"*Vince in a club,*" He mocked in a whining child-like voice. "You're right you didn't meet either one of those girls at a club, but are you with them today? No! And will you *please*, for the love of God, stop looking at the club as if it's full of losers. Everyone there isn't looking for a quick hook up. Your job is to find the one who's looking for you. And you can't do that if you're limiting your search. Trust me on this one."

"Yeah, well, maybe you're right. But change takes time. And besides—" I stopped suddenly noticing one of my favorite stores. "Oh shit I almost forgot I need an outfit for Thursday. Let's go in Banana for a second."

"An outfit for Thursday? For what?"

"I'm going to see *Beauty and the Beast.*"

"With Toni Braxton? You didn't tell me you had tickets bitch? Who you going with?"

I sucked my teeth. "Jason."

7

"Really…" he smiled, "are you two finally getting serious?"

"Kevin," I huffed, "honestly I don't know what's going on with us. I mean I like him. I do. But at the same time, I'm not going to deal with his shit you know?"

He shook his head. "So he's still playing hard to get?"

"I don't know what he's playing man, but this show is it. Afterwards, if I don't feel right, or have a clear indication as to where we're heading, I'm out. I don't have time to deal with a man who doesn't know what he wants."

He sighed. "That's too bad; I actually thought you guys made a cute couple. But nonetheless follow your heart."

Immediately upon entering Banana I felt completely out of place. I had gone to work earlier that day, so basically I woke up, threw on anything, and headed to the office: a sweatshirt some jeans and a pair of Tims. I figured since it was Saturday no one would see me before I had the opportunity to change. But when Kevin called and said, *"Let's go shopping, it'll be fun"*, I was like *"cool"*, and forgot all about how I looked.

"Welcome to Banana Republic Gentlemen!" The well dressed caucasian bellowed upon our entry into the brightly lit franchise.

"Thank you." Kevin smiled showing all thirty-two.

He is much more cordial than I am in situations like this. You see I have a problem with salespeople. They talk too damn' much and, they're way too helpful. *Do you need any help? Can I help you find your size? Oh that looks great on you!* Ugh! That shit kills me! I grunt when I walk in so they'll know right away *not* to fuck with me. They usually get the message and hover five to ten feet away folding shirts or, doing some other menial task until I motion for their assistance.

"Can I assist you gentlemen with anything this evening?" He asked politely.

"No thank you." I grunted, then turned and walked over to a rack of pants.

Kevin, on the other hand smiled politely and said, "We're just looking for now," then turned and followed me. "Bitch!" He howled as soon as he approached me. "Why are you always so hostile? Ooooooo I can't *take* you New Yorkers for that! Y'all always have an attitude about something!"

"Kevin, what are you talking about?" I asked studying a pair of slacks.

"What am I talking about?! *Bitch* you *know* what I'm talking about! I'm talking about the way you walked in here and threw shade at that salesman! That's what I'm talking about bitch!"

8

"Kevin please. You know that man don't give a fuck about you or me. He has a job to do, and that job is to sell something—anything for that matter in this goddamn store so that he can get a fucking commission. Plus, they always—"

"Can I help you gentlemen with anything today?" Another salesman asked.

"No thank you!" I hissed, causing him to eyeball me before casually walking away. "See what I fucking mean, they *always* interrupt you! When I figure out what the hell I want then I'll ask for help."

Kevin shook his head in disbelief. "Jared my friend, you are *one* piece of work."

"Thanks." I said ignoring his sarcasm while simultaneously holding up a find. "How do you like these pants?"

"Oh those are cute bitch, how much are they?"

"A hundred and forty-five dollars."

"That's not bad. What else does it come with?"

"The hanger!"

"Lies!" He shrieked. "Banana is coming up! They're trying to cash in on all the girls coins!"

"Yeah I know. But I like them. Help me find my size."

Kevin put his left hand on his hip and rolled his eyes. "You see what I mean about your trifling ass? You *read* the people that work here, and then ask me for help. Now tell me, does that make any sense?" He asked, while at the same time motioning for a salesman.

"Hey, have you guys made up your mind about your purchase?" The salesman asked approaching us.

"Yeah," I said flipping through the rack, never once looking up, "I was wondering if you had these pants in a size thirty-two. I don't see any here on the rack."

"Sure, we probably have some downstairs. I'll check."

"Thanks." I whispered, still searching.

He hadn't moved two feet away before Kevin began his commentary.

"*Oooo* Jared! Did you check him out? Girl he's *cah-ute* for you!" He said in his *"I'm about to hook you up!"* voice.

"Yeah whatever," I said, still searching through the rack, "he's okay."

"Okay?!" He flinched. "Bitch you kill me. You really should get your eyes checked for glasses! You make sure you take a good look at that man when he comes back. *Squint* if you have to. I know your type, and that boy is it, *trust!*"

9

Sure enough minutes later as the salesman made his way back with my slacks in hand, I noticed the way he seemed to glide across the floor. There was a sort of cockiness about him that screamed, *"I am the man!"* And for the first time I noticed him. He was a strikingly handsome man with a very defined manicured appearance. He was wearing a black cashmere v-neck sweater, with black trousers and black square toe shoes that fit his five feet nine inch muscular frame perfectly. His chocolate brown skin was smooth and flawless. His lips—*damn'*! They looked perfect for kissing. Kevin was right. He did have the look I wanted. But did he have the mind? *Damn'* him for knowing me so well!

"Here you go man. That was a size thirty-two right?" He said handing me the pants I had requested.

"Yeah. Thirty-two. Thanks," I muttered, studying his handsome face.

"No problem, that's what I'm here for. And uh, if you guys need anything else just let me know, I'll be right over there." He said, then turned and walked away just as confidently as he had strolled over.

"Damn' Kevin that boy is PHINE! Did you check out his disposition? It's off the fucking hook!"

He laughed reveling in the moment. "See look at you, I told you bitch now you're all in!"

"Kevin you're right, you're right, but this time you've out done yourself. Did you hear how smooth his voice was? My God!"

"Calm down bitch, you don't even know if he's down!"

And then, it hit me. "I didn't even think about that." My body slumped. "You see that's the problem with this fucking lifestyle, too many goddamn complications!"

"Oh stop tripping bitch, he might be down. I saw the way he smiled at you when he handed you those pants."

My eyes lit up. "For real? Don't play Kev."

"I'm serious girl! My gaydar was beeping like crazy."

"*Gaydar* Kevin? I'm not about to embarrass the shit out of myself because your fucking *gaydar* decides to beep!" My eyes traveled the store searching for him. I located him standing on the other side of the floor unfolding then refolding a group of red sweaters. The bravado this man gave off arrested my curiosity and held it captive. At that moment I decided I had to know who he was, and for what team he was batting. "Listen Kevin," I said eying my prey carefully, "I have my own way of finding out these things. Watch this."

I casually walked towards the salesman that had just assisted me.

"Excuse me but, is there a dressing room around here I can use to try on these pants?"

He smiled. "Sure, right this way".

I followed close behind as his slightly bowed legs led me in the direction of the fitting rooms.

"Oh Jared?" Kevin called out softly. "Try this shirt on with those pants, I really think it'll make a nice outfit." He tossed me an off white collarless shirt that would indeed match the khaki colored slacks perfectly. "And make sure you come out afterwards so I can see how it looks on you."

The salesman looked at me and smiled.

Great! I thought. *If the boy is down, now he's going to think Kevin and I are an item.* Pissed, I shot Kevin the nastiest stare I could manage. Unmoved, he returned a look as if to say, *'What Bitch!'*

You see my plan was simple. Straight men can usually care less how another brother looks in clothing. To them it's all competition, so they would never go out of their way to big another brother up. Gay men on the other hand, will look, look again, approve, and then, compliment. Plus, straight or not, I had to show him and everyone else in that damn' store, I wasn't some bum off the street trying to buy class. I knew how to wear clothes. It's just that day I hadn't gone through the trouble of selecting a death-defying outfit.

While in the dressing room, I overheard Kevin chit-chatting with the salesman, at the same time I'm sure, checking the read out on his gaydar. Which in a way wasn't such a bad idea; between the two of us, one of us was bound to figure out his tea.

Minutes later I emerged from the fitting room *(looking dapper of course)*, and was greeted with smiles from Kevin, but more importantly, the salesman. It worked. He was checking me out.

"So what do you think?" I said confidently, knowing damn' well the compliments I was about to receive.

"Wow you look great man," the salesman smiled, "neutral tones really does compliment you!"

"Thanks man, beige is one of my favorite colors." I faced Kevin and winked, "Well, what do you think?"

"Oh I like it man! It looks real nice. I'm sure Ms. Braxton will appreciate you dressing up for her performance."

"You're going to see Toni Braxton? Really? Is she in concert?" Quizzed the salesman.

"No, she's performing on Broadway in Beauty and the Beast." I said styling my wears in the mirror. "I want to look my best for her. I have orchestra seats, and uh, I'm hoping she'll notice me sitting out there and meet me after the show for dinner and a movie." *(Rule # 4,720: If they are down, you never want them to know* you are *right away. Keep them guessing. It's that old game of cat and mouse.)*

11

"Ah man, that would be great! But uh, it looks like I have competition in the Toni Braxton department. We may have to talk about this further."

I laughed nervously. *(Uh-oh, now who's fooling who?)*

"No, but seriously," he continued, "if you're going to the theater, you may want to switch shirts," he reached and grabbed another one from a nearby rack. "Try this maroon one on with the collar; it'll dress up the outfit a bit."

"Sure." I said heading towards the dressing rooms. "Oh Kevin," I stopped suddenly, "did I show you my new tattoo?"

"Nah man, let me see it."

I removed my shirt.

"Damn' Jared!" Kevin exclaimed. "Have you been hitting the weights again man? You're getting big!"

"Yeah...I just started back. But yo," I said pointing to my tattoo, "check it out!"

"Man, that's a nice ass tattoo!" The salesman exclaimed. "Where'd you get it done?"

"In Brooklyn." I said showing off my prized possession. "One of my best friends took me to a friend of his and he hooked me up."

He moved in closer to study the design. "Cool. What does it mean?"

"I call it frustration," I said, then went about defining the design in detail. "The lightning bolts and the clouds up here by my shoulder, represent the storms brewing in my life. And as you can see the storm descends down. This image of a man right here represents life. See how the lightning is striking him? Well that's me. It shows how I feel when all of life's problems are hitting me at once."

He nodded. "That's deep man. Did you design it yourself?"

"Nah, I told the artist I wanted lightning and chaos and shit, and explained how I was feeling and he just drew it. Then, we edited it and," I pointed, "here you have it, the finished product!"

"That's cool man but, if you don't mind me asking, did it cost a lot? I mean cause, it looks like it did."

"Nah, it didn't." I said smiling realizing my plan was working better than I had anticipated. "Like I said since my boy took me down there I didn't have to pay that much, he only charged me like one seventy-five."

"Get out!" He blinked in disbelief. "I have this fly ass tattoo I had drawn for me, and it's nowhere near as detailed as this, and the lowest I've been quoted is three fifty!"

"Man, like I said, I'm sure this one would have been more if I hadn't gone with my boy."

"Damn." He paused studying my arm. "Do you think maybe you can get a quote for my tattoo?" He asked, his full lips breaking into a smile. "I mean if it's not too much trouble?"

My heart warmed. "Nah man, no trouble at all. Do you have it on you now?"

"No, actually I don't, but I can get a copy to you. Do you work around here?"

"Yeah right up the street, Fifth and 43rd."

"So look, maybe Monday during your lunch you can stop by here, and I could give you a copy."

"Sure no problem man." I smiled. *Damn* I worked that shit *out*!

"Cool. So listen, do you still want to try on that maroon shirt?"

"Oh yeah, I forgot all about it. I'll be right back."

After trying it on, I decided to go with my original outfit despite the salesman's insistence that the maroon shirt and khaki slacks would be more appropriate. I explained to him, the last time I went to a Broadway show I dressed in a suit and tie, and by far out shinned everyone in the theater. This time I planned on playing it safe.

"I didn't catch your names," he said handing me my credit card and bag.

"Oh my bad, its Jared, and this is my boy Kevin."

"Nice to meet you both. My name is Michael." He extended his hand. The chemistry we shared must have transferred through our handshake because both his hand and mine were extremely warm. He blushed. "So Jared, I guess I'll see you Monday?"

"Sure thing. I'll stop by during my lunch."

"Great, and again, it was nice meeting you two. Make sure you guys enjoy the rest of this weekend, the weatherman said this heat's not supposed to last."

"Thanks, and you too." Kevin said as we exited the store. We barely hit the cement before he began his commentary. "Alright bitch for going shopping and picking up a man!"

I laughed. "I haven't got him yet my man, but I think he was checking me out in there. Did you see it?" I asked hoping I wasn't imagining things.

"Yeah I saw it. And I think you two will make a tight couple."

"What makes you say that?"

"Because, he won't take your shit." Kevin said bluntly.

"My shit? What's that suppose to mean?"

"Jared, you know how you are, *Mr. Control Freak*. You want everything your way or no way. And well, he just seems as if he can handle himself. There's an air of confidence surrounding him."

"Confident he is," I said envisioning him gliding across the floor once more. Yes, he was most definitely confident.

"Listen, just make sure you take your time." Kevin warned, noticing my distant gaze. "You know how you like to rush into things."

"I know, I know..."

"I'm just saying Jared..."

I raised my hand and stopped him before he began. If there was one thing I hated, it was somebody telling me how to live my life. Kevin knew this.

"Anyway," he said grudgingly changing the subject, "what are you doing later?"

"That's right, I forgot to tell you, Ron is throwing a 'tee shirt and panty party', and I'm helping him out with the door. You wanna come? *There should be some cuties there.*" I said trying to peak his interest.

"Nah, I don't want to go to that party and dream. The men there don't want me. Besides, I don't feel like playing straight tonight. Maybe Aaron and I will catch a movie or something."

"Okay, but if you two change your mind you know where to find me."

I learned a long time ago, not to try to convince my friends in the life to come with me to any of my straight friends' functions. Gay people were just as prejudice as straight people. Neither wanted to party with the other outside of necessity.

"Yeah well," he said pulling me into an embrace, "just make sure you tell me about all the cuties there tomorrow."

"I'll have a complete run down of the evening's events prepared before dawn." I held him tight. "Get home safe."

On the train I replayed my encounter with Michael over and over in my head. I must have watched him cross that floor a thousand times. I envisioned his smile, the way he looked right before he laughed, and yes my God, those legs. He was handsome, charismatic, sexy—*unbelievably sexy*—and—and—

I stopped myself. What the hell was I doing? I couldn't believe I was spending this much time, thinking about someone I had just met! Someone I didn't even know! Who didn't know anything about me! I hated getting myself all worked up and excited only to end up disillusioned. Besides, there was still Jason. Even if Michael was down, I was still seeing someone. I was already involved. So why even go there?

Regardless, Michael managed to consume my thoughts for the rest of the ride.

I once heard Bill Cosby say, *"If you know what you want, you will recognize it when you see it."*

Damn, had I just seen my dream?

14

TWO

Kevin

I T'S NOT AS EASY AS IT LOOKS. And it damn' sure ain't as glamorous. Girls kill me running around talking about: *"I can't find a man!"* I only have one question. When you get one, will you know how to *keep* him? *Okay!* Because, any girl can get a man, but only a fierce one knows how to keep him!

Take me for example. When I first met Aaron, I was a shitty mess! You heard me, a shit-ty mess! I was looking for a man, but for all the wrong ones, in all the wrong places. Honey, every Friday night I'd be up in Miss Keller's standing at the bar watching the cuties *(and a few dragons!)* pile up in that rat trap. And whenever opportunity presented himself, I'd gradually work my way around that crowded, cramped, tired ass bar, until we came face to face. Of course, my face would always be flawless, my outfit o-vah, and my body laced! Eventually, I'd strike up a conversation, and if I like what I heard, it was on!

But I didn't stop there! Oh no! Saturday was the night! Honey, Miss Sound Factory Bar never disappointed. I mean never! She would always serve up the choice trade for me to feast on. Back then, I use to get paid once a week. So you best believe every Friday, Miss Macy's or Miss Bloomingdale's would get all my coins if necessary for one fierce old outfit! Chile, Sound Factory Bar had it going on! I couldn't just go in there wearing some old tired ass ensemble! I had to represent!

As soon as I got dressed I'd run out the house and hop on the A train.

Not to digress, but let me share some helpful info with you girls out there looking for a man. The "A" train honey! RIDE THE "A" TRAIN! *Trade—down!* Girl...the A train is better than some clubs I've gone to, and believe me when I tell you honey, they're ready, willing and able! Trust me on this one...

But anyway girl, like I was saying, I would hop on the A train, and hit it to the club. By the time I got there, usually around 1:30, 2:00 in the morning, it would be pumping. I'd put on my club face, and submerge myself in the music. Usually, I'd hang out downstairs devouring the sounds of hip-hop, one beat at a time. My favorite at the time was Method's and Mary's *"You're all I need to get by"*. Whenever it came on, no matter what I was doing, the beat would consume me, pulling me in, possessing my mind. Immediately, I'd start to dance, giving into the rhythm. Half the kids on the dance floor couldn't take me! *Jealous bitches!* Because my body, unlike theirs became the instruments, lyrics and essence of that song. I was alive! I was free! Honey, I was fierce!

Once the song ended, and I came down from my high horse, acquiring attention was usually a piece of cake. All eyes were on me, and the choice of men was mine. I'd survey the room flashing my signature smile, searching for the one I'd dreamed of. A six foot, light skinned, thugged-out trade ass niggah! Every *once* in a while, I'd stumble across one of those thugged out real ass niggahs, because as I'm sure some of you girls know, most clubs are filled with *ladies* dressed as *niggahs* perpetrating a fraud! *Okay!* But, like I said, *every-once-and-a-while,* I'd find a real one…and honey, I'd latch on like a leech!

But you know, something always went wrong. It took me a long time to realize that a type is nothing more than a type. There is no flesh and blood, no give and take, no…nothing. It was simply an image I created in my head, and completely unfulfilling. You see, I wanted a Method Man. But every time I got a Method Man, I realized I wanted more. A beat face and a beat body is all good, if all you want is sex, but I wanted more.

I wanted a mind.

I wanted a friend.

I wanted a partner.

Honey, I wanted someone who could speak! *Okay!* And my quote unquote type was providing none of that.

So one day I asked myself, I said, *"Ms. Girl, what's more important? The external superficial components of a man, or, the internal heart and soul of a man?"*

Needless to say after thinking long and hard, *(and I do mean long and hard),* the latter won.

Now I'm happy to report I have a man, and I love him dearly. He's not NY trade, but he's a man. He doesn't have a beat out body, but he's a man. He doesn't dance and party like I do, but he's a man. He's good looking, well groomed, well mannered, honest, independent, trustworthy, and sexy! He's everything I've always wanted. And I never would have found him, if I hadn't opened my eyes and mind, and moved passed looking for a type, and started looking for a man!

But it wasn't easy, because *chile,* once you got your mind set on some fine wine, and somebody offers you last year's ripple, something's got to give! I went on a few dates with some "ordinary" guys, but honey, they just didn't do it for me. They were either too stuffy, too laid back, or just too damn' boring!

I was about to give up, and go back searching for *"that niggah"*, when I met Aaron. At first, I wasn't too interested in him because I knew a few of his friends very well, and they were *pre-ten-tious!* And anyone that knows me, knows I can't take no *high* sidity girls! But after we talked on the phone for about a week, I realized that he was down to earth, and nothing like I had imagined.

I still remember our first date. We went to the movies, and afterwards, walked around the city. The evening was magical, almost mystical. The stars were out in unbelievable numbers, which was extremely odd for New York City. A light summer breeze cooled us as we strolled through Central Park.

"So, are you originally from New York?" He asked. His diction was impeccable, and quite to my surprise, a turn-on.

"No." I answered. "Actually, I'm from LA…land of the stars."

He paused, his eyes twinkling. "Really, which part?"

"Orange County. Why? Do you know someone out there?"

"Why yes. I have family in Long Beach."

"Really, get out! My best friend Vince is from Long Beach. Do you travel out there often?"

"No, I haven't been out there in years, maybe *ten*, or *twelve* years. I used to go every summer when I was younger, but after my parents divorced I spent most of my summers on the bus between my mother's house, and her new man, and my father's house and all his quirky girlfriends." He pointed to a bench. "Do you mind if we sit and talk for a while?"

"Not at all." I said taking a seat. "So why did your parents divorce?"

"Well, the papers said irreconcilable differences, but the truth is they were both too lazy to work at staying together. It was easier to just call it quits."

I sighed. "Marriage sucks."

"Sometimes, but if you go into it with an open mind, it could be the best thing that happens to two people." He paused. "Are your parents still married?"

"No. My father died years ago."

"I'm sorry to hear that." He whispered sincerely.

"Don't be. He was an asshole." I leaned back and watched the stars. "It's a beautiful night isn't it?"

"It is. I love nights like this, especially when the stars are out."

"Yeah, this is pretty unusual for New York. Now in California it's a different story altogether. A night like this, I could lie out and watch the sky for hours." I sighed. "I really miss being there sometimes."

"When was the last time you went home?"

"Wow, home..." I said drifting. It had been some time since anyone asked me about home. California yes. Home, no. It was too painful to remember, so I chose to forget. I had no choice but to forget. "I haven't been there in years." I said staring, remembering then forgetting again. "I guess you can say I've adopted New York as my new home. My home away from home."

He tilted his head, "So you have no family in California?"

"None living." I lied, feeling the pain well up in the bottom of my soul. I fought hard that night not to cry. I was determined not to. He must have sensed the pain his question raised, because he immediately changed the subject.

"Kevin I have to admit, I'm somewhat taken by you. I don't know what it is, but I have this...this feeling in my stomach that I've never felt before." He let out a soft laugh.

"This morning," He continued, "when I woke up, I did something I never did before. I knelt down by my bed and I thanked God for leading me to you, and you to me. Now, I pray all the time. It's just I've never thanked God for a "date" before." His eyes roamed my face. "I know you think I'm crazy..."

"No. Actually I think it's sweet." I said shyly. "And if it's worth anything, I'm a little taken by you too. But I have to be honest with you Aaron," I said making eye contact, "I like to take things slow. I'm not saying I'm going to date other people while we're talking, or that I don't believe we can make this work. It's just, I don't want to put all my eggs in one basket and risk losing them all. I've seen way too many of my friends do that, and get hurt."

His face softened, as he stared deep into my soul. "Kevin I totally understand, and I agree we should, no, we will, take our time. I've been burnt a few times myself, and I'm not looking forward to getting burnt again. But I will tell you this, what I feel for you is pure. It is honest, and it is real. I know we met for a reason. And if you are as willing as I am to discover the meaning of that reason, then let's not waste another moment worrying about tomorrow. There's absolutely no harm in trying. If you're ready, I'm ready."

As I looked at this man, this beautiful man, I realized that everything he had just said, I completely felt. And for some reason, I knew I was ready to take that next step. I looked straight into his eyes and told him, I was ready to discover the purpose behind our meeting, and I meant every word. That night, on that bench, in the middle of Central Park, we ignited a fire that has yet to diminish.

Do we have a perfect relationship? No.

Do we get on each other's nerves? Yes.

Believe me it's trying as hell some days. But, it's not all our fault. We are doing the best we can to make it in a world that's constantly knocking us down, every time we try to stand. But you know what? We're winning. We're beating the odds. It's been two and a half years of blood, sweat and tears that I wouldn't trade for the world.

Some of my friends, especially Jared, often ask me what made me change. And, truthfully, I haven't changed. I'm still the same old crazy Kevin that likes to party with the best of them. I still love cruising fierce trade, and I still love dancing to Method's and Mary's *"You're all I need to get by"*. The only difference is now I have a *man* to sing it to.

So, to all you girls out there searching for love, I'll give you the same advice I so often give Jared. Hold on, and don't give up, it's gonna happen. But when it does, make sure you're ready to give a little and take little. Because it's not just about getting a man, it's about *keeping* that man.

THREE

Jared

MONDAY MORNING I AWOKE tired and cranky from a weekend that seemed to begin, right as it was ending. I opened my eyes and stared blankly at the ceiling contemplating a reason to call in sick. I hated my job, and today, any reason would be good enough so long as I did not have to suffer through one more day of endless meeting, after meeting on shit I really could give two shits about. But then I remembered Michael and our agreement, and within a matter of seconds I was up and in the shower.

Afterwards, I made my way to the closet hoping the fashion fairy had left me something new and enticing to sport to work. But as I stood in the nude sifting through the suits and ties, I realized she had passed my place once more. What the hell I was going to wear? I couldn't just wear anything! I needed to make an impression; one that stayed with him long after I'd gone so that if he was indeed down, he'd have something to think about.

I searched and searched and searched until finally I found the outfit: A navy blue pin stripped suit with an evening blue shirt and a gold Kenneth Cole tie. Once dressed, I realized that perhaps the reason why the fashion fairy always neglected my closet was because I really didn't need her help at all. As usual, I was looking tough.

On the train, while grooving to the sounds of James Ingram's *One Hundred Ways*, I revisited my encounter with Michael on Saturday.

'Maybe its infatuation,' I reasoned trying desperately to make some sense of my erratic behavior. *'Maybe when we meet up today, I won't feel as strongly as I had on Saturday.'*

At the time that reasoning made perfect sense because, we all do it: Meet someone and immediately make up in our minds that they're the one—when the reality is, we don't know shit about them. I knew I was getting ahead of myself, and doing the things Kevin warned, and I, secretly promised I would not do. But no matter how many times I tried to abort the system sending rush messages to my heart, I could not force a shut down. It seemed to have a mind of its own, and my job was to follow its lead.

And so I decided not to fight it, but instead, see where it would lead.

As I approached the job I thanked God for life, health and strength, and secretly asked that lunch come quickly. I had a date to keep.

Christopher David

A FTER FINISHING UP BREAKFAST, my first most important task of
the day, I checked my e-mail, the second most important task of the
day. I love e-mail, and honestly, if it weren't for e-mail, I doubt I'd even go
to work. It was one of the few luxuries my job offered. *(Besides of course
the bi-weekly paycheck...)*

When the inbox downloaded, there were three new messages. The
first was from Jason:

```
What's up Jared?

how are you on this blessed day?  fine i hope...i just got n
and thought i'd send u some of my good vibes.  btw how was the
party saturday?  sorry I couldn't make it, but herman and i
went shopping to pick up some thangs and we sort of lost track
of time.  u know how that goes...anyway, take it easy 2 day
and remember God loves u.

Peace & inner blessings, Jason
```

Ugh! I hated Jason! God knows I did! I know you're like,
"Why...he seems like such a nice guy." But trust me, you don't know him
like I do, or rather, the way my heart does.

We had been dating for about four months at the time, and were
going absolutely nowhere meaningful. He was caught up in his own little
egotistical world and based on his lackadaisical attitude regarding our
togetherness hell would freeze over, before he would commit to a
relationship. For months I tried unsuccessfully, of course, to woo him. I
played all my trump cards, but to no avail. He was not giving in. My
patience had begun to wear thin, and so too was that thin line between love,
and hate.

Kevin introduced me to Jason. That bastard! He's always making a
quote unquote *Love Connection*, every friggin' chance he gets. One day out
of the blue, he called me up and was like, "Jared, I've got the *puuurrrrfect*
guy for you," he hummed, sounding hauntingly similar to Eartha Kit's *Cat
Woman.*

"Okay Kevin," I sighed uninterested, "what's *this* one like?"

"Well, he's really cool and, he works in the music industry..."

'Great!' I thought, *'Another one!'* Both Vince and Kevin were in
the music industry when I met them five years earlier. I never could figure
out why people in the music industry were so arrogant—especially the gay
assistant to the assistant of the assistant.

"…He has a great sense of humor. A strong belief in God—I think he's an Israelite or something—"

"He's not one of those *'kill all the white people'* cat's on 42nd Street right?"

"Now bitch. Would I be calling you to hook you up with *one of those* assholes?" He asked irritated. "You know I can't take those girls!"

"I'm just saying Kevin I have enough issues of my own. The last thing I need is a niggah holding a bunch of hate rallies in my apartment!"

"Jared, there's no need to worry about that, Jason wouldn't hurt a fly."

"Cool. So what does he look like?"

"Oh, he's *very* handsome!" He said with no hesitation. "The boy *takes care* of himself. I've *never* seen him without a line-up, and he can *dress* his ass off!"

"Oh yeah, so why is he single?" I asked suspiciously. "Is he some type of misfit or something?"

He sucked his teeth. "No Jared, he's not! Like I said, he's a nice guy. He just happens to be single, and you happen to be single so I thought *'hey two nice people, why not hook them up'?*"

"Is he a queen Kevin?"

"No girl! You think I don't know your type!?" He snapped. "Trust me you <u>will</u> like him, and you <u>will</u> hit it off!"

I sighed hesitantly. "Okay Kevin, so when do I meet him?"

"Well actually, you could meet him right now. I mean, I could get him on the three way—"

"Kevin I don't know about that—"

"Oh hold on bitch, it'll only take a second."

Before I could protest further, he clicked over.

I love Kevin. Believe me I do. But it was times like this when he frustrated me the most. I didn't mind meeting his friend, but not like this. I had my own way of doing things. But with him, it was his way, or no way.

"Jared are you there?" He asked returning to the line.

"Kevin look," I said in my most serious tone, "I really don't want to meet this guy this way. Give me some time to think about—"

But it was too late. My mystery date had answered the phone.

"Jason speaking. How may I help you?"

"Hey what's up Jason, its Kevin. Got a minute?"

"Not really. I'm busy as hell, over here." He paused. I heard a number of telephones ringing in the background. "Is it important Kev?"

"Yeah…sort of. It'll only take a minute."

He sighed. "Alright Kevin, what is it."

23

"Well," Kevin said excitedly, I imagined him sitting in his office twitching with glee. "Do you remember me telling you about my friend Jared?"

"I think so…" He replied as if trying to recall the conversation. But knowing Kevin, there probably wasn't one.

"Remember the one I said I thought you two would make a good couple?" He said trying to jog his memory.

"Oh yeah, what about him?"

"Well, he's on the line. Jared are you there?"

For a moment I sat in silence, trying to figure out how I got to this point. There's nothing worse than a blind hook-up. What may be perfectly acceptable for someone else may be all wrong for the next man. Besides, I'd seen some of the people Kevin thought were cute!

"Yeah I'm here Kevin, what's up?"

"Well then speak up girl! I'm trying to introduce you two here!" He barked and immediately went into his introductions, "Okay, Jared this is Jason. Jason this is Jared."

"Hey what's up man?" I mumbled.

"Nothing much, what's up with you?" Jason asked sincerely. I liked that, calm under pressure.

"Ummm—I'm cool. But, right now I don't know how comfortable I am conversing with you and *you know who* on the phone."

Kevin sucked his teeth. "What's that suppose to mean!"

"No offense Kev, but you've done your part. It's pretty much up to us now."

"Well excuse me for being in the way!" He spat. "Girls kill me. You hook them up one minute, and then the next they're kicking your ass to the curb!"

I laughed. "Yo, Jason, is there a number I could reach you at?"

"Sure." He said, and rattled off the number.

"Cool, I'll call you in a minute. Peace Kev."

He sucked his teeth and slammed down the phone.

It's not that I felt uncomfortable with Kevin on the line. It's just he always had to be in the know; and at times that little trait of his could be so aggravating. I kind of wanted him to suffer a little bit. I knew it was eating him alive not knowing what Jason and I were discussing. And I also knew, as soon as he *thought* we were off the phone, he'd be checking in with one of us to see how the conversation went, what we talked about, but most importantly, when we planned to fuck. He would eventually get all that information and more but for now, he'd just have to wait it out.

When Kevin first introduced us I was at a good point in my life. I was growing both spiritually and mentally, and discovering the inner me I had long abandoned. For the first time in my life, I was somewhat confident and secure and becoming aware of what I wanted and did not want in my life, and in a relationship. It was a major accomplishment for someone who had battled severe bouts of depression and low self-esteem for a number of years (mainly due to my sexuality). But it seemed finally life was starting to make sense to me.

The first time we hooked up, I realized how accurate Kevin had been when he said, *"Oh, he's very handsome"*.

Jason had the appearance of a regular guy with extremely masculine features. He stood about five foot ten inches tall with a defined muscular build and a rich mocha complexion. His best attributes by far were his eyes, *(a golden brown, with hazel highlights just about the pupils,)* and yes, his lips *(full, succulent, sensuous kiss-able lips shaped and molded by God himself)*. Sometimes, when he was happy, his eyes would dance, and his lips would form the beginnings of a smile—so sweet, so pure, so innocent, I dreamed of waking to them every morning. It was times like these, I found myself in a wonderland, dreaming a dream only dreamers dreamed. Living a lie. Lying to live in a place I constructed in my mind, filled with fear, masqueraded as love. Truth strangled by love, or, rather, a variation of love. It was there, in my mind that I learned, the truth can and will take on many different meanings for many different people.

To this day, a part of me believes Jason and I would have made a beautiful couple if only he were more honest with himself and open to the possibilities. But like many people, Jason had been wounded by love, and this wound prevented him from sharing his true beauty. Not only with me, but with everyone he came in contact with.

Once, over dinner, I asked him why he held back so much, and without skipping a beat he answered: "Nothing lasts forever. I learned that lesson the hard way." He paused then added, "What people don't realize is that the end of a relationship is always closer than it seems. So, at the beginning, I prep myself for the end. I know its coming. It's inevitable. My job is to be ready."

Confused, and intrigued at the same time, I asked him to clarify his point: "It's simple." He said. "I loved innocently once. I gave everything I knew how to give. Everything I imagined a person should give when in love, and he took my love; all of it." His words drifted off somewhere painful. "Then," he chuckled, "I find out 2 years into our relationship that he never really loved me. He never even cared. Out of curiosity one day I asked him why was he with me, and he said, *"Because, when we met you were new on the scene, and everybody else wanted you."* I couldn't believe he said that shit to me right to my face. Here was the person I trusted with my heart and soul basically telling me I was *fresh meat*."

25

A deep agonizing pain filled his voice. His eyes normally bright and vibrant revealed the hurt his actions often refused to show.

"But you know" he continued, "when you think you're in love. When you think you've found the one that completes you, the one you've searched for your whole fucking life, it becomes so hard to think clearly. After he said that shit I knew I didn't belong there. I knew it. But I stayed anyway hoping things would get better. Deep down I knew they wouldn't.

"And then one day he just left, and I lost it. At some point during our relationship, we had become one, or rather, I had become him. And I couldn't imagine living my life without him—without us. So I stressed him, and the situation out. I kept asking him over and over, *how could you do this to me—how could you just up and leave me like this*? Instead of accepting the truth about us and moving on, I begged and pleaded with him to take me back and give me a second chance. But he never did. He moved on without me as if we'd never been together. To this day that shit still eats at me.

"But then one day, after praying for answers I got one. And I stopped crying just like that." He said snapping his fingers. "From that day forward, I vowed never to go there again."

"Why?" I asked.

"Because," he said sipping his drink, "when I needed love, he let me down."

"But, don't you see, it wasn't love that hurt you, it was your ex. He's the one that sold you false dreams, not love."

He nodded. "Maybe, but in the heat of the moment, they're one in the same."

After dating Jason about four months I realized the day he stopped crying, he stopped caring. He stopped believing in the power of love. On that day he built a wall around his heart and policed it around the clock. No matter what I did to prove to him my feelings were genuine, the wall never softened. He had Herman, his family, his job and shopping, to him that was all the love he needed, and, all the love he wanted.

I read his e-mail once more, and grew angrier. This guy! He always found time to hang out with his friends. But whenever I asked him to do something, work was crazy, he had to go to the gym or some other tired excuse would take precedence over me. I often wondered why he and Herman had never made a go of a relationship. After all, they spent half the day and night together. But hey, what did I know, maybe they already had!

I hit the reply button.

What's up Jason,

Thanks for sending me those vibes this morning. I needed that.

The party was a success. Actually, I didn't think so many people were going to show up in their underwear. But quite to my surprise they did.

Coincidentally, Kevin and I went shopping as well on Saturday. We had a great time. You know how crazy he is...I was cracking up the whole while.

By the way, how's Herman's job search going?

Anyway, hope all is well in your camp...when you get a chance hit me up. I should be around all day.

Peace Jared...

Asking about Herman's job search was heavily sarcastic. He had been searching for a permanent gig for more than two years and still no luck. I imagined he never really wanted a job or for that matter needed one since Jason always managed to pick up the tab. Without question, I knew Jason had bought Herman at least two outfits on Saturday or more.

If you asked me, Herman knew how giving Jason was. And if it were left up to him, Jason would never have another friend, never mind a boyfriend! He was more watchdog than friend; everywhere Jason went, he followed. He was Jason's confidant, personal stylist, piece approver, eyes, ears, voice, and *constant* cock blocker! No one got to Jason, except by him. If he approved, Jason proceeded. I swear, in all my life, I had never witnessed such a friendship, and I doubt for as long as I live I never will.

The second message was from my cousin...

Jared...

I just got back from Paris, visiting one of my old college buddies. Can I tell you we were drunk every night! I hadn't had that much fun in what seems like forever. You've got to plan a trip out here. I know you'll love it!

But anyway, I just got your e-mail and I'm sorry to hear you sound so down about love man. What's up with that? Aren't you the one usually carrying cupid's bag around? Has this new dude—what's his name—Jason got you singing the blues? Listen, people are people Jared...and no matter how much you try, you will never change them. If he doesn't know what he wants or recognizes what he has...fuck him! Soon, he'll realize what

27

he's throwing away, and by then, it'll be too late. Don't let anyone steal your spirit cuzzo. It's just not worth it.

I've got to run, I have a class in about 4 minutes, and if I'm not there soon all my students will cut out!

Peace! (And stay up yo!!!!!!!!!!!)

Ant...

    My cousin's timing could not have been better. I needed that advice after reading Jason's e-mail. It's like he knew exactly how I was feeling. But before I could reply to his e-mail and thank him, the telephone rang.
    "Jared Covington, how may I help you?"
    "What's up son?"
    "Ha-ha! What's up Sean?"
    Sean D. Phelps was one of my very best friends in the life. He was by far one of the most honest, straightforward brothers I knew. Which mind you, is extremely rare in this lifestyle. If Sean didn't like you, he didn't hesitate to tell you. If he thought you were lying, he didn't hesitate to tell you. If he thought you were trying to get over on him—*or for that matter any of his boys*—he promptly stepped to that ass, ready to *beat* that ass! He was a man's man and swore by God, he was the last man standing. If you let him tell it, no one was harder than him—no one tougher. His only quirk? The niggah could gossipppppppp...
    "Nothing's much man." He replied. "Just taking it one day at a time. You know, chilling. How was the weekend bruh?"
    "Ah man, the weekend was sweet. Friday night I just sort of chilled out at the house. Saturday, I went into the office for a while and knocked out some work. Then later on that afternoon I hooked up with Kevin and did some shopping. *And yo!* I met the flyest niggah in the world working at Banana!"
    "Get the fuck out of here!"
    "For real man. Only thing is, I'm not sure if this cat is down."
    "Hmm...you're playing right?"
    "Nah I'm dead serious. Neither Kevin nor I could figure it out."
    "You two dumb bitches!" He laughed. "You know half the mother-fuckas working in *Banana Republic*, *Club Monaco* and the *Gap* are down! It's like *fashion training camp* for faggots and shit! How you think most of them get all that gear they wear? Discounts baby! Discounts!"
    "You're stupid—you know that, right!" I said, trying to prevent my laughter from escaping my cubicle. "But seriously Sean, the boy showed no signs of being down. *You know me man!*" I said hitting my chest to

emphasize the point. "I'm the first person to peep the kids! But this cat's shit was tight! If he is down, he didn't let on at all."

"Still my man, I don't know what the fuck you're worrying about. If he's working there, then nine times out of ten, the niggah's down—or has at least messed around before. And I'm almost positive he won't mind doing so again."

"Well, my goal is to find out. I'm stopping by there today during lunch."

"Oh?" He asked suspiciously. "For what? Got a date already? Or, *stalking?*"

I laughed. "Come on man you know I ain't going out like that at least, not this soon. But seriously, on Saturday he noticed my tattoo and asked me to price one for him. So, I'm picking up a copy of it today."

"*Hmm*...cause I was about to say—"

"Yeah well, I straightened it up so it doesn't matter what you were going to say, so dead it. Anyway, what about you, what did you do this weekend?"

"Nothing much, just went to the Warehouse Saturday with Dio."

I leaned back in my chair. "Word? So you guys had fun?"

"*Hmm*..." He said suspiciously. "Dio did."

I sat up. "Don't tell me he met someone!"

Dio'genes or *Dio* as we called him is the Editor-In-Chief of WARES, a men and women fashion magazine he created. Dio prided himself on his accomplishments, and always criticized me and Sean for placing relationships, before our careers. He felt nowadays, love was overrated, and chose his flourishing career over it. *"At least with work, you can see the benefits!"* He would argue. But, I always found his stand odd because he loved music—especially, sappy love songs! It was he who first introduced me to the likes of Will Downing and Dianne Reeves. There were days he would come by the house and we'd spend hours on end listening to Dianne and Will. He had every album both had ever recorded, and knew every word of every song. *"Still Pump-kin,"* he once commented, *"I wants no parts of the kids today!"*

"Now Jared," Sean said, "you know that niggah meets somebody every time he bats those fucking green eyes and loosens those dreads. But this time, he ran into some cat he used to talk to back in the day. All I know is his eyes lit up like a fucking Christmas tree when he saw him. Trust me when I tell you son, it was a *very* strange moment. I'd never seen him look so intensely at anyone, except of course when he was about to read their ass for points!" Sean said chuckling.

"Later that night," he continued, "when I was teasing him about how he was acting and shit he told me it wasn't no love thang. That they just used to kick it back in the days."

I was dumbfounded by Sean's report. It wasn't that I didn't think anyone would be interested in Dio, because he definitely had it going on. He was a cross between Allen Houston and Allen Payne, with deep green eyes, and shoulder length dreads. It's just Dio never showed interest in anyone! At least not romantically! Because, according to him no one was "*good enough*". Ever!

"Wow. So, you think it was serious?"

"Hell fucking yeah! You should have seen the way they embraced. It's like they *held onto* each other. I'm telling you I don't give a fuck what Dio says, I *know* there was something between those two. I could feel it."

"Damn', for real man? I can't believe it! Dio was actually moved by someone!"

"Believe it..." He said.

"You know, I always thought it was strange the way he put all his energy into his work. I mean—*come on*—I've heard of workaholics, but damn'! It's like Dio is married to his fucking job!"

"I've thought the same shit man. I really think somebody hurt his ass real bad before..."

"You're probably right. But, what about you, did you run into any old flames or meet any new ones?"

He sucked his teeth. "Man Jared I'm so fucking sick of these niggahs out here! It's like they're all losers—Grade A Certified MOTHER FUCKIN' LOSERS! Everyone I meet is either emotionally dependant, fucked up in the head, or fucking broke! What I wouldn't give to meet a MAN, instead of all these bitch ass niggahs. On the real Jay, this shit is stressing a niggah the fuck out! I'm telling you I'm about to give up on this shit in a minute!"

"Ah man, you can't give up. He's out there."

"Yeah well, I wish he'd hurry the fuck up! A niggah is getting tired as a motherfucka!"

Through the phone I heard someone barged into his office. He tried to cover the mouthpiece but I still heard everything he said. *"What the fuck do you want—didn't you see my door closed?"* He barked at the intruder. *"You must don't like your fucking job!"*

I laughed. Typical Sean. Of all my friends, I was probably most proud of him; particularly because of his career advancement in the music industry. When he first started out some year's back, he was an intern at a major hip-hop label. But with perseverance and hard work, he moved up the latter rather quickly. In less than three years, he was offered the VP of Publicity position at **HUNGRY AZZ NIGGER'S** Records.

Once I remember him telling me, *"Jared if you want something in life, I mean if you really want something, you have to sacrifice. Sometimes, it's going to be hard as hell…and people are going to put all types of shit in your way, but you've got to keep going man…even when you feel like giving up. I'm saying, look at me! If I could make it—a niggah straight out the fucking projects—anybody can!"*

Sean grew up in the heart of Fort Greene Brooklyn in the buildings just off Myrtle Avenue. He lived in the toughest neighborhood, and went to the toughest schools. He fought almost everyday of his life until finally his parents moved the family out of the housing projects and into a two-bedroom co-op in the Clinton Hill section of Brooklyn. It was there, another side of Sean was born—the rapper.

From the early age of 15 Sean aspired to be a rapper. He studied the best of them: *Rakim, KRS-1, Chuck D.* and yes, *LL Cool J.* Of them all L by far was his favorite. He rocked a *Kangol* like L, wore a fat ass rope like L, and yes, even licked his lips like L. Eventually, people started commenting on how strikingly similar he was to the hip-hop superstar. He loved the compliments, and always took them to heart. Somehow, they made him feel even more connected to L. But it wasn't until much later he discovered his admiration for L was much more than he had ever imagined.

On his nineteenth birthday, a couple of his friends took him to a concert with all the latest hip-hop acts, when a stunned audience was greeted to a surprise performance by the master himself LL Cool J. When he took the stage, the ladies went buck wild! From every corner of the Beacon Theatre, they emerged nearly trampling the fifty or so solidly built bodyguards protecting the superstar on stage.

The Theatre was pumping with the sounds of LL and *LeShaun's* mega hit, *"Doin it"*. L graced the stage like a professional, moving from one end to the other, never missing a beat or an opportunity to drive the star-struck females crazy. His name was being yelled by hundreds of horny women desperately trying to capture his attention.

"LL I Love You!"
"LL I want to have your baby!"
"LL! LL!"

Not a soul in the theater was seated. The power this man emitted excited Sean, in ways he never imagined. He watched his idol rock the house one verse at time. He watched as normally reserved looking females, who wouldn't, if their *lives* depended on it, sweat out their hair, throw themselves at the feet of this icon not at all embarrassed by the words they screamed, or the antics they exhibited.

That night, while he slept, he replayed LL's performance in his dreams. He imagined himself alone in the theater with L on stage performing, *"Doin it."*

He imagined L performing this song for him.

He imagined L, shirtless, sweating, dripping.

He watched as L licked his sensuous sculpted lips, making them moist and wet. He then watched as LL danced, and gyrated his hips as if he were indeed, *doing it*. He watched as L slowly reached into his sweats, and touched his shit. The next thing Sean knew, his body was pulsating, his sex spilling juices so forceful, so powerful so creamy he was suddenly awakened by an orgasm so *intense*, he yelled out L's name.

When he came to and realized what had happened, he sat stunned…lost for words…lost for emotions but more so, ashamed; ashamed of his feelings, ashamed, of his dream. Angry, he remembered.

He stopped listening to L. He stopped rapping. He stopped dreaming.

He started dating females with a vengeance, in hopes that one of them one day would quench the thirst he had acquired for men, but to no avail. Depressed, and nowhere else to turn, he took to weed and alcohol. His nights were a constant blur; his days spent recuperating.

Three years ago, after beating his girlfriend down in a drunken rage in the middle of Times Square, he sought help. And for the first time since that fateful night, he spoke about his dream with his therapist. He spoke of his fears. He spoke of the nightmares that followed. The feelings he could not control. The loneliness he felt and the pain in his heart. His therapist worked diligently for months to uncover all the issues weighing heavily on his soul and eventually, Sean began to understand. He wasn't a freak of nature. He wasn't a disease. He was actually a decent, normal, human being with something to offer the world. Weeks later for the first time, he let down his guard and experienced the longings his body desired. To his surprise he found peace in his life. Since then, he's grown comfortable with his sexuality. But still to this day, I can't help but think he lost a piece of himself that night in his room he'll never be able to reclaim.

"Yo son listen," he said returning to the line, "I've gotta go. There's a situation over here. It seems we have a pissed off artist on the line."

"Go ahead man, handle your business, I'm about to head out to lunch anyway."

"That's right, you're hooking up with shorty." He chuckled. "Don't worry he's down! But, call me later anyway and let me know how everything went."

I hung up the phone and checked my last e-mail. It was Kevin wishing me luck with Michael. I smiled, closed the e-mail, grabbed my coat and headed towards the elevator. As soon as I pressed the call button I was hit with a wave of nervousness. Was I really going by there? When the hell did I get so brave? I didn't know shit about this cat. Did I really want to play myself? What the fuck was wrong with me?

These thoughts haunted me until I stepped off elevator and into the cold. I buttoned my coat and threw caution to the wind. What did I have to worry about? This wasn't no *love* thang.

It was about a tattoo.

A simple ass tattoo...

BANANA REPUBLIC WAS BUSTLING WITH PEOPLE. Sales reps were scattered everywhere helping the throngs of shoppers who piled into the store during their lunch hour, all desperate to find a sale. I scanned the store for Michael, but soon realized he was nowhere in sight. *'Damn!'* I cursed. *'Maybe he went to lunch. I should have asked him what time was good for him before leaving Saturday.'* Slowly, my heart began to break at the thought of not seeing him. I'd done what I hated to do, gotten excited, and now the let down was coming on strong.

I was too embarrassed to ask any of the other sales reps if he had come to work that day. So, dejected I scanned the floor once more before finally giving up.

Walking down 42nd Street I cursed myself for getting so hyped. I knew this feeling all too well, and each time I experienced it, I promised never to do so again.

Love. Why was I searching so desperately for it? Why was it such an issue in my life? There was so much more I should've been, or could've been concerned about—besides, hadn't I learned from past experiences that love and relationships just didn't work, at least not in this lifestyle. Why couldn't I just accept the fact that I would most likely grow old alone? I mean sure, you have people in this lifestyle that have been in relationships for years. But there's nothing holding them there. At any point your partner of ten years could decide that this isn't for them, and leave. Then you have a lonely fifty-year-old man sitting at the end of a bar, at some punk club, looking for love—attention—somebody—*something*—*anything* to hold on to, desperate to recapture his life. I saw it every time I went out. And the truth is, I never wanted to be that man. I knew there was somebody out there for me. There had to be. And so, I couldn't give up. I *had* to keep searching.

After walking and thinking for about a half-hour, something urged me to walk back past the store. At first I resisted, but eventually gave into my hearts desire to see Michael again. When I entered the store the second time the pace had settled considerably, which allowed me to notice him immediately. He was in the women's section helping a young lady with her selections. He was as beautiful then, as he had been on Saturday, if not more. He wore a gray button-up stretch shirt that showed off his chest, with black trousers that fit his ass just right. His rich flawless cocoa skin radiated under the track lights. My heart fluttered when he looked up, smiled that smile, and mouthed the words, *'one moment'*.

Instantly my sex began to stiffen. Damn'! Why'd he have to move his lips like that? It was as if he was beckoning to be kissed. I turned and began browsing through a rack of shirts as not to stand there with a semi, staring lustfully at him.

Before I knew it, the vultures had surrounded me.

"May I help you find your size?" The chipper red-haired sales lady asked.

"No thank you, I'm just looking right now." I said and noticed Michael walking towards me.

"Jared! It's so good to see you man!" He said extending his hand. "I thought you had forgotten about me?"

"Forget about you—*shit*—I could barely get you off my mind!"

That's what I wanted to say, but instead I smiled, and settled on a less direct approach, "Nah man, I couldn't do that. I'm a man of my word." I said as the warmth of our hands collided.

"I see." He said warmly. Our eyes met and locked. And for just a split second, it was as if I were seeing my future all at once. I saw the house, the car, the kids—okay, maybe not the kids but you get the picture. I saw my life. Feeling the heat, he quickly released my hand. "Um, I," he stammered, blushing. "I got that copy for you in the back. Give me a second and I'll get it for you."

"Copy?" I said still lost in his smile. Damn' this man was fine!

"Yeah..." He said raising his left brow. "Remember, the copy of the tattoo I asked you to price for me?"

"Yeah! Yeah! The tattoo!" I said nervously as tiny beads of sweat began forming. *'Asshole!'* I cursed myself, *'How could you fuck up like that! You came here for the tattoo! Now get your shit together!* "I didn't forget, it's just—man you gotta excuse me." I found a napkin in my coat and wiped my head. "I haven't had lunch yet, and my brain is on E!"

"Ah don't worry 'bout it man, that shit happens to me all the time. Hold on, I'll get the," he paused, then smiled, "*tattoo* for you."

"Alright, alright..." I smiled bashfully, "enough of the jokes..."

"I'm just playing. Hold on, I'll be right back."

No sooner than he had disappeared did the vultures return and slowly move in for the kill. The first one spoke.

"May I help you sir!"

"No thank you." I offered calmly.

The next one spoke, "Good Afternoon sir, but would you be interested in applying for the Banana Republic credit card?" He asked, as his eyes traveled my body, paused momentarily at my crotch, and without skipping a beat, returned to my face. He seemed impressed.

"No thank you. I'm fine." I offered politely, and attempted to walk away.

"Are you sure?" He growled, his eyes returning to my crotch. "I mean cause, uh, you get ten percent off your purchase today if you're approved..."

Annoyed that he would stare so hungrily at my dick in a public place, I snapped, "Did you not just hear me say no, or are you that hungry for some?!"

Just as he was about to answer and I was about to reach out and grab his skinny ass, Michael returned and grabbed my arm.

"Yo, let's step outside for a minute." He chuckled. Once through the doors, he turned and laughed, "I'm sorry about that. I hope he didn't say anything too harsh to you. That guy has a wicked tongue."

"Yeah well, I've got a wicked uppercut!" I said buttoning my coat against the wind.

"Relax," he said handing me a piece of paper, "and check this out..."

"Ah man, this is sweet!" I said studying the tattoo. "Where'd you get it from?"

"I had this lady design it for me. It's a combination of African symbols found on, I think its Adika—Adrinca—"

"Adinkra Cloth?" I laughed.

He smiled. "Yeah, that's it Adinkra Cloth. It's from Ghana."

"Michael this is really nice. What does it mean?"

"Well, like I said, it's a combination of symbols. Each one has a different meaning. I don't really remember what each one means separately, but collectively, I call it Determination."

"Determination. I like that." I said studying the piece. "Don't be surprised if I get this before you, this shit is hot!"

A frightened smirk graced his face. "You're kidding right?"

I laughed. "Of course I am. I wouldn't do that to you. If anything, I'll wait until after you get yours, then..." I shrugged, "I don't know, a brutha may just have to bite."

He smiled, "After I can deal with," and let out a relieved laugh. "But seriously, from the looks of it, how much do you think your boy's gonna charge?"

I studied the piece closely before answering, as if what I was about to say was law. Truthfully I had no idea what he would charge. But shit, what the hell: "Guessing, I'd say a hundred to hundred and fifty dollars."

His excitement overtook him. "Ah man! That'll be great if I could get it even close to that!"

"Yeah but," I said folding the paper and stuffing it in my pocket. "I'll check it out and let you know for sure."

"Cool," he said, then licked his lips. "Listen, wait right here. I wanna give you something, before you go."

He turned and disappeared into the store. When he returned he handed me a business card. "On the front," he pointed, "is the number here to the store. And on the back, I wrote my home number. I live alone so, you can call me anytime. It doesn't matter."

"Cool." I said beaming.

"Then I'll speak to you soon?" He asked extending his hand.

"Definitely," I said, grasping it firmly, "without a doubt."

I FLOATED BACK TO THE OFFICE, lost in the world of Possibilities. Having met with Michael the sky seemed brighter, people happier, and the world a better place to live. When I reached my desk my whole being was radiating from the experience.

"What the *hell* did you have for lunch?" Vicky asked surveying my big kool-aid smile.

"He must have met some chicken head out there in the street!" Lisa chimed in.

"Why are you two *always* in my business?" I asked barely able to contain my excitement. "Can't a brother be happy once in a while without being frisked?"

"No!" Jordan said standing to see what was going on. "Not unless he's dating me!"

"In that case he'd want to get *frisked*, *locked up*, and *put to death*!" Lisa said laughing in her usual high pitched tone.

"*Shhh...*" I whispered trying to contain both Lisa's laughter and now my own. "You know if John hears us he's going to run out of his office to see what's going on."

"Now Lisa..." Jordan said with both hands on her curvaceous hips, "what man *you know*, wouldn't want me? *Especially* with a figure as sleek as this?"

"I can name a few!" Vicky said raising her hand.

"Well, nobody asked you!" Jordan said snapping her fingers. "And for the record, I wouldn't want any of the men you know anyway!"

"You two are so crazy..." I said spinning in my chair.

"So why are you so happy?" Lisa grilled. "It ain't payday, and it doesn't look like you went shopping."

I smiled as she searched my cubicle as if therein lied the evidence. "You won't find anything." I said. "I'm happy today simply because the sun is shinning, I have good health and I'm surrounded by good friends!"

"Oh Lawd!" Vicky moaned throwing her hands in the air.

"Cut the bull Covington!" Jordan barked.

"I'm serious, no bullshit. Life is good for me right now."

"Yeah well, I still think it's about some woman." Lisa said folding her arms. "Every time you *think* you're in love you get that *same* look in your eye."

"*What look?*" I asked shocked. If there was a look, it was definitely news to me.

"That look!" She pointed. "Like you've floated from where ever you were, here."

"Yeah...Lisa's right." Jordan agreed. "You get that look—then you go out and spend your entire paycheck!"

"Lawd...why can't I meet a man like you?" Vicky said shaking her head. "All the ones I meet are always asking *me* to borrow *'a few dollars'*."

"That's *precisely* why I don't want to meet any of the men you know!" Jordan scoffed.

"Vicky please, *you know* you don't want no man." Lisa said.

"How you figure?" She asked curious, both her eyebrows raised.

"Because," Lisa said, "you're always doing for yourself. And you know you have to play on a man's ego. You have to make him *think* he's doing something for you so he could feel useful—needed. But you..." she paused, eyeballing her pupil, "you do everything yourself. And you know damn' well a man's not going to hang around feeling unneeded."

"Ain't that the truth!" Jordan sneered. "They're just like a bunch of puppies—always needing attention!"

Vicky rolled her eyes. "Well, if he can't find something to do with himself, then I don't need him in the first place!"

"I hear you girl!" Jordan said slapping her five. "Ain't nothing like a tired shiftless man sitting around looking dumb! That's why I make sure my men, do *everything* a man's *supposed* to do!"

"*Supposed* to do?!" I bellowed. "What's he *supposed* to do?"

37

"For starters, take me out to dinner. Open the door. Propose. Buy me a house, and feed my kids!" She said, counting each characteristic on her fingers.

I shook my head knowing she was dead serious. "You have some serious issues woman. Some serious issues. And what may I ask are you giving him in return?"

"Everything a wife's supposed to give! Trust me when I tell you, my man won't have to want for a *thing*! Of course now, I plan to keep my job—because a sister has *got* to have her own source of income nowadays. But as far as everything else is concerned, I'll make sure the house is maintained, he and my kids will be well taken care of—food and clothing wise and, I plan to keep a *home. Not* a house—a *home*! There is a difference."

"What's the difference?" Lisa asked.

Jordan narrowed her eyes in thoughtfulness. "A home is full of love. A home is where you come after a long trying day of work—*or school*—and feel completely comfortable, peaceful. A home is where you can talk to anybody about anything. No matter the topic."

Vicky laughed. "Well, I guess none of us was raised in a home then!"

"I guess not." I added, thinking of all the times growing up how I wished I could've talked to somebody—anybody about what was going on in my head.

"Some of that I can relate to," Lisa admitted, "but some I can't."

"Well, it's really not that hard to get if you think about it…" Jordan reasoned. "I just want to make sure my husband and children feel special when they walk through the doors of our home. That's important to me. So, every night when I tuck my daughter into bed, I make sure I kiss her on the forehead and tell her how much I love her, no matter what. That way, she'll *never* have to wonder."

"I remember when I use to tuck my son in," Vicky sighed softly, "but then the day came when he told me, '*Mommy I'm a big boy now, I can do it myself*'. It hurt like hell. I guess because I felt I had lost a part of him I'd never be able to get back. But at the same time, it was good to see him growing up and becoming a young-man."

"Let me ask you guys something…" I asked motivated by the conversation. "Do you believe in love at first sight?"

Lisa jumped to her feet. "Ah-Ha!" She pointed. "See! *I told you* it was about some chicken head! All right out with it J.C.! Where'd you meet this one?!"

I stared at her in utter disbelief. "First of all, I told you before I don't mess with chicken heads! And *further* more, it was a general question. Something I was simply thinking—"

"I don't believe in it." Vicky answered. "I have to see where and how you live first, and then maybe—"

"Girl please!" Lisa snapped. "All that ain't necessary! You mean to tell me you've never been walking down the street and bumped into a *phine ass* man and thought, *'Damn' I could love you!*"

"Hell no!" Vicky yelled.

"Lisa, all that walking down the street stuff is for *dreamers* like you and Covington." Jordan interjected. "And for probably the first time in history—*somebody please make a note of this*—I completely agree with Vicky. Nowadays, you have to know *something* about a person before you start falling head over heels for them. *Especially* when you have children.

"For example, let's say you fall for someone. You know he's feeling you, and you're feeling him, and then he finds out you have children, and because of this, all of a sudden, he doesn't want to get serious anymore. What do you do then?"

"Well see first off I can't relate to that question, because I don't have children." Lisa said. "But if I did, I would've mentioned that from Jump Street. Still, kids or no kids, nothing should hinder one's ability to fall in love instantly. That's just an excuse. People are always trying to attach rules to love when there are no rules. If its one thing I've learned, choosing *who* you fall in love with is not an option."

"So you're saying you believe in love at first sight?" I asked.

"Yeah I do. When I met Emanuel, I knew immediately I'd love him. I hadn't been involved seriously with anyone for years. But all it took was one look..." Lisa smiled, "and the rest was history."

"*Well,* you should have looked twice!" Jordan sneered.

"What's that suppose to mean?" Lisa asked visibly annoyed.

"Lisa, you know what it means." Jordan spit. "You and Emanuel have the strangest relationship! How could you be with someone for over three years and still not have a commitment? And to make matters worse, still refer to each other as friends! Come on! But, *I'm sorry girl*, it makes no sense!"

Lisa nodded her head considering Jordan's words. Then, without a hint of malice she folded her arms across her breast and spoke. "Opinion noted, but contrary to what you may believe Jordan, my relationship does not require your stamp of approval. When Emanuel and I first met, I approached our relationship from a whole different perspective entirely. In all my prior relationships, I basically dictated the course of the relationship. As a woman, I decided *when* we went out for the first time, *when* we kissed for the first time, and *when* we made love for the first time. You know," she paused, pulling us all in, "all the things women control—*oops*—I mean, determine today. Well, with Emanuel, I made the decision to give up my need to always be in control and allowed him as the man, to dictate the course of our relationship. And so far, it's working."

Jordan sucked her teeth. "Yeah well still, I think it's strange. I'm saying, three years Lisa? And still *just* friends?" She shook her head. "But you're right girl, it is your relationship."

"So Lisa, are you happy?" I asked.

She tilted her head. "*Over all?* Yes. Of course deep down I wish we could change the title from *"friends"* to *"lovers"*, but what are titles anyway? Say we change it; will that make him love me any more? I doubt it. Let's just say I'm content in knowing he's the only man I'm sleeping with, and I the only woman he's sleeping with."

Vicky's eyes lit up. "Humph. You seem mighty confident with that last statement chile…"

"I know right!" Jordan laughed. "Girl you don't know *what* that man does when you ain't around!"

Lisa nodded. "True. But I can't spend my time worrying about that now can I?"

"I guess you're right." Jordan said half-heartedly. "But again, it is your relationship, and, if it works for you, and you're happy, I'm happy."

"Thank you." Lisa said right as my phone began ringing. "Uh-oh!" She laughed. "There goes the hot-line! Must be that new chick-chick-chicken head!"

"Covington. Why does your phone always seem to ring every time we're in the middle of a good conversation?" Jordan asked annoyed.

"I don't know; it's not like I plan it that way." I said reaching for the receiver. "Jared Covington. How may I help you?"

"Yes. I have some papers over here I need you to—"

"Hey Jason, what's up man?"

"Nothing, working hard as usual. What's up with you babe?"

"The same, nothing. Over here talking to a few of my co-workers and, thinking about Wednesday." I leaned back in my chair. "I read some of her reviews yesterday, they seem pretty good. Are you ready?"

"*Am I ready?!* Man, I've been telling everyone I know—*and don't know*—I have front row seats! I know she's gonna kill it Thursday!"

"Yeah I know. I still can't believe I scored those tickets. But you just make sure you show up on time or I may have your backup take your place!"

Jason had an awful habit of showing up thirty to forty-five minutes after our scheduled arrival time. That little quirk *irked* my last nerve.

"Oh don't worry, I'll be there! A brother is excited. Anyway, how's your day going?"

"It's going okay, nothing special." I lied.

"Really?" He replied. "They must not be working you hard enough over there?"

I laughed. "Not to worry, they're working me just fine!"

"Good. How was lunch?"

A flash of Michael popped in my head. "Interesting..." I said smiling.

"Really?" He laughed. "The chicken was that good?"

I laughed. "Nah, nothing like that."

"So what was it? Or do you not want to talk about it?"

I hesitated. "Not really. But, question: I thought you said you were going to call me back last night?"

"Oh, my bad. Herman stopped by unexpectedly, and we sort of kicked it for a while. And by the time I took him home, and got back, I was exhausted, so I went straight to bed. Sorry about that."

"Nah, don't worry about it. I was just curious that's all." I said trying my best not to sound annoyed. I hated that. Why leave a message, saying you're going to call, and you never do! If you're not going to call, don't say you are. And then again, there was Herman ruining my fucking relationship! No wonder Jason couldn't focus on me; Herman kept blocking his fucking view!

"You didn't wait up did you?"

Wait up? Wait up?! Who the fuck did he think he was? *Larenz Tate?* Like I was going to lose sleep waiting for his dumb ass to call! Please...

"No, not at all. I fell asleep around ten, ten thirty."

"I figured so," he said, totally oblivious to my budding anger, "that's why I didn't bother to call back when I got in."

"Like I said no problem. But listen, I've got to go. I have people at my desk." I lied.

"Alright then. So, I'll talk to you later?"

"Yeah, whatever, I gotta go." I mumbled and hung up the phone.

I could see it happening. We were unraveling, slowly, but surely. The sad part was he probably didn't even care enough to notice. I needed more from a partner, and if he wasn't willing to give it freely, I wasn't about to ask for it. And, like my cousin warned, by the time he realized what was going on, I would be long gone.

LATER THAT NIGHT after ascending the four flights to my apartment, sleep weighed heavy on my mind, though I knew it was completely out of the question. There were bills to write, phone calls to make and at least a forty-five minute run on the treadmill.

When I entered the living room, my answering machine blinked indicating two new messages. I hit the play button and flopped on the sofa.

Message 1
"Jared! What's up this is Dio! Sean tells me you met some boy working in a store! A Banana Republic at that! I hope that's not true darling because, I'm constantly trying to uplift this family, and you kids are constantly dragging it down! I don't know what I'm going to do with you...anyway *sweety*, hollah at me when you get this message. We need to talk."

Message 2
"What's up pussy mama? This is Kevin. When you get this message you <u>better</u> call me back girl! And don't have me waiting up all night to find out what happened with you and Michael today!"

Exhausted, I decided to call them both later. I needed to gather some major energy before I spoke to either one of them. Trust me when I tell you, you needed energy when speaking to those two. Instead, I fixed myself a drink, settled into the sofa and browsed through the day's mail. I got through two before I blacked out. An hour later, I was awakened by the incessant sound of the telephone ringing.

"Hello?" I yawned.

"Did you get my message or have you chose to ignore it?"

I stretched. "You mean the one you left *trying* to let me have it in?"

"*Trying, Pump-kin!?* Diogenes does not try! If anything *Sweety* you let yourself have it!"

"What's that suppose to mean?"

"It means, how could you go shopping and pick up the *"man"* bagging your garments honey? That's like me asking the *"boy"* bagging my groceries at the supermarket out! Haven't you learned *anything* from me?" He moaned dramatically. "Has *all* my teachings been in vain?"

Dio was love, pretentious, but love, ostentatious, but love, over-dramatic, but love. I knew he was only looking out for my best interests. As usual, he was probably thinking of the countless times I complained of spending money on guys who couldn't afford to do the same for me. But it's not like I expected anything in return when I gave gifts or offered to treat. It was just in my nature. The problem: it seemed no one else shared my unique trait.

"Listen Dio, I feel you, but you know I could careless what someone does for a living. As long as they have a job and can provide for themselves, it's all good to me."

"*Soooooo* young, *soooooo* naïve," he moaned. "Haven't you learned how the kids operate yet? Or are you not at all concerned about their tactics?" He paused, allowing his words to settle. "Once they see you're handling, they latch on like a leech, and suck as many coins as they can from you. Why do you think I tell half of the girls I'm a struggling artist, and the others, I'm a freelance photographer? If half those bitches knew I was the CEO of WARES, honey, I'd have to beat they're grimy hands out of my pockets!"

"Dio, first of all, I'm not handling like you! And if I were, I'd watch my back too. But, come on, not everybody's out to get paid!"

"You keep walking around with blinders on if you want to *Pump-kin*! These young kids nowadays ain't trying work. All they want to do is sleep all day and party all night! And each time they go out, they make it their business to scan the clubs for trade with money. Once they find you, watch out! Next thing you know they're asking for jeans and sneakers! Then *Prada* this and *Gucci* that! And then," he huffed, "when they've really reeled you in, it's—*I need a hundred dollars to hang out with my friends tonight, or, I saw this really hot coat at Barney's today!*"

The tension in his voice caused me to burst out laughing. "Yo Man! What's the matter with you?! Why you tripping? You need a hug or something?!"

"*Pump-kin* you're the one that needs the hug! Out there picking up them kids in *bargain basement* stores! *Have things really gotten that bad?* Next thing I know, you'll be as bad as Sean picking up children on AOL!"

I laughed so hard I started to cry. "Now you know I ain't that desperate—*damn' niggah*—you are one vicious bitch!"

"I keep telling you and Sean about trying to come for me *Pump-kin*! Remember I'm *legendary—from* the old school. Ya'll young bitches don't want none!"

"You're right..." I managed, having finally pulled myself together. "So listen, Sean tells me you ran into an old boyfriend this weekend. What's up with that?"

He sucked his teeth. "You know, that bitch kills me always telling other folks business. I don't know who's worse, you with your questions, or him with his gossip!"

"Anyway, is it true?"

An unnerving silence filled the lines. Dio was not one to discuss his personal life. He thrived on the business of others, but kept his strictly confidential.

"No," he finally answered, "I wouldn't call him a boyfriend. An acquaintance maybe, but definitely not a boyfriend. We used to talk briefly some years ago but it wasn't serious."

"How long is brief?"

"About three months or—*my aren't we nosey?*"

"Not nosey. Curious. Aren't friends supposed to discuss each other's lives?"

"I see." He paused. "Friends. Then, why—if you don't mind—*friend,* are you suddenly after all these years, so interested in my personal life?"

"First of all, it's not all of sudden. As a matter of fact, I've waited patiently for years for you to share pieces of your life with me, yet you haven't. Besides, I just wanna know 'cause, Sean said you guys kind of *"held onto each other"*, when you hugged; and that there was some kind of, *"chemistry"* between you two. At first I couldn't believe it, because I've never seen or heard of you even remotely connected to anyone on that level!"

He was quiet. Uncharacteristically quiet. So quiet, that for a brief moment I thought he had hung up. "That bitch told you everything didn't he?" He asked in disbelief. "I don't believe this. He is one gossiping son of a bitch!"

"Dio you know Sean didn't mean any harm in telling me. But now, I'm sensing maybe he was right. Was there a connection?" I pushed, hoping he'd cave in and tell me.

Several moments elapsed before he spoke.

"I *guess* you can say there was a connection." He sighed heavily. "We use to talk back when I was a fashion stylist—a long, long time ago darling, way before all the glitz and glam you know today. I met him at a photo shoot for some hip-hop clothing line account I had at the time. There were so many, I can't really remember which one exactly. But anyway he was one of the models.

"I'll never forget the day we met. I had had a *dreadful* morning. One of those days when nothing seemed to go right: I couldn't find my keys, couldn't catch a cab, and by the time I *finally* made it to the set, half the models, including my assistant were late. Then, *Miles* walked in. He had the kind of smile Jared that could light up any room. He marched right up to me, shook my hand, and said: *"It's such a pleasure to be working with you Diogenes! When my agent told me you were styling this shoot, I got so excited!"* He said, gripping my hand firmly. *"This really is an honor!"*

"Wow! Thank you!" I said fully absorbing his statuesque six feet curly haired frame. Jared, the man was beautiful. By far the most beautiful man I had *ever* laid eyes on. Everything was on point! His eyes were a

44

haunting chestnut brown, with eyebrows so thick and masculine, they seemed painted on. His complexion was a light caramel with just a hint, of a summer's tan. And his sideburns and goatee were trimmed to perfection. I was stunned—which doesn't happen often—by his beauty. "And you would be?" I asked, catching my breath.

"Oh I'm sorry. My name is Miles, Miles Coleman."

"Well Miles, it's great to meet you." I said staring into his perfect mouth. "It's obvious you're familiar with my work."

He nodded. "I am. I've followed you—I mean—your work for some time now. Plus, you've styled a few of my friends who model, and can I tell you, you work miracles!"

"Thank you. Thank you." I said trying my best not to blush. I couldn't let this guy know he was getting to me—after all, I was Diogenes!

He smiled, I imagine aware he was reeling me in. "Your style..." He continued, "comes across so fresh—so clean—so new! A lot of stylists go for what's hot. It's like they're afraid to take risks. *But not you!*" He said sizing me up. "You're out there *creating style* as oppose to *mimicking* current trends."

This guy was good! I was smiling my ass off basking in his compliments. "That's pretty much what pushed me into the business." I admitted. "I wanted to give the fashion world something it was lacking, something new." I paused, still taking in his beauty. "But often times, when you're a rebel like myself compliments are few and far between, so believe me my friend this is a welcomed surprise."

"You deserve it." He said staring deep into my green eyes, and, after a few heated uncomfortable moments, continued. "But, anyway, here I am late, and running my mouth. Where should I change?" He asked surveying the set.

"The dressing rooms are in the back." I replied. "Check with my assistant Neale, he should be back there by now—*I hope*, and should have everything set up for you. Your agent did call in your sizes right?"

"Yes. He's pretty reliable so, I'm sure he took care of all the details."

"Great! Then you should be all set! I'll see you in a minute."

When he turned and walked away Jared, my heart screamed! AHHHHHHHHHHHH! This boy had it going on! He was confident, well spoken and, *obviously recognized talent when he saw it!* After the shoot he asked if I'd like to join him for a bite to eat and I consented.

We went to the Soul Café and enjoyed cocktails while waiting for a table. The women by the bar, obviously taken by the beauty we exhibited, couldn't figure out which one of us to stare at. Whenever one made it obvious she desired conversation I'd look the other way, but to no avail.

Honestly, I don't know what it is about women and their inability to be ignored? My cold shoulder somehow always, in some strange way, made me more desirable to them. They stared. I ignored. Eventually, with mega shade, and a few flicks of my wrist, they got the hint: I was not to be bothered.

When we were finally seated we must have hit on every topic imaginable. I guess you could say we just sort of clicked. Then out of nowhere he said, "I hope I'm not being too presumptuous by asking this, but, are you seeing anyone?"

I hesitated. "Presumptuous no; but, might I ask where this is coming form?" I said curiously perched, while waiting for his reply.

He smiled bashfully. "Forgive me if I'm prying, but it's just, well, uh, at the bar, all of those ladies were checking you out, and you, well, you barely even noticed them."

Jared I gagged! I didn't know what to think! So naturally I thought the worse. Did he think I wanted him—I mean yeah he was beautiful—but how dare he! He had invited me out! I could see if it had been the other way around! *Pump-kin* I was just about to light into him and let him know, it was none of his *damn* business what my sexual preference was, when it hit me. When we were perched at the bar sipping our cocktails, I didn't see him checking out any of those young ladies either.

They gawked.

He ignored.

What was his excuse?

I tilted my head ever so slightly, "Well," I said rather boldly, "If my memory serves me correct, you didn't seem to notice them that much yourself."

He leaned his head back and laughed long and hard. Some of the restaurants other patrons looked in our direction trying to figure out what was so funny. Wondering the same thing, I too stared at him in disbelief. Had I made a joke? If so, when did he plan to let me in on it? Annoyed, I sat back in my chair and sipped my drink. At the exact same time he leaned forward and whispered, "That's because I don't date women."

Pump-kin, I spit that martini all over that table! He jumped back narrowly missing my accident then jokingly asked: "Are you okay?" Embarrassed, I assured him I was, then proceeded to tell him the reason I disregarded the women at the bar was because, I didn't *do fish* either. And for a moment that seemed to stretch on forever, we shared a gaze that could have moved mountains. Afterwards our conversation went even deeper.

Later that night after filling ourselves on countless apple martinis, we strolled back to his hotel on Lexington Avenue. Once in the lobby he smiled seductively.

"Would you like to come up for a night-cap?" He asked swaying back and forth.

"I—I don't know about that…model man." I laughed.

He hiccupped, "Why not? I promise to be on my best behavior." He raised his right hand. "Scouts honor."

I swayed. "That's what I'm afraid of."

He laughed and grabbed my arm. "Come on man. One more drink, then I'll call a car for you."

We never had that drink. It began in the elevator. A kiss. A feel. Before we knew it, we were groping each other like madmen as we traveled the floors. When the doors opened, an older white couple watched in horror as we exited the car with pulsating erections. Both recoiled and threw their heads in the air in disgust. Unashamed, we walked quickly by them to his room. Once inside the loving making commenced.

He placed his bag in the closet, told me to make myself comfortable then entered the bathroom. I made my way to the oversized windows and peered into the night. The Manhattan skyline had never looked so beautiful. From where I stood, I could make out the top of the Empire State building, all lit up in red. I smiled, the color of love. I had never been there, and for some years managed to avoid its lure. But tonight for some reason *love* danced in my soul. And as I gazed out into the night, I silently wondered, *could he be the one for me?*

Seconds later I felt his warm hands wrap my waist and his lips gently grazing my neck. His pelvis, hard and firm, pressed strategically against my hips. I closed my eyes and imagined us together this way forever.

Was this love?

He turned me, and filled my mouth with his tongue. I allowed him to explore it freely, and for the first time in my life tasted love. Suddenly without warning he stopped, walked towards the desk, and placed a CD in the stereo. He grabbed my hand and led me to a chair in the corner of the room. There he stood before me and began seductively unbuttoning his shirt. I watched in amazement as bit by bit, his flesh was revealed to me. My heart pumped faster than normal and I knew for sure, it would give way to its desire to love this man. While Luther Vandross, and Cheryl Lynn crooned, *"If this world were mine"*, Miles stripped. It wasn't long before he stood before me as naked as the day he was born into this world, only I imagined, more beautiful. I walked to him and allowed my fingers trace the curves of his body. Beautiful, is the only word that best describes the sight. His arms, chest, legs, and ass: all beautiful. I grabbed his sex, and watched as his lips quivered and released a low powerful sigh filled with delight.

"I prepared a bath for you." He whispered. "Shall we?"

I removed my clothes and followed him. I was surprised to find several scented candles burning through the haze of steam. He was a true romantic. I eased my body slowly into the warm water and relaxed as he took to bathing every inch of my body. I returned the favor. Fifteen minutes later, fully showered and refreshed, we returned to the room.

Joe's, *"All the things your man won't do…"* filled the air. And to this song, we created the most loving erotic video imaginable. We pleasured each other one by one. He led. I led. He gave. I gave. There was no awkwardness to our rhythm, or hesitations in our positions. At the time, I wasn't use to this type of love making so it wasn't long before I exploded something wonderful. He followed. Afterwards, we lay there lost in the after glow of satisfying love.

He lit up. "You're wonderful, you know that right."

"I aim to please."

"You please very well." He coughed, exhaling the sweet smells of marijuana.

We both laughed.

"Do you always smoke after sex?" I asked, taking a drag.

He propped his head on his arm. "Only when it's good; you should feel honored."

I smiled. "I do."

"Good." He said flashing those perfect teeth. "Let's get showered. We've got a lot of weed left."

That was the beginning of the end. I fell in love with him Jared. I did. It was the first time anyone made me feel whole…complete… special…"

"What happened to you two?" I asked stunned.

"You know how the industry is *Pump-kin*," he said, as his cell phone began breaking up, "are you still there?"

"Yeah…I'm here." I said hanging onto his every word. "Go ahead."

"Like I was saying, you know how the industry is, busy as hell. I was flying from coast to coast from gig to gig, and he was doing the same modeling. It just so happened we were hardly on the same coast at the same time. We each had telephone bills amounting to six, seven hundred dollars a month easy. Still, distance can kill a relationship. You can't get that hug you need over the phone, never mind anything else. So one day after not seeing each other for about a month, we accepted the truth. Time and space were keeping us from making it work, and so, we said our goodbyes and sort of lost contact over the years."

"Damn' man! Why you never shared this with me before?" I asked annoyed.

"Because you never asked."

"Okay bitch," I said sarcastically, "how am I supposed to ask about something I know nothing about?"

"Jared you should know me by now darling, I don't run around telling folks my business. It's all on a need to know basis. And when you *need to know Pump-kin*, I'll tell you." He said laughing.

"Ha, ha, ha. Always the jokester aren't you? You know what I mean! I always thought you didn't believe in love, or relationships."

"*Sweety*, I don't know where you got that idea from! I believe in love. I always have and I always will. But what I do not believe in is all the shit the kids go through nowadays to be *in* love. Besides, half the men out there ain't about shit anyway, and, the ones that are, are straight, married, or involved! And trust *Pump-kin*, I'm not about to lose my mind over them!"

"Whatever. I'm out there, and I don't fall into any of those categories."

"You *Pump-kin* are a rare exception to the rule. Remember, with all things in life, a few exceptions are allowed."

"True. So tell me, have you seen Miles since Saturday?"

"You don't stop do you?" He asked in an exasperated huff. "Always the little reporter!"

"Come on man—have you?"

"Yes I have!" He bellowed. *"Why are you so concerned?"*

"Because I love you, and I'm happy for you!"

"Well there is simply no need to get all giddy *Pump-kin*, because this ain't no love thang, and I'm not falling. I have too much on my plate right now to the point there's absolutely no room for love. It's simply not an option."

I laughed. "You'll be surprised my man, what happens when your heart begins to speak, you may not be able to shut it up."

He scoffed. "Trust and believe darling, as sure as my name is *Diogenes,* I will not be falling!"

"Okay," I relented, "but at least relish the moment…"

"Oh trust darling I will, but listen, I have to go. I've reached my destination. I'll talk to you later. And oh Jared…"

"What?"

"Lose the store boy! If you need assistance finding someone *suitable* darling, just ask. I'll be more than happy to introduce you to a few of my former pieces!"

"Whatever Dio, you know I don't do leftovers!"

"Ha! That's not what I heard!" He laughed and hung up the phone.

I sat on my sofa blown away. I could not believe Dio had actually been in love. It all made sense now: the love songs, the evasiveness, the "no relationship" rule. This Miles must be some guy if he managed to snatch Dio's attention. Many had tried, but none were successful. The ones he did allow in, purely for entertainment purposes, he would drop without hesitation. If they sneezed wrong, they were dismissed. If they questioned his sincerity, they were dismissed. God forbid if one of them *ever* used the "L" word! War would commence!

Once, I watched as a young man cried desperately on his hands and knees for Dio to love him. Dio, unmoved by the theatrical gesture, stepped over the kid, walked to the door, held it open and demanded he get up and get out! The young man, pained and embarrassed retrieved his coat and left in a huff. Afterwards, I asked Dio how he could be so cold! Classic Dio replied, "Please chile, she's an actress! A tired one at that! No wonder she can't get a gig!" We both laughed. But now, after all these years the missing pieces of Dio's life was finally coming together, and I was convinced this Miles character would somehow complete the puzzle.

FOUR

Diogenes

WHEN I ENTERED MAROONS' I spotted him instantly. He was sitting patiently on one of the sofas sipping what appeared to be gin and tonic, while browsing through a magazine. As usual, he was dressed well in faded jeans, a chocolate brown suede shirt and the original beef and broccoli timberlands.

The years had treated him well. He was still a study in grace. When I approached him, I was surprised, and at the same time honored to discover it was my magazine he was reading.

"Great magazine," I commented, "read it often?"

Startled, he looked up and smiled. "Often enough. A very good friend of mine is the editor."

"Get out of here!" I joked, filling the vacancy beside him.

"It's true..." he smiled. "As a matter of fact," he squinted, "you kinda remind me of him. You both have the *finest* green eyes I've ever seen on a man."

His words perfectly timed as always, caused me to blush. As usual, he knew exactly what to say to throw me completely off guard. I laughed. "You're good you know that right?"

"Am I really?" He smiled seductively.

"You question my judgment?"

"Not at all, it's just one would think otherwise considering how long it's been."

I glanced at my watch purposely ignoring his last comment. It had been some time. "So, have I kept you waiting long?"

"No not really, I've been here about ten minutes."

"Good. I would've been here sooner but I was speaking to Jared. And once he gets to talking, you can't shut him up!"

"Jared..." he said considering the name. "Is he one of your friends?"

I smiled. "The best."

The host, a tall attractive dark skinned brother, approached us as we talked. "Excuse me gentlemen," He said politely, "but your table is ready."

We stood and followed him through the restaurant. Maroons' is by far one of my favorite eateries. It's small, cozy and extremely romantic. The menu is a combination of Southern and Caribbean cuisine, prepared with the love and dedication of a home cooked meal. The atmosphere is less stuffy than that of other black owned establishments, like *Justins*, *The Soul Café*, and *The Shark Bar*. Here, the ego is checked at the door, and people are allowed to be themselves.

Immediately, upon being seated, the waitress introduced herself, recited the specials of the night, and took our drink orders. Ten minutes later, she returned with our drinks, and asked whether or not we had decided on dinner. I nodded and ordered jerked chicken with plantains, rice & beans and steamed vegetables, while Miles had barbecued chicken, yams and macaroni and cheese.

"Would you gentlemen care for anything else?" She asked cordially.

"No thank you." Miles smiled warmly before turning his attention back to me.

"So, how was the show today?" I asked referring to the runway show he was in earlier.

He rolled his eyes in an exaggerated mock. "Hectic! I don't know how I've made it eight years in this profession! Modeling has got to be the most trying job in the world!"

"Yeah, but you love it." I said sipping my cocktail.

"I do some days, but then again, some days I don't. It all depends."

"On what?"

"The show, the designer, the models; most are professional, and that's cool. But it's that one unorganized, unprofessional son-of-a-bitch that drives me crazy!"

"So, what about acting?" I asked. "Have you gone on any auditions lately?"

He nodded. "Some. My agent claims he's busting his ass trying to get me a decent part every time we speak." He chuckled. "But he claims I'm too talented to play the typical black role."

I laughed. "What the hell is the *"typical black role"*?"

"You know, the crack head, the gangsta, the rapist—all the roles that stereotype us as the scum of the earth. And he's right. I don't want to get typecast. If I'm going to have a successful acting career, I need not start accepting those types of roles."

"That's understandable." I mouthed, just as the waitress returned with our food. After surveying the plates and nodding our approval, Miles reached over grabbed my hands and offered up a word of prayer.

"Most heavenly Father...I thank you today for life, health and strength. I thank you for everything you have done, and will do. I thank you for my family and friends. I ask that you keep your loving protective arms around them as they come and go. I ask that you fill their hearts and mind with love. I ask that you fill my heart and mind with love. Let me be an example, a light, so that I may show others how beautiful it is to know you. Keep me grounded in love, your love." He paused momentarily, sighed, and then gripped my hands tighter.

"Father God, I know all things happen for a reason and according to a divine plan. I know that you provide me with the very things I need to live, and I know that everything happens according to your plan. Just as I know, Dio has come back into my life to share with me all the beauty your love represents. I thank you Father for answering my prayer. I thank you for sending him back to me. But, not just that Lord, I thank you for all things, great and small. Bless this food we're about to eat. Let it provide nourishment to our bodies, as your word does for our soul. In your name I pray, Amen." He shook my hands smiled and said, "Enjoy your food."

I fought hard to hold back fear. To play it cool. But I couldn't help *but* panic and wonder whether or not I heard clearly. *Did he just thank God for sending me back to him? Why...what was that about?*

A nervous energy formed in my stomach as my head overflowed with question after question, thought after thought while Miles, sat calmly across from me savoring his meal, completely unaware of the war going on inside of my head.

Was he serious? How could he be? It's been years—a lot has changed. Does he think he can just pop back in my life and pick up where he left off, like he has it like that?! Well he doesn't! I can't—I'm not going to do this to myself! I'm not just going to let him come in and rock my world again! I have too much shit to think about right now—way too much!

"Dio are you alright?" He asked, noticing I had barely touched my food.

"Um, yeah, everything is, um, everything is fine." I lied. Nothing was fine.

Our eyes met. "Dio I know you. Something is bothering you, you're just not telling me."

"What do you mean?" I asked defensively. "I said I'm fine."

He pointed to my plate. "Then why have you barely touched your food?"

"Because um, I um..."

"Listen Dio, something's wrong I know it. You're one of the sharpest brothers I know. You're never lost for words, unless of course something's wrong." He replied knowingly. If anyone knew me, the real me, it was definitely Miles. "Plus," he continued, "whenever you start stuttering, I know something's troubling you. So what is it?"

He was right. Something was wrong, terribly wrong.

"Did you, mean what you said in your prayer?"

He paused somewhat puzzled. "Yes. I pray very honestly Dio, of course I meant it."

"Oh…" I said playing with my vegetables.

"Oh? Oh what Dio? What is this about?"

"Miles listen I just don't think I'm ready."

He shook his head. "Ready for what?"

"Ready for this relationship. Ready to rekindle this old flame." I grew angry. "Ready to get hurt again!"

By the look in his eyes, I could tell I had hurt him, not so much by what I said, but how it was said. Almost immediately I regretted it.

He sat back from the table. "Is that what you think?" He squinted. "Do you think I want to hurt you? Do you honestly think I'd do something like that to you?"

"Miles I didn't mean it like that—"

"Well then how did you mean it?!" He snapped as the first sign of tears glistened in his eyes. "Or rather, how am I supposed to take someone telling me they don't want to get hurt by me again?!"

"Miles, baby listen, I'm sorry. I didn't mean it that way, let me explain—"

"What is there to explain Dio? You think I'm going to hurt you, you just said it!"

I reached for his hand. "No, no, no, I phrased it wrong. I know you would never do anything intentionally to hurt me. It's just…" I paused, choosing my words carefully. "It's just these relationships I don't trust nowadays. They're so, well you know, superficial."

He snatched his hand away. "What does that have to do with me? Are you calling me superficial?"

"No Miles! I would never say that about you! You're so real…and beautiful…and," I didn't want to say it, but I couldn't help it. It just sort of slipped out. "Perfect."

The word felt strange falling from my lips. I felt it in my heart, but I had never said it aloud. Miles looked deep into my eyes and offered a thankful smile. My heart beat wildly. I loved him. I know I did…but I was scared. Scared of falling in love with him again, but more so, scared of losing him again.

"Dio, do you mean that?" He asked nervously, his eyes aglow. "Do you really think I'm perfect?"

"Yes." I admitted. "You are, in so many ways. You're the only person ever to capture my heart. And, you're the only person I've ever allowed this deep into my world. I remember the first day I met you on the set. As a matter of fact, I was just talking to Jared about it earlier. You were so beautiful, and you, you had this innocence about you that was

54

simply irresistible!" My voice fell to a whisper. "I fell in love with you that day."

His eyes lit up. "You did? You never told me that…"

"I know. I was too awestruck to tell you. I thought perhaps if I said something that night while we lay cuddled in bed, I would scare you off. And that's the last thing I wanted to do! So I kept it to myself."

I paused watching him internalize my words. Was this the feeling Jared was always talking about? Was this, true love?

"You were my first love Miles, my only love. And when we broke up I closed off that part of my life. I didn't want to love anybody else if I couldn't love you. I didn't want to cuddle, kiss or hold hands with anyone, if it wasn't with you. It meant nothing if it wasn't with you."

"Dio, I never knew you felt like this…I mean, you never returned any of my phone calls, or answered any of my letters after we broke up. Don't you remember we promised each other that we would keep in touch, and that we would not let anything or anyone come between us? What happened?"

The lines in my face hardened. "Fear. Jealousy. Anger. Choose one." I picked up my cocktail and sipped it slowly. "Miles, I never wanted to let you go." I said returning the glass to the table. "I never wanted it to end. And when it did, it cut deep. The thought of not seeing you again killed me. And then, it settled in just what breaking up meant: I couldn't hold you anymore, because someone else would be holding you! I couldn't whisper things in your ear, because someone else would be doing that! I grew jealous, angry, and bitter. I hated everyone and everything that reminded me of you. I wanted to forget you. I wanted to wash away all memories of you, and I did. I forgot about you, for years. That was the only way I was able to go on with my life. And it worked…" I paused, my heart thumping, "until I saw you last week at the club. Then, out of nowhere, it all came back. The memories, the feelings, the love—everything! Did you feel the intensity of our hug that night?"

"Yes Dio…I did."

"Did you see the tears in my eyes?"

"Yes Dio, I did."

"Those tears were for you Miles, because I love you, I always have and I always will. But I'm afraid that if I go too deep into this with you again I'm going to get hurt. And right now, honestly, I don't think I can handle that again. I love you Miles, but I love myself more."

He sat quietly. Staring off into space, his arms propped on the table holding his face. The waitress removed the plates and asked if we wanted dessert. We both declined, and instead, ordered another round of drinks. We sat silently until she returned. Miles sipped his then calmly spoke.

"Dio…when we first broke up, honestly, I thought it was best. We hardly saw each other, and when we did, it was for only a few hours at a time. You had your career, and I had mine. We were a lot younger then, and I guess we put everything else before each other." He paused, deep in thought. "Looking back over the years, I can honestly say that it was a mistake. It was stupid. But then we were young so, again I understand why we did it." He paused once more, allowing the silence to grow full and thick, and my imagination wild. "Dio I have loved others before you, and since you."

Defeated, I sank lower in my chair and stared sadly at the table.

"But," he continued, "I have never loved anyone, as much as I have loved you. Since we broke up, I have compared everyone—and I do mean everyone—to you. No one measured up. No one made my heart pitter patter the way it does when I'm with you. No one made me feel complete like when I was with you. No one. That's why when I saw you in the club last week I lost my composure. I held you so close, because I missed you so much! And believe me when I tell you, I didn't want to let you go…

"But, I don't want to cause you any confusion Dio, I really don't. I don't want you to feel like I'm coming back into your life to hurt you, because that's not why I'm here. I want to love you. I want to be with you. I really do." He paused and fiddled with his napkin for a long while. "Listen, I've had the chance to look at both sides now, life with you, and life without you. I know them both very well. But right here, right now, with your permission, I hope to choose life with you. I love you man, believe me I do."

I sighed heavily overwhelmed by the words he spoke. Words that both settled and alarmed my soul.

"How do we do this?" I whispered.

"I don't know…"

"Where do we start?"

He shrugged. "I don't know…"

"I'm scared."

"Me too." He said reaching for my hand. "Me too. Let's just take it one day at a time, and see what happens. We owe each other at least that."

I nodded my head in agreement, but inside there was a war going on. Do I let go and let love run its course? Or, do I bottle up my feelings, and lock them all inside?

Eventually, I'd have to make a decision.

FIVE

Jared

I HAD JUST FINISHED SEVEN POINT FIVE MILES on the treadmill when the telephone rang. I checked the caller ID. It was Kevin, and I was not in the mood to talk. While running, I thought about Jason. I thought about Michael. I hated one, and desired the other. I thought of ways to end my relationship with Jason, to be with Michael, but without hurting him. That angered me even more. *Why should I care about his feelings? Why should I even consider them? Had he fully considered my feelings—my emotions—while he entertained Herman?* I ran with furious pain-filled strides as my body dripped in sweat. I snatched the phone from its holder.

"Hello."

"What's up pussy mama? Didn't you get my message? Why didn't you return my call? Did I do something to you?" He rattled off, without taking a single breath.

"No Kevin, you didn't do anything, and I'm not upset with you." I said dryly.

"What's wrong with you?" He snapped, sensing the stillness in my voice. "I know you don't want me to come over there and beat that ass! Cause you know I will, so what's going on?"

"Nothing..." I lied. "I just finished exercising and I'm tired. What's up with you?"

"I was calling to see how things went with Michael today, since you didn't bother calling back like I asked you in my e-mail. Did you go by there?"

"Yeah...I did." I said nonchalantly.

"So?" He quizzed.

"So, what?" I snapped.

"So did you find out whether or not he's down bitch?!"

"No! I told you Sunday I wasn't going to stress it, if he is, he is. I'll find out when the time is right."

"Well alright bitch for having an attitude!" He barked into the phone. "What's really up with you!"

"Nothing!"

"Well you damn' sure ain't acting like it!"

"Forgive me *Queen Mother* for not acting the way you would have me to act, next time I promise to do better…"

"Whatever bitch, I forget your time of the month comes around sooner than the other girls. So how's Jason? Did you speak with him today?"

"Yeah, I did." I said bitterly recalling our conversation.

"Me too. He sounds excited about seeing Toni on Wednesday."

"Yeah, well I'm sure he'd be a lot happier if he and *Herman* were going!" I hissed.

"Whew bitch…you are on fire tonight! What was that about?"

"I'm just so sick of Jason and his bullshit! He's really starting to get to me."

"What did he do now…"

"It's what he didn't do, that's the problem this time. When I got home from my sister's last night, there was a message from him, indicating he was by his folks, and that once he got home he was going to call. But he didn't! So I paid it. But today, I asked what happened right, and he tells me Herman stopped by un-expectantly and they hung out. But wait, *that's not it!* He had the audacity to ask me if I waited up for him?"

"Did you?"

"Hell no! What the fuck do I look like? I don't wait up for anybody!"

He sucked his teeth. "I don't know what's up with Jason. Ever since he and Herman started hanging out he's been acting weird. He wasn't like this when I first met him. He was genuine, sincere—a man of his word. But it's like now he's all caught up in some make believe world with Herman filling up his head with all types of nonsense! Telling him how to act, what to wear, how to wear it—"

"Oh! And did I tell you he and Herman went shopping on Saturday too?"

"No. But I bet you Herman picked out two outfits for Jason, and one for him in every store they went to!" Kevin said with a mouth full of laughter.

"I said the exact same thing! As a matter of fact, I sent him an e-mail today asking him how Herman's *so called* job search was going."

"And what did he say?"

"Nothing. And he didn't mention anything about it when he called either. I guess that was his way of saying it was none of my business."

"Please, Herman's smart, he's never going to get a job as long as Jason's footing his bills."

"How about that? And why should he? Especially if someone's stupid enough to take care of him! Shit, I work too fucking hard to be supporting another adult—*especially* another grown ass man!" I said gazing out the window.

"I know what you mean girl...oooh, hold on one minute, someone's on my other line."

While on hold, I located Mary's *My Life* CD and placed it in the stereo. I thought about Jason and how great we could have been if only he was open and receptive. At one point, I was willing to place it all on the line for him *(And you know how difficult it is for a **man** to put it all on the line!).* But he had shown little interest in me, and what I had to offer. Some days I would sit for hours on end gazing out the window, contemplating ways to bring us closer. As a result, I had taken him out to dinner, to movies, and now, after mentioning he wanted to see Toni Braxton in Beauty and the Beast, I purchased the tickets and spared no expense in doing so. But, I was giving more than I needed to give, and settling for less than I deserved, and it was beginning to take its toll on me. I had become irritable, anti-social and desperate, and I hated those emotions! Sooner or later something, or, someone would have to give. It was only a matter of time.

"Hello!" Kevin said sharply, returning to the line.

"Yeah...what's up, who was that?"

"Aaron!" He barked. "He gets me so sick!"

"Oh God, what are you guys arguing about now?"

"We're not arguing!" He yelled. "We're having a disagreement!"

"My bad, a disagreement!" *(What the hell is the difference?)* "What are you guys *disagreeing* about now?"

"He wants to hang out with this guy I don't like."

"And? Why are you concerned with who he hangs out with?"

"Because he's my man bitch! Wouldn't you be concerned about who *your man* hangs out with?"

"No, not particularly."

"Well then explain the whole Jason and Herman situation!"

"That's different," I admitted, "I don't care *who* Jason hangs out with. That's his choice. Herman was his friend *before* he met me, and they'll be friends *after* I'm gone. My problem with Herman *is not* that he hangs out with Jason, it's that I believe Herman manipulates and controls Jason."

"Well, I heard about this guy, and from what I've heard, he's a *shitty-mess!*" Kevin huffed. "And Aaron is way too gullible and naïve to hang out with him! He could influence him—"

"Now Kevin, how is he going to influence Aaron? Isn't he a grown ass man?! Don't you *think* he can take care of himself?"

"It's not Aaron I'm worried about bitch! It's this guy!"

I paused, trying to follow the logic of this conversation. "Okay, so what's wrong with this guy Kevin?"

"First of all, he's single—"

"Kevin I'm single!"

"So!"

"*So?*" I asked in disbelief. "What if Aaron decides he has a problem with you hanging out with me simply because I'm *single!*"

"Bitch *that's different!* You were my friend when Aaron met me. He knows that. He understands that. He, on the other hand, just met this guy about a year ago, when his friend Donté used to date him—and as a matter of fact, I spoke to Donté about it the other day and he has a problem with Aaron and him being friends too!"

As usual he had done his research and had sufficient evidence to back up his case.

"Amazing!" I spit.

"*What?*" He quizzed.

"This is *exactly* what I don't want to deal with in a relationship! It's like people think once you get together with someone, your life ends! What...Aaron's *not allowed* to meet and greet openly anymore? He *can't* make any new friends?"

"Jared *I'm not saying* he *can't* have any new friends. All *I'm saying* is, I don't trust this guy. That's all."

"Well Kevin the truth of the matter is—it's not up to you! Until this boy does something to jeopardize your relationship, you have absolutely *no reason* to distrust *him* or *Aaron*. It's just that simple, that is, *if* you want to keep him!"

"You know what," he sneered, his voice filled with rage, "bitches kill me always trying to give advice, when they ain't even in a relationship! Why don't you do me a favor Jared, and wait until you *get a man*, before you start telling me how to keep one!"

"Kevin, please, *just because* I'm not in a relationship doesn't mean I don't know how to think rationally, and it doesn't mean I've forgotten what it's like to function in one! Its people like you, with all your control dramas that give relationships a bad name! And for the record, just in case you've forgotten, this is the *first* relationship, count it, the first one, you've had that's lasted more than *three days!* I, on the other hand have two relationships and five years of experience under my belt"

"That's cute honey, you can count. Still, that gives you no right to tell me how to handle my man!"

"You're right. But, that's not what I'm doing. I'm trying to help you see it from a different angle—*but you know what*—see it your way! It's your relationship, and it's your fucking life!" I snapped and slammed down the phone.

Ooooo I was so fucking angry! Kevin *always* took me there! It's people like him and his fucked up way of thinking that made love and relationships so arduous! I'd be damned if I got involved in another relationship and started worrying about *who the fuck* my boy hangs out with! To me that shit was nothing but insecurities! It's hard enough dealing with someone in the first place; adding babysitting duties to the fucking list only made a challenging situation worse. Kevin should know that.

One part of me wanted to pick up the phone and find out why he was being so fucking bull headed about the whole thing. But then, I thought about it—*it wasn't my problem*—it was their fucking problem. Let them figure it out!

Shaking with rage, I sat defiantly on the sofa listening to Mary sing, *"Be with you"*. There was something about the way she sang the lyrics that made me reminisce on my days with Vince. I remembered how I use to play that song over and over. As she sang *"Does he love you—Does he want you—Does he even care?"* I remembered how I use to ask myself those very same questions over and over again. I remembered how desperate I was, how lonely I was, how my whole world was built on the stability of that relationship. *"Now I can't sleep at night—why'd we have to fight?"* Mary was singing *my* song, my life… *"It seems like each and every time I come around, you don't want me there—and it's beginning to make me so scared—so scared that I might lose you…"*

At the time I thought that's how relationships were supposed to be. All I wanted was to be with him, nothing else…

Was that love? Was this the way God intended it to be?

Love. People. Relationships. My head was spinning, thinking of all the times I had tried hopelessly to make *the impossible,* possible. *Was I going to spend the rest of my life searching for "the one"?*

I wanted so bad to experience the bliss so many others were experiencing. I too wanted to come home after a long day of work, and kiss my love on the forehead. I too wanted to lay close at night and feel the presence of my man snuggled up beside me. I too wanted happiness.

While sitting drifting further and further into a self-induced depression, the telephone rang. I checked the caller ID box; it was Jason. *'What the fuck does he want?'* I mumbled ignoring the irritating sounds invading my depressive state. He had aggravated me enough for one day. I didn't need to hear about him and Herman anymore. If they got along so got-damn' well, let them fucking hook up! I was *tired* of the games, *tired* of the bullshit, and *sick* and *tired* of being the fucking good guy.

61

As the winds of *"Be Happy"* began to hum through the speakers, I left the sofa and took my all too common place near the window, gazing out at the trees. I watched a single leaf, battered and alone, try desperately to hold it's own against the harsh winter winds of the night. Moments later it lost its battle and floated helplessly to the ground.

The liquor took me deeper into Mary's world. It took me deeper into the lyrics. Soon, I began dancing around my living room. *"All I really want is to be happy, and to find a love that's mine, it would be so sweet."* I had made a promise to myself years ago that I would not settle for less than I deserved. And as I danced, I re-affirmed that statement. I knew happiness would only come when the time was right. Maybe that time had come— *maybe* happiness was Michael, but how could I know for sure?

Before I knew it, heavy streams of tears lined my face. I drank. I danced. I cried. Burdened, I looked towards the heavens and sang to God, *"All I really want is to be happy..."* I've come this far Lord...please, just help me the rest of the way...

SIX

Kevin

IF THERE'S ONE THING I HATE, it's a bitch telling me how to handle my fucking relationship! *Who the fuck does Jared think he is?* He acts like I'm one of them young bitches out there running around trying to keep a man! I know how to keep a man—*okay!* I've got one, does he? Hell no! Yet, he's gonna tell me how to handle my damn' relationship! *Shit!* Friend to friend really, does that make sense? You know what, as a matter of fact, keep your opinion, because it doesn't matter! The point is he should learn to mind his business, and so should the *rest* of you bitches out there trying to judge me!

I don't have a problem with my man meeting new people, never have, and I never will, just as long as I know what's going on. I'm really not the jealous type, but the girls are fierce nowadays! Honey they will steal your man right from under your nose! You'll be sitting around, thinking, *"oh they're just friends"*, and behind your back, they're justa humpin' and a fuckin'!

How do I know? Honey 'cause I've played that scene before.

I remember back in L.A. I had this one ole' fine piece of trade! *Whew!* Girl she was TDH! Tall Dark & Handsome! And had dick for days chile! I mean a big ole' chocolate thang! We use to get down and nasty any and every chance we got—and it didn't matter where, just as long as we didn't get caught. Umm chile, just thinking about that man, and all that dick, is making me hot!

I met him one day while shopping at the Beverly Center. I walked into Crate n' Barrel to buy some candles with my friend Hector, when I noticed this vision of manliness strolling my way. He had on a charcoal gray velour sweat suit with Nike tennis shoes. First, I noticed the b-boy walk, then the face—but honey, as my eyes traced the curves of his body, I noticed the imprint of the dick that would forever change my life! He wasn't wearing underwear so his dick was just a swinging back and forth, and forth and back! I almost had a heart attack right then and there! I couldn't help but stare! *But* when our eyes met, he gave me the nastiest look like, *"what the fuck you looking at faggot!"*

I paid it, because honey, first of all I don't look like no faggot! I may cut up with you girls and talk this way, but out in the streets, I know how to represent—*okay?* So don't get it twisted! Second of all, I work out faithfully! I got body *downnnnnn*! If she would've even *thought,* about stepping to me with some bullshit I would've beat that bitch with a bat!

Anyway chile like I was saying, she screwed her face up, and I just looked at her like, *"what, got a problem?"* He pretended not to notice my defensive stance, paid for his shit, and left the store. Hector and I purchased the candles and continued about our shopping spree. About an hour later we were walking through the parking lot, when I saw Ms. Trade be-bopping to his car. He stopped, turned, smiled, and then kept walking. I looked at Hector like, what was that about? He shook his head and brushed it off. So again, I paid it.

Honey, as I was preparing to pull my Toyota Corolla out of my parking spot, a fierce black convertible BMW 328i with twenty-inch rims pulled up and blocked my exit. Annoyed, I blew the horn to let who ever it was know I was trying to leave. But they didn't move, so I blew the horn again, yet still, no response. Mad as hell, I put the car in park, jumped out, and stormed to the car. Quite to my surprise it was Ms. Trade.

"What took you so long?" He asked in a comfortable masculine voice.

"What?" I frowned, annoyed by his directness. "What are you talking about? Could you just back up so I could get the hell out of here!"

"First of all niggah, take it down a notch ah-ight!" He demanded.

Honey, my pussy got moist! He was a man! A real man! A man's man, and he wasn't taking no shit!

"Now…" he continued. "I saw you checkin' me out back there in the store…" He spit, his voice dead serious. "What was that about?"

I swallowed hard as I surveyed his position. He was sitting with his left hand on the steering wheel, but his right one was between his thighs, holding something. I couldn't tell if it was a gun or a knife or what, but I knew it something.

"I don't know what you're talking about man…" I said backing up from the car, my heart beating a mile a minute. "But right now, all I want to do is get out of this space. I don't want any problems."

He laughed, revealing his pearly whites. "Chill man…I ain't gonna' hurt you, I just wanted to know if you're feelin' me, that's all."

The tone of his voice changed drastically causing me to laugh quietly to myself. Ms. Trade was cruising me.

"I guess you can say that." I smiled, feeling my confidence return.

"I thought so." He asserted. "So listen, let me get the digits so I can hit you up lata."

I looked back at Herman, and winked. "Sure, you got a pen?"

"Yeah right here, what is it?" He said revealing the hidden object. After taking the number, he smiled and said, "I'll call you tonight", then sped off.

True to his word, he called at exactly 1:57 am. I had just drifted off to sleep and was in the middle of one of my recurring dreams with Tupac, when the telephone rang.

"Hello?" I yawned into the phone.

"What's up niggah?" The voice boomed. "You sleep?"

Shocked that he had actually called I sat up in the bed. "Nah, not at all." I lied.

"Good, you up for company?"

"Now?" I asked surveying my apartment. It was a mess. Clothes, dishes and CD's were everywhere.

"Yeah now! Why? You got somebody else over there?"

"Nah, not at all, it's just that," I paused searching for the clock, "it's 2:00 in the morning!"

"So what! It's Saturday night!"

"Well...I don't know—"

And then I thought about it—fuck principles! So what if I just met him! This man was fine, and he called at two o'clock in the morning to spend time with me. And here I was about to kick his ass to the curb—a fine one at that. What if he never called again? This could be a once in a lifetime opportunity, and I was about to let *pride* stand in the way?! Besides, what was the worst he could do? Kill me?

"As a matter of fact, yes," I said suddenly, "I do want company. Let me give you directions."

A half-hour later, there was a knock. I sprayed on some cologne and rushed to the door. Standing in my doorway, Ms. Trade looked better than I remembered, taller and definitely sexier, with his tank top and see through nylon shorts. He smiled as he walked in.

"What's up man?" He said in his now familiar deep voice.

"Nothing," I smiled, "just waiting on your ass."

"Cool, cool. You got a nice place here." He said taking in my studio.

"Thanks."

"You hooked it up yourself?"

"Basically. You want something to drink?"

He paused. "Yeah what you got?"

"What you want?"

"Some Maddog."

"Some who?" I shrieked.

He laughed. "Some Maddog? You know, the malt liquor?"

I shook my head. "Look, I have some Vodka one of my boys left by here if you want some of that, but I know I don't have any Maddog."

He laughed. "That's cool. I'll take it"

We sat on the couch and talked for about an hour and a half. During which time, I learned a lot about him. His name was Hakeem Johnson, he was twenty-four, and lived in Compton with his girlfriend. He had two kids by his ex-girl, a daughter She'kira, four, and a son, Ja'keel, two. He loved his kids, and did everything possible to ensure, they'd never want for a thing.

He loved music, specifically, hip-hop and he talked extensively about his collection of Too-Short, Ice Cube, and Easy-E CDs. One day, he hoped to manage his own rap group and, to ensure his future plans he was taking night classes at El Camino Community College in Business Management.

His favorite pastime was playing basketball with his boys from around the way, and spending quality time with his kids.

The more he talked the more I learned, and the more interesting he became. He was smarter than he led others to believe, which he felt gave him an advantage. His reasoning, if people think you're stupid then they're prone to explain things in detail. The more they explained, the more he learned, and thus, the smarter he became. I thought it was bullshit, but hey, if it worked for him, it worked for him.

After about four drinks he leaned over and kissed me. For the next few moments, I allowed his tongue to explore my mouth. Confused, I stopped him.

"What about your girlfriend?"

"What about her?" He asked kissing me gently on my neck, causing every hair on my body to tingle.

"Aren't you in a committed relationship?"

He stopped abruptly and stared deep into my eyes. "Look, I love my girl ah-ight. And ain't nobody gonna take her place. But at the same time, you offer me something she can't."

"And what's that?" I asked curious.

"This." He said grabbing my dick. "She can't give me what you can give me." With that he leaned over and let his tongue explore my mouth once more.

Gently, he began massaging the shaft of my dick and with each pull it grew larger and larger. I moaned in excitement, as I thought of how I met this man—this beautiful, beautiful masculine man. A part of me knew it was wrong to mess around with him, but then, the other part of me longed for the pleasure I knew only his strong muscular body could provide.

Before long we were both naked making out on my carpet. He gently kissed my body starting with my lips, then my neck, then my chest, pausing momentarily at my erect nipples. His lips, thick, full and sensuous created sensations I never knew my body could feel. As they made their way lovingly down my stomach, I anticipated their arrival on my dick. With the grace of an angel, and the determination of a pro, he took my piece in his hand and gently guided it into his warm mouth. The feel of his tongue on my dick sent my hormones rocketing. Chile, Ms. Trade knew how to suck some dick! He caressed, and held it as if it were a long lost friend; one he missed dearly. Feeling myself nearing climax, I pushed him away.

"Whatcha you do that for?" He asked disappointed.

I smiled. "I'm not ready to cum yet."

"So what you want?" He asked seductively. "Some ass?"

Honey, can I tell you something? There is nothing like a trade *down*—thugged out—masculine ass—motherfucker, asking you if you, want some ass! Especially one as phine as Ms. Trade! My dick throbbed at the thought of pumping his tight ass. He felt it, grabbed his shorts, pulled out a condom and a small tube of lube, and proceeded to fit my piece into the rubber. Once done he turned over on his belly and added, "Handle your business daddy!"

Honey! I wore Ms. Trades' ass out! I had him climbing the walls, screaming all types of obscenities at me! Motherfucker this, Motherfucker that—you name it he yelled it! The sight of this man doggy-style clawing my carpet in excitement nearly caused me to nut. But, before I did, I pulled out. He wasn't getting off quite that easy.

"What the fuck you do that for?!" He yelled, annoyed I had fucked up his ride.

I smiled. "I'm not ready to cum."

"What? Why?"

"Because, fucking you like that has made me hot. I want you to hit this." I said tapping my ass.

He smiled, retrieved another condom, and squeezed, let me reemphasize that, *squeezed* his fat dick into a magnum condom. Then, he laid on the floor, and began stroking it, as I readied my ass with lube.

I mounted him cautiously, then slowly—very slowly—slid down his massive dick. With only one third of it inside me, I felt both pain and pleasure I had never experienced before. He moved to slide the rest in, but I jerked, letting him know, not so fast girl, mother can only take but so much at a time! A few minutes later, the fucking began.

Honey, I thought I knew how to fuck! I thought I knew how to smack it up, flip it and rub it down! But, that man, with that dick, wore-my-ass-out! He had my legs crossed, bent and pinned in positions I never

67

thought they could do! My body trembled with pleasure with each stroke. We hit about eight different positions before I demanded he take it out! He obliged, removed the condom, and laid next to me. Within minutes we both jerked our dicks to climax, shooting warm cum all over each other's body.

We dated for a year and a half, and the sex just got better and better. During that time, I met his two children, his ex-girl friend, and his live in girlfriend. I was even the best man in his wedding. His wife thought I was crying out of happiness for them. If she only knew, I was crying because I was living a lie and so too was the man I loved.

When the priest bellowed, *"Is there anyone present, that knows of any reason why these two should not be joined together in holy matrimony, let them speak now, or forever hold their peace..."*. I wanted to scream out to the top of my lungs *nooooooooooo!* But knew I couldn't. Hakeem watched me with knowing eyes. I had promised him the night before I wouldn't say anything when that part of the ceremony came. Through tears I told him how I felt about him. I told him how difficult it would be for me to stand next to him, and watch him dedicate his life—our life—to another. I told him, I could no longer go on with this charade. I could not keep pretending, and hiding my feelings from him, and the world. I explained to him how every kiss, every touch, every moment spent with him had been recorded in my heart, and that the pain of loss, was causing it to break in two. I told him how it pained me to lie to his children, to his mother, to his fiancé! I wasn't ashamed to tell the world that I loved him, but he was! He was ashamed of our life and, our love—but I wasn't.

Regrettably, I agreed to honor his day. But in my heart, I knew that, that night was the last night we'd spend in the dark, sneaking around. It was time for a change.

I dated him, when he had a girlfriend. I accepted that. But I refused to date him with a wife. My father ran around on my mother for years, and I saw the pain in her eyes whenever he came home with the scent of another on his breath. I watched her as she hung her head in shame every time someone informed her of his misdeeds. And I watched in horror as he denied her claims, time and time again. I watched as she cried, and he laughed.

So there was no way in hell I was going to continue participating in this secret rendezvous' if he chose marriage. Enough was enough. I wasn't going to hurt his wife, the way my father hurt my mother. I told him, but he didn't believe me. That is, until I stood to give the Best Man toast at his wedding. All eyes were on me as I spoke.

"Today, we're here to honor a beautiful couple, Hakeem and Sharese Johnson, on their decision to become one, in holy matrimony." The words pained me as they parted my lips. *How could he do this to me? How could he choose her over me?* Emotionally distraught, I continued, "Many people today, don't seem to understand the importance of marriage, or the symbol for which it represents, and that disappoints me, because marriage, is an important step in a couple's relationship. It announces to the world, that they have found *the one*. The one that makes all their dreams come true. The one that finally completes them.

"Marriage is a way of saying: I could possibly love you always. It is a way of saying: you are my best friend and I *choose* to spend the rest of my days with you; come what may through it all, you can always count on me.

"That is why Hakeem and Sharese stood before us today. To announce to all of us, that their love is a mighty love, and nothing, and I do mean nothing, will pull them under. Nothing will stand in their way—simply because, nothing else matters. At least not when you have love.

"I commend them for taking such a courageous stand, because it says something about them, and, about their love."

I paused and wiped the steady stream of tears streaming down my face. "Hakeem and Sharese, I honor you, and I love you, and I hope you two have many loving years ahead of you. I wish you love, and I wish you happiness in the years to come. And," I paused, grabbing Hakeem's attention, "I will miss you both."

Hakeem stared at me with tearful eyes. Both he and Sharese were crying uncontrollably. She because of my description of their love, and he, because he knew what the words meant.

"This is both congratulations, and goodbye. Tonight I will be moving to New York, but not to worry, I will carry you both in my heart. So," I said raising my glass, "congratulations and much happiness for your future."

I placed my drink on the table and left. Hakeem rushed after me, and caught me in the lobby. He hugged me tightly and whispered, "Why baby why?"

"Because it's time for me to move on Hakeem, you've found the one that brings you happiness, it's time for me to do the same."

"But you can't leave me Kevin!" He said hysterically, embracing me tighter. "You can't! What am I suppose to do without you?!"

"Love that beautiful woman you just married in there, that's what."

We stood there quietly for a long while, holding onto the moment, afraid to let it pass. "I love you Kevin," he cried into my flesh, "and I always will."

"I know you do baby, I know you do." I said rubbing his back. "Now get back in there with your wife, before everyone thinks we ran off together."

We both laughed.

"Yeah you're right." He said releasing me slowly. He wiped his face and stared into my eyes. "I'm gonna miss you boy...I really am. Promise you won't forget about me when you get to New York."

"I promise."

He smiled. "And promise me you'll keep in touch. Cause, I don't wanna have to come to New York and kick some niggahs ass, if he tries to keep you away from me!"

"There won't be a need for that Hakeem. I will always carry a special place in my heart just for you man...just for you."

That was the last time I saw him. It's been eight years. I still think about him from time to time, and I wonder how he's doing. I wonder if he's still as fine as he was the day I first saw him in that gray velour sweat suit...and yes, I wonder whether or not Sharese ever really learned the truth about us. You see because, to her, we were *"just friends"*, but to each other, we were much, much more.

SEVEN

Jared

THE NEXT MORNING I awoke sprawled chaotically across the sofa. The intensity of the sun indicated that I had over-slept my alarm by at least an hour and a half. Almost immediately I went to jump up to call my job, but soon realized getting up would not be as easy as initially thought. An army of pain, determined to take no prisoners, marched defiantly throughout my skull. Delirious, I considered my plight: I had to call the office. But, in order to do this I had to locate the phone, which at the moment required movement. Damn, call my job, or get fired. Get fired, or call my job. For a while getting fired seemed reasonable, though I knew without a doubt it was not an option. I had to call.

In time I lifted myself from the sofa and painstakingly began searching the room for the cordless. Five minutes into what seemed like an endless hunt, I stumbled over the bottle of Absolute I had finished off the night before. The sight alone caused my stomach to twist, and nearly sent me scurrying to the bathroom. I could not believe I had finished off a fifth; an entire fifth. What the fuck was I thinking?

Fifteen minutes later, buried in the sofa I located the phone. Relieved, I dialed my office, reported my absence, and resumed my position on the sofa. At some point, despite the sun's annoying rays beaming in my face, I managed to drift off to sleep.

When I opened my eyes the second time my head felt much better. I gathered enough strength on my first attempt to make it to the bathroom in one piece. Once there I brushed the horrible stench of liquor and sleep from my mouth. While doing so I studied myself in the mirror and wondered why the hell I put myself through all the drama. After finding no reasonable answer, I walked to the shower, turned on the water, and stepped inside. As the warm beads caressed my aching body question after question filled my head, each one it seemed, more pressing than the next. *Life...was it really that deep? Everyone has their share of problems; was I merely blowing mine out of proportion? Or for that matter, did I even have the right to gripe? I had everything any man in his right mind could want: clothes, jewelry, a decent paying job, a hot apartment, family and friends who not only loved me, but constantly sought time to spend with me—and shit, the list went on! You name it, I had it. What the fuck did I really have to complain about?*

A half-hour later while fixing a makeshift breakfast the telephone rang. *Unknown Number* flashed across the caller ID box. Assuming it might be Kevin or Sean calling from work, I answered.

"Hello." I mumbled.

"Hey, what happened to you this morning? Why aren't you at work?"

It was Jason. Had I known, I never would've answered. He was by far the last person on earth I wanted to speak to.

"I overslept this morning." I said, scrambling my eggs.

"Oh." He replied somewhat dry. "Did you get in late last night? I called, but you weren't there, did you get my message?"

"Message? You left a message?" I lied knowing damn' well I heard it when he left it.

"Yeah, about nine, ten-thirty…"

"Really? I wasn't feeling well last night, so I guess maybe I didn't hear the phone ring."

"You weren't feeling well? What's wrong?" He asked genuinely.

How cute. He was concerned.

"Nothing really, I just had a headache that's all. How are you?" I asked hoping he'd change the subject. And as expected, he did.

There had been a time, not so long ago I loved hearing his voice, but those days had long passed. Now frustration and anger replaced excitement and anticipation. Did he not understand what his indecisiveness was doing to *me*—to *us*? His calm, unconcerned temperament obviously proved that he didn't fully consider my reaction, to his actions. Just months ago, I would have moved mountains to be with him. I believed in him—*in us*. But that was before I learned he and Herman came as a package. Standing there listening to him go on and on about his day, and his life, and Herman, *and his life*, irritated the shit out of me. *Who the fuck did he think I was—his friend?* I had enough friends! What I needed was a partner! I thought I made that clear from the beginning.

"And guess what, I finally got me and Herman's tickets for Atlanta this weekend." He said in between breaths.

"Tickets? Altanta? This weekend?" I quizzed.

It was Martin Luther King's birthday weekend, a.k.a., the official Gay Pride kick off for men of color across the country. Men of all shapes and sizes from coast to coast would convene in Atlanta for a festive weekend filled with drinking, partying and of course, sexing. Naturally I was upset when he mentioned this. One, because it came three days before his departure, and two, because he and Herman had just returned from Chicago celebrating New Years. The initial impulse to curse him out and slam down the phone came on quickly. But then, I thought about it, accepted it, and finally let go. I wasn't going to compete anymore. There was no need to put myself through it. I needed a man that wanted to spend time with me, not trek off to every punk event around the country.

"Yeah..." He paused. "Don't you remember me telling you about it last week?"

"No I don't." I said furiously. "When did you guys decide to go?"

"About a week ago..." He said gently, sensing the sharpness of my tone. "I thought for sure I told you. Are you *sure* I didn't mention it?"

"Jason," I snapped, feeling the army return, "I'm sure I would've remembered something like that. It's not like you *forget* your lover's going off to Atlanta for the weekend!"

"I could have sworn I told you..."

"Well you didn't. But hey, it's cool. I hope you guys have lots of fun. From what I've heard, it's sure to be quite entertaining. But yo, I gotta go."

"You're upset *aren't you*?"

"No. Why would I be upset? I'm saying—what reason would I have to be upset about how *you* choose, to live *your* life?"

"I'm right!" He bellowed. "You *are* upset! What's the big deal? It's just one weekend!"

"*Look*, I'm not upset—ah-ight—but your *telling* me I'm upset, is *making* upset! I've already told you, it's your life, and I really don't care *what* you do with it. But right now, in *my* life, I don't feel so hot so, I'll talk to you later."

"Well I really don't see what the big deal is?" He continued, despite my request. "If you told me you were going away with one of your friends I wouldn't get *all* upset. *God,* it's just a trip Jared!"

At that moment I hated him. I hated him for taking me on this emotional roller coaster! I hated him for choosing Herman over me! I hated him even more for leaving me alone; mentally and physically. And to him, it was just a trip?

"You're right." I lied, masking my rage. "Forgive me. I don't know where my head was. It must be this headache."

"That's okay...I understand. We all make mistakes." He said, totally oblivious to my cynicism. "I just hope you're feeling better tomorrow though. I wouldn't want to miss the show."

"I'm sure you wouldn't." I spit.

"*You* would?" He asked defensively.

I sighed. "No Jason, I wouldn't..."

"I thought not. So listen, get plenty of rest, drink lots of fluids, and I'll check up on you a little later."

It took every piece of strength I had to keep from cursing him out. I could not believe I actually thought that one day we'd get this shit together! That one day we'd *actually* be a couple! How fucking stupid was that?

I threw the eggs away and made my way to the sofa. As I sat there alone, tears lining my face, I begged of God for probably the millionth time in my twenty-six years, *"Why'd you make me this way?"*

As usual, there was no answer.

A FTER SITTING SULKING FOR ABOUT AN HOUR I decided to escape the confines of my apartment with a trip to the barbershop. A fresh cut always cheered me up. Outside I was surprised to find the first signs of snowfall. Throughout the course of the day, the sun had given way to heavy clouds that threatened to blanket the city. I smiled, knowing something magical was on its way. As I made my way down the street I watched as adult after adult hurried to their destinations all anxious to avoid the approaching storm. Their children, on the other hand, were probably sitting in school silently waiting for the dismissal bell to begin terrorizing the neighborhood and each other with snowballs.

When I reached the shop my barber Tone unenthusiastically mumbled, *"What's up"*, and continued cutting. He wasn't one of those social barbers that talked and talked and talked. But then at the same time, he wasn't all that quiet either. He picked and chose his moods like one chose their underwear. Some days he felt like talking *(loose like boxers)*, and then some days he didn't *(confined like briefs)*. Usually he'd let you know right away, as soon as you walked in, whether he was wearing briefs or boxers. After patronizing his shop for about five years I could pretty much tell his mood by his first three words; today it was most definitely boxers.

Honestly I completely understood his temperament at times. Since their inception, barbershops have been a staple in the community for both interesting conversation, and people. So naturally the shop would attract all sorts of individuals, as the owner, he had to deal with every personality that walked through the door. Everything and everyone would have its turn in the shop: sports, politics, gossip, even late breaking news like the crack head up the street that *just* hit the number for $500.00 and spent every last cent of it on a hit! Some days he would join in and laugh along with the nonsense, and then some days he wouldn't.

After greeting the heads I knew in the shop I settled into a seat and listened to the various conversations going on around me. One guy was talking loudly about this chick he had sexed the night before and another about the Los Angeles Lakers and New York Knick game happening later that night. The four or five women in the back getting their hair and nails done were glued to the television set, watching *All My Children*. A few people were gazing off into space with perplexed expressions on their face. I assumed just as concerned about their life as I was about mine. It wasn't long before the first peddler made his way into the shop selling imitation *Calvin Klein* socks. "Two for five-dollahs!" he repeated over and over sounding just like Otis from *Martin*, "Two for five dollahs!" A few patrons studied the merchandise as if they were about to purchase a pair but eventually handed them back with a disapproving stare. Everyone else ignored him as he made his rounds. Luckily before he could ask me Tone called me to the chair.

"What's up man!" I asked taking a seat. "How you feeling?"

"Tired Jay tired." He said shaking his head. "I was in here last night man 'til about one thirty in the morning."

I studied him through the mirror. "When you gonna take some time off man? I keep telling you, you work too hard!"

"Man and I keep telling you, I don't get paid like you do when I stay home! *And speaking of work niggah,* what are you doing here in the middle of the day? Shouldn't your ass be at work?"

I laughed. "Tone man, it's a long story…"

"Yeah I bet!" He replied knowingly. My reputation of taking time off preceded me. "But even still, this is what I'm talking about—I couldn't do no shit like this! Take off, just like that, whenever I wanted to! That's that *Big Willie* shit!"

"Nah man—*you* the *Big Willie!* This is *your* shop. If you don't want to work, you don't have to work. It ain't like you got somebody breathing down your neck like I do."

"Yeah I do niggah! Look at all these customers? I can't be fucking up, taking off and shit and expect to keep this shop filled like this! Come on…"

"I feel you, but still, when it comes to *Willying*, you my man take the cake—*I* ain't got no Benz parked outside."

"True, true. But if I banked mine, like you bank yours, I wouldn't be worrying about car notes and shit! And for the record, just 'cause a niggah's driving a Benz, don't mean he's a Willie…"

"No doubt." I nodded.

"But yo kid, how did the party turn out Saturday after I left? Did those two Spanish chicks ever take their shit off?"

"Yeah man, they thought I was playing! I told them: *it's a tee shirt and panty party! How the hell are you going to come up in here, fully dressed and shit, and expect to stay that way!?"*

75

"Yo, I don't know why bitches be doing shit like that!" He said laughing. "They knew what type of party it was right?"

"Yeah, Ron told me he explained the whole concept to them when he invited them."

"Word? Speaking of Ron," he chuckled, "it looked like that niggah was having a *good* ass time!"

"He was." I laughed. "That tee shirt and panty shit was his idea. He had to convince me, 'cause I was like: *How are you gonna get people to take their clothes off in the middle of January?*"

"From what I saw niggah, you ain't have to convince that many people to get butt ass!"

I laughed. "True, True. So yo, what happened to you? Why'd you break out so early?"

"Cause man, my girl ain't having that shit!" He said brushing my hair. "If she even *thought* I was somewhere around tits and ass—*that weren't hers*—she'd start flippin'!"

"She's jealous *like that* man?"

"Nah not at all. She just knows how *shy-stee* bitches are nowadays. Plus," he grinned, with a hint of pride, "she likes to protect her turf."

"Ah-ight!" I laughed slapping him five. "That's what I'm talking about! But what about you? Would you be jealous if she went to a party like that?"

"Honestly Jay—yeah, I would. It's not that I don't trust her and shit, it's just, well you *know* how *niggahs* are man. They'll try to pick up your shorty with you standing right there in front of them! Imagine if a niggah *ain't* around! It's like free range and shit—no holds barred out this motherfuckah!"

I nodded my head in agreement. "So, let me ask you something? You care who she hangs out with?"

He paused. "No. Not really. Not if she's hanging out with positive people. But if she's hanging out with birds that ain't about shit—*fucking chicken heads and shit*—hell yeah I care! I tell her all the time, she gotta be about something! I can't be with nobody who ain't thinking about tomorrow. *On the real Jay,* you know how much I love cuttin' hair and shit, *but,* I don't want to be doing *this shit* when I'm fifty years old man!" He stopped suddenly and placed his hands on his hips. "Can you imagine that shit?! By the time I reach thirty, a niggah like me only wants to be working four days a week! And, if she's gonna be with me—*she's gotta be with me*—you feel me?"

"Definitely man. I feel you." I said fully absorbing his words. I too wanted someone who was bout it bout it: A shorty about *getting* a house, *two* nice rides, and *traveling* the world. "You think you guys will ever get married?" I said looking up at him.

He sucked his teeth. "Maaaaannnnn, she talks about that shit all the time but I'm like, for what? What's the point? We've been together now for—like what—five years! What the fuck is marriage gonna prove?"

"That she's the one niggah!"

"Well, I don't know if I believe in all that *the one* bullshit. I mean, don't get me wrong I know I love her. And right now I know I ain't going nowhere, but marriage?" He sucked his teeth. "I just don't get it."

"What's there to get?"

"That's exactly my point." He replied. "What is there to get? Half of the motherfuckahs out there that get married *consider* divorce, or, actually get one. If all them motherfuckahs married *the one*, then, why split? Why even think about splitting?" He stopped suddenly and stared at me. "Wait wait wait wait, why you asking anyway? Don't tell me you're thinking about getting *married* Big Jay! Don't tell me you're about to sell out niggah? Come on—"

I laughed. "Hell no! I can't even find a shorty that's down for theirs! Marriage?! Nah man, that's definitely out of the question!"

He laughed. "Yeah, you say that shit now! Let the right bitch come along and put that thang on you, you'll be running down the aisle!"

"Well uh, it ain't happen to you yet so, I ain't worried!"

"OOOOOOhhhhh!" He stepped back and covered his mouth. "You got jokes today niggah? Huh? How about I fuck up your hair *Chris Tucker*—or is it *Jared the Entertainer?*"

I threw back my head and laughed hysterically. His girl, who had been engrossed in her stories looked up and asked what was going on. He waved her off and told her to mind her business.

"Look Jay," he whispered outlining my beard with alcohol, "let's dead that marriage shit before she overhears us and starts getting funny ideas!" He held a smaller mirror behind my head and allowed me to critique his work. "So, yo," he said after I nodded my approval, "did you pick up your girl Faith's new album? That shit is *tight* man!"

"Now you know I had to get that. As usual she's doing her thing. Did you check out track number six? That shit's off the hook!"

"Yeah I know, but I can't stop listening to number twelve. Babyface did his thang!"

"No doubt," I said handing him a twenty. "He hooked Whitney up on her album too. Did you check out number eight on her shit? It's tight."

"Yeah, my girl let me hear it, but I ain't pick up it up yet."

"Get it man. It's a good CD."

"Yeah I will. But, if I don't, I'll just take hers."

"Ah-ight Tone," I laughed giving him a pound, "I'll see you on Saturday."

"Yo Jay man—thanks." He said prepping his next customer. "As usual, it was good kickin' it with you!"

When I exited the shop, I immediately realized how much better I felt. Getting out of the house was precisely what I needed to take my mind off of all the bullshit, and focus entirely on the problem at hand, me.

I wanted a relationship so bad that I was beginning to act desperate. If Jason wasn't ready, Jason wasn't ready! And it wasn't my job to make him ready. Sure I cared about him—*as a matter of fact*—I loved him. But that didn't mean I had to hate him simply because we couldn't get it together. I was bigger than that, way bigger than that.

As the kids began filtering into the streets, the snowball wars began. While walking, I watched as they ran and played oblivious to the problems that awaited them in the years to come. I watched in disbelief as one kid got pummeled by five or six kids at once with snowballs! Afterwards, he laid there and laughed. Instantly, it struck me that adults had forgotten *how to laugh* in the face of adversity. Unlike children, we lie there and wallow, and pose questions like *why me*? From experience I had learned that situations, regardless of their nature, made me stronger, wiser. So why did I greet each new day with uncertainties? Why was I so afraid? I used to laugh, I used to believe, *but now*, life seemed so serious. Why?

Watching that kid laugh, made me laugh. And suddenly, I couldn't hold it in any longer. All of the hurt and pain, I had held onto for years and years, I let go. Happiness is a decision; and at that moment I decided that with or without someone, I was going to be happy. And for the first time, in a long time, I was.

As I neared the house my cell phone rang. I answered on the first ring.

"Are you still upset with me bitch?" Kevin said sharply.

"No, I'm not." I said actually glad to hear his voice. "What's up?"

"Nothing." He replied. "I left you a message at your job this morning. And after a while I figured either you were still upset and wasn't returning my calls, or, that you weren't in because I kept getting your voicemail."

"Yeah, I woke up late this morning and was like fuck it!" I said unlocking the front door.

"Bitch, you always say fuck it!" He laughed. "I don't know why those girls ain't fired your trifling ass yet as much as you call out!"

"Niggah they ain't fire me because I'm irreplaceable!"

He laughed. "Alright bitch—we'll see just how *replaceable* your ass is when you're standing on the unemployment line! *Okay*!"

78

We both laughed.

"So what did you do today Ms. Girl, call over a fierce piece to keep you warm and cozy in all this snow?"

"I wish." I said, lying across the sofa. "The only thing I did was go to the barbershop."

"Umm hmm, I should have known! You make sure you keep your wig snatched! A girl may end up jobless, with bills up the ass, but trust the hair will be done!" He said with a mouth full of laughter. "Anyway Pussy Mama, I spoke to Jason today. And he swears up and down that you're pissed that he's going to Atlanta this weekend."

I stood and crossed the room. "Initially I was upset, but honestly Kevin, now I could care less." I said gazing calmly out the window. "Jason has to do what's best for Jason, and I, what's best for me."

"I hear you girl besides, now you'll have more time to research Michael. Have you spoken to him today?"

"Nope, but you just reminded me, I was supposed to give John a call to find out Dee-gee's number to get that tattoo priced. But knowing John, he's probably out of town somewhere."

"So you haven't called him at all?" He asked raising his voice. "Girl you sure don't seem all that interested in seeing what this man has to offer!"

I thought about it. "Well in a way I am, and in a way I'm not. I don't want to confuse shit. Plus, what if I play myself, hit on this guy, and then find out he's not down."

"Well, what if you *don't* play yourself, and you find out later you missed out? The only way you're going to find out for sure honey is if you talk to him. That is, if you really want him."

"Yeah I know, but I have to find out about this tattoo business first. By the way, how are things with you and Aaron? Are you still mad at him?"

"No. I thought about what you said last night. And later, when I talked to him I apologized for not trusting him. A lot of it was my shit—*you know?* And you were right, I have to start trusting him, because if I don't, why am I even with him?"

"True, that's very smart man, and a very good move on your part. At the rate you guys are going you two will be married in no time."

"Girl I don't know about all of that, you know how I feel about marriage. But, if I were to pump down that aisle one day you know you couldn't be my matron of honor bitch. I've already promised Kay-Kay he could wear the second *most fabulous* gown of the ceremony." He said laughing. Kay-Kay was one of his childhood friends who had relocated to Atlanta.

"Good! Who said I wanted to be in your tired ass wedding anyway? Knowing your *country* Californian ass, all the gowns would be plaid!"

79

"Bitch you kill me always trying to come for me! Anyway hoe, I gotta get back to work. I'll talk to your tired ass later, bye!"

After hanging up with Kevin, I located John's cell number. As expected he didn't answer. I left a message and quite to my surprise he called back almost immediately. After kicking it with him for a minute about this and that, I explained my predicament. He got Dee-gee on the three-way, and arranged everything. I thanked them both, told John I would call him later and hung up.

Now I had a reason to call Michael. I checked the time. It was 4:53. I retrieved his number from my wallet and dialed his job hoping he was still there.

"Good Afternoon. Thank you for calling Banana Republic. How may I help you?" The sultry female voice asked.

"Yes, may I speak to Michael please."

"Michael? Sure, hold on." She said placing me on hold. Sade's *Kiss of Life* played softly in the background. As soon as I began humming the words, Michael answered.

"This is Michael, how may I help you."

"What's up man, this is Jared."

"Hey hey, what's up Jared?"

"Nada Mucho. I was just calling to let you know I spoke with the tattoo artist, and he said whenever you were ready to just come in and he'll take care of you."

"Ah man thanks!" He bellowed. "That shit is so cool! I've got to find a way to repay you!"

Silently I thought of a million ways, or rather a million positions, but opted to keep them to myself. "Don't worry about it man. I'm just glad I could be of service. Do you have a pen handy? I want to give you the directions to the shop."

Silence, then: "You're not going to take me?" He asked, his voice falling to a whisper.

My heart slammed against my chest.

"Sure—I mean, yeah—I can take you," I stuttered, stumbling over the words, "that's no problem."

"Great, but listen I can't talk right now. My boss is signaling me to hang up. Give me your number, and I'll give you a call later on tonight so that we can arrange everything alright?"

"Cool…" I said and rattled off the number.

My heart was doing cartwheels! He wanted me—*me*, to take him to get his tattoo! Was this really happening? He must be down! Why else would he want me to go with him when he could go by himself, or even, with his girlfriend?

Suddenly a rush came over me—what if he wanted me as much as I wanted him? The thought alone sent my hormones skyrocketing! I ran and retrieved Sade's *Love Deluxe*. Kiss of Life, had been playing in my head the whole time we spoke, and I needed to hear it!

As Sade crooned *there must've been an angel by my side,* I once again began dancing around my living room. Only this time with a smile on my face and a new beat in my heart. It was hard to believe that a day that had started out as stressful and as painful as this one had ended up so beautifully. Outside as the sun began to set, and the winter winds blew hard against my window, it appeared another storm was approaching. But all I could think about was Michael, and how I couldn't *wait* to dig deeper into his world.

A FEW HOURS later while engaged in a heart felt episode of *Sex and the City*, the telephone rang. "Hello..." I mumbled.

"Whatcha doing *Pump-kin?*"

"Watching Carrie fall for Mr. Big. Why, what's going on?"

"Nothing. Sean and I are right by your house, and we were wondering if you were up for company? *That is* if you don't already have company *Sweety!*"

Both he and Sean erupted into a bout of laughter.

"You niggahs kill me! Why am I always the assumed playa? Especially when you know you two munch more trade than anyone I know!"

"What-ever *Pump-kin,* open the door, our cab just pulled up."

Before I could fully unlock the door, Sean pushed his way in. "It's about time niggah! It's cold as shit out there!"

"Now Sean," Dio sneered, pulling me into an embrace, "you know this bitch had to beat her face before she opened the door!"

"You two don't stop do you?" I said hugging them both. "No—*how are you Jay—is everything all right Jay*—no, you two bitches come in reading!"

"Whatever niggah. What you got to drink?" Sean said ignoring me, heading towards the kitchen.

"I don't know look in the cabinet. I think I have your drink in there."

He looked back. "Some Henny?"

"Yeah, but Sean listen," I paused, making eye contact, "go easy on the bottle man, I just got it."

He smiled devilishly. "Don't worry son, I'll make sure I take real good care of it."

"So how's life?" Dio asked flipping through a stack of CDs. "Anything new and interesting happening I should know about?"

"I wish."

"Come on, something's has to be—*Jared*!" He yelled unexpectedly, causing me to flinch. "How long have you had this CD?"

"What CD?" I asked annoyed.

"This Miles Davis, *Kind of Blue* CD?"

"For a while, why?"

"The other day, I was talking to a friend of mine and he mentioned Erykah sampled one of her hooks from her first album off of this CD."

"She did. She used it in her intro."

He frowned. "You know, that shit really pisses me off. All these years I thought she was creating music not stealing it!" He said placing the CD in the player. "She's just as bad as all the other tired ass artists coming out today!"

"Ah come on Dio give her some slack, everyone samples nowadays! That doesn't mean she's not a good artist."

"You two bitches stay talking about that bullshit!" Sean said returning to the living room. "I'm saying, what's up with the hip-hop?"

"*First of all Pump-kin!*" Dio spit eyeballing Sean. "How *dare* you take your hip-hop ass in that kitchen and make only *one* cocktail when you know damn' well there are *two* other bitches in here besides yourself! *Second*, if you'd take your head out of the ghetto long enough to gain a reasonable amount of common sense, you'd know that there is a time and place for everything—right now, this very moment, it's time for *jazz*. When we hit it to the club on Saturday night, you can have all the *hip-hop* your non-speaking-ah-English ass can handle. But until then, I'll take an absolute and cranberry on the rocks, with a twist of lime, thanks."

Sean stared at Dio in disbelief. "I'ma slap the shit out of you one day you know that right?"

"*Sweety* please, that *butch-queen* shit don't work on me! What, am I supposed to be scared? Please, anytime you're ready bitch, bring it on, bring-it-on!"

Sean stood motionless staring heatedly at Dio. Somehow he found the strength to let it go. "Dumb bitch..." he mumbled, and returned to the kitchen.

"*Soooo* Jared darling. What's going on with you and that *store-boy*?" Dio buzzed as Miles began to fill the room. "You know I want to know all the dirty little details!"

"His name *is* Michael." I spat, trying not feed into his sarcasm.

"*My bad sugar*, wait, let me rephrase it." He cleared his throat. "What's up with you, and that *store-boy*—Michael? *Did I get it right this time sweety?*"

I couldn't help but laugh. Dio despite his ways was still love. "He's fine Dio. At least he was when I spoke to him at work earlier."

"That's not what I was talking about bitch and you know it! Have you found out whether or not he sucks dick?"

I laughed. "Nah. I spoke to him briefly today about his tattoo, and he said he'll call me later on tonight when he got home but—"

He gagged. "You mean he has a phone?"

"Here." Sean said practically tossing Dio his drink. "Does who have a phone?"

"This isn't what I asked for!" Dio snapped shoving it back.

"It's a drink bitch so drink it!" Sean retaliated, his eyes daring him to protest further. "Now..." he continued, "does who have a phone?"

Dio looked at the glass, sniffed it then mumbled, "His new store-boy."

"His name is Michael." I spit.

Sean narrowed his eyes in confusion. "Why wouldn't he have a phone Dio?"

"Sean please, don't pay any attention to Dio, you know how *bourgeoisie* he—"

"*Bourgeoisie?!*" He bellowed. "Bitch, what does being *bourgeoisie* have to do with anything?"

"My mama always told me," Sean warned, "not to ask questions I didn't want answered!"

"Fuck that bitch!" Dio spit. "Like she's some philosopher and shit..."

"Look man, don't be talking about my mama. I'll kick your ass! Plus you don't want me to start ragging on your mama's stankin' ass! Her welfare recipient havin' ass—"

"Don't try it bitch!" Dio said cutting his eyes.

"Alright fella's..." I said breaking up their catfight. "Enough about everybody's mama. What I wanna know is, what's up with you and Miles Dio?"

Dio calmly sipped his drink then placed it on the coffee table. "Why?" He asked nonchalantly. "What's up with him?"

"*OOOOhhhhhh*, I get it! You want to know everything about me and Michael, but at the same time, you and Miles are off limits!"

He smiled. "No, it's not that at all *Pump-kin*. It's just there's simply nothing to discuss. Now Sean on the other hand, might have some tea. That bitch went on a date last night!"

I raised my brows. "Oh? Sean you didn't mention you had a date last night. As matter of fact, I don't remember you saying anything about meeting anyone! Don't tell me you're keeping shit from the family?"

"Now come on Jay," he said defensively, "you know that ain't my style! And for the record, it wasn't a date!" He said shooting Dio a nasty look. "It was more like a booty call, with the same shorty I met two weeks ago at Will's party—as a matter of fact—" he pointed, "I told you about him son!"

"That's right, that's right!" I nodded. "Congrats on getting some bruh. Was it good?"

He shrugged. "It was ah-ight."

"Well," I said slapping him five, "look on the bright side, at least you got some."

"True that. But you know with me it's not just about getting some—"

"I know, I know. I'm just saying—at least you're getting some. A niggah like me has been on a drought for a minute now."

Dio's face lit up. "Really?" He leaned forward. "What about Jason? Aren't you two still an item?"

"Yeah—and? Like I said, a niggah like me has been on a drought for a minute!"

"Why?!" Sean yelled. "That cat's got the ill body! Don't tell me he's *whack* in bed!"

"I'm not saying that Sean—but—I'm not denying it either. Let's just say, I've had more fun lately watching porn."

"So why the hell have you been with him for *so* long?!" Sean asked puzzled.

"Okay!" Dio chimed in.

"Because, he was interesting at first, and, I don't know, I liked his mind."

Dio laughed. "That's all well and good *Pump-kin,* but I'm sure you see now a *mind* can't get you off!" He said snapping his fingers.

"True, but still, I don't want to be with him, or anybody for that matter, simply because the sex is good!" I argued.

"I feel you Jay. That's why I said earlier it ain't just about getting some. But my man, when I *do* get it, I want it to be good!"

I nodded. "Alright so question, how important is sex to you in a relationship?"

"What!?" Dio howled in disbelief. "What kind of question is that? It's VIP! *Very Important Pump-kin!* I will *not* under any circumstances subject myself to *horrific* sex!"

Sean laughed. "I'm with you D. Sex is a major part of a relationship! That shit's mad important. It's right up their with hygiene."

"Okay...okay." I nodded eagerly. "So let's say you meet this phine ass cat! I mean he's got it going on, nice body, good conversation I mean everything is on point! But, you find out about a month into the relationship, that the sex is whack. Would you still date him?"

Sean shook his head. "Not on your life..."

"Hell no!" Dio asserted. "She'd have to carry her ass somewhere else, 'cause she won't be laying up in my bed dishing out no junk dick!"

We all laughed.

"Even if he was everything you ever wanted in a man?" I argued. "I'm talking about the shit you've dreamed about."

Sean shook his head. "Nah, I still wouldn't date him. Because *in my dreams* the sex is *Off The Hizzy*! And besides, it'll only create problems."

"How?" I asked.

"Because! Here I'd have this fly ass niggah I'd *hate* having sex with. Why, because the shit sucks! And eventually you *know* what I'm going to end up doing right?"

"What?" I quizzed.

"Cheating! *You dumb bitch!*"

"Ahhhhhh, don't give me that shit!" I yelled brushing him off. "Niggahs are always looking for an excuse to cheat! Trust me when I tell you, if a niggah wants to cheat, he's gonna do so whether or not the sex is whack!"

"*True...*" Sean agreed, "but still, if the shit is whack, that's just one more reason why, without a doubt I'd be cheating!"

I shook my head. "But I'm saying—"

"Niggah will you take this jazz shit off!" Sean yelled rubbing his temples. "It's fucking up my high!"

"Take it off then! Dio only wanted to here one song!"

Dio shook his head at the scene we were making. "You girls are too much!"

"Anyway, like I was saying before I was so rudely interrupted..." I said shooting Sean a nasty look. "You don't think it's possible to be in a relationship—have *so-so* sex and not cheat?"

"Sure niggah, *anything's* possible." Sean said thumbing through the CDs. "But how happy would I be?" He paused reading a few. "And knowing me," he said selecting one, "I wouldn't be happy at all. Because, for me, good sex, coupled with a *brain*, defines the perfect man."

"Bitch! Would you *hurry up* and put some music on before *I knock you*! Now you're fucking with my high!" Dio screamed.

85

"Niggah I am!" Sean shot back as Mariah's *Butterfly* began to play. "And I'm only gonna tell you this shit once more: you better stop yelling at me like I'm your fucking son and shit ah-ight!"

Dio sucked his teeth. "Well, you better be glad I like this song bitch—"

"Yeah—*or what*?" Sean replied.

"Yo, will you two calm down? Damn. I don't know why you guys always go at it like this?" I said staring at them both. It never failed. Put these two in a room together, and watch out. "Now Dio," I said once they stopped glaring at each other, "you still haven't told us anything about Miles. What's up with you two?"

He sat back and crossed his legs. "You know what *Sweety*, this year I'm going to buy you a little *Diane Sawyer* news kit for Christmas, since you *stay* pumping people for tea!"

"Come on Dio, why you gotta take it there? It's a simple question!"

"Jared, you know how this niggah is,*"* Sean interjected. "I don't know why you keep asking him shit."

"And what's *that* suppose to mean?!" Dio spit.

"It means what *it* means." Sean retorted.

"*What—ever...*" Dio said rolling his eyes.

He knew what it meant. For some reason, he always avoided direct contact. Of all my friends, I knew less about him. At times it frustrated the shit out of me, but then, at other times, I could care less. This time however, I was determined to crack his code of silence. After all, what could he possibly be hiding?

"Come on Dio, we're your friends. If you can't talk to us, who else can you talk to?"

He slammed his drink on the table, nearly spilling it and yelled, "What?! What do you bitches want to know?! I swear you're no better than everybody else! Every time I turn around somebody is all up in my face trying to get in my fucking business! I'm of sick it! I swear to God I'm sick of this shit! What is it Jared! What do you want to know?!"

Sean and I looked at each other, and then back at Dio. It was obvious neither one of us cared at that moment. If pulling teeth was the only method left to induce this man to open up to us, personally, I wanted no parts of it.

"Nothing Dio. Nothing at all." I replied.

He huffed. "You know what, *fuck* this shit I'm out of here! I can't take anymore of your fucking attitude, and this fucking interrogation!" He stood and glared down at the two of us. "Sean are you leaving, or staying?"

"I'm staying." Sean snapped. "I ain't finished talking to Jared yet."

"Fine. Stay." He spat. "I know what you're going to do. But trust, it's okay. You two bitches can sit up here, like two tired ass queens all night long and talk about me all you want—but trust and believe it doesn't matter. You're not the first, and you *damn'* sure won't be the last."

He snatched his coat from the closet and disappeared down the stairs. For a moment Sean and I sat in silence, dumfounded by what had just occurred.

"What-the-fuck is his problem?" Sean asked bewildered.

"I don't know, but he'd better check himself!"

"You know what I'm saying? He's got some deep rooted issues my man and he's taking them out on the wrong kats!"

"I know. What do you think it is?"

He shook his head. "I have no idea! That niggah keeps everything bottled up inside and never lets anyone know when something's bothering him..."

"I know but, one day he's gonna have to remove the mask. And hopefully, after shit like tonight, he'll have friends around to help him pick up the pieces."

Sean stood and stretched. "I feel you son, but yo, I need to get out of here, I've got a long day ahead of me tomorrow. Are you going to work?"

"Yeah, I can't take off anymore days this week. I've got too much shit to do. Besides, tomorrow I have that play to go to."

He chuckled. "That's right, with Jason. Man, I still can't believe that niggah's garbage in bed..."

I hugged him and laughed. "Believe it my man, believe it."

EIGHT

Diogenes

I STOOD OUTSIDE MILES' HOTEL ROOM debating whether or not I should go through with my verdict. After leaving Jared's, I jumped in a cab and headed home. I was so annoyed and upset with him and Sean for putting me on the spot I didn't know what to do. As soon as I reached my apartment, I fixed a drink and recounted the events that had led to my current state.

I loved Miles. There was no question about it, none whatsoever. But this wasn't supposed to happen! I wasn't supposed to rehash feelings for someone I had *clearly* gotten over! That is, I thought: if I ever really got over him in the first place. Had I? Had I been holding onto him all these years? Silently praying he'd return, to rescue me...to love me?

"What am I thinking!?" I said aloud, fixing my fourth drink at the bar. *"There is no way in hell that I could still be in love with him six years later! The pure idiocy of it makes me laugh!"*

And I did. I laughed until my sides ached. I laughed until I could laugh no more, and yet somehow I managed to laugh again. I laughed until my laughter turned to tears. Tears that streamed heavily down my face, burning my eyes, blurring my vision. Tears from a heart filled with uncertainty, loneliness and the truth: I loved Miles. I did. He was the best thing that ever happened to me. And my love for him was the only thing that ever *really* mattered.

This realization sent me further into hysterics!

I could not love Miles! How could I—*Diogenes*—love someone that broke my heart? Someone that took my breath away literally and figuratively! Someone who opened me up to the world of love and desire and then without warning, without the *slightest* hint whatsoever, slam that same door in *my* fucking face?! Was this love? Was this the feeling everyone was searching for? *Jared* was hoping for? Dying for? If it was, I fumed, then, I wanted no parts of it! Not if it meant I had to suffer in order to have it!

Angry, confused, frustrated and drunk I decided to call Miles and tell him I would not love him again—no—I would tell him, I could not love him again! Not now, not ever! I would not permit him back in my life so that he could destroy me once more! It took me three years to get over him.

Three years of solitude and lingering questions with no answers as to why it did not work—or rather, why it could not work!

I picked up the phone and dialed his number but slammed it down just as it began to ring. What the hell was I doing?! I couldn't let him know how much he hurt me! He'd think I was stupid, or worse, weak! And I couldn't let him think that!

Out of nowhere a voice from deep within whispered, *"So what if he thinks you're weak?"*

Pissed, I through the phone violently across the study and howled, "How did I fucking get here!?"

An awkward silence filled the room, and all at once it seemed cold, very cold—cold, and hollow.

Through tears I screamed again, "How did I get here?!"

The words pained me as they parted my lips. I swore I would never fall in love again. That I would never allow love to bring me to a place of uncertainty. I made a pact with myself one night along with Janet that we would both grow old alone before we'd ever have another lover.

That promise gave me strength through the years, and it helped me believe I had it all together. Yet, here I was again, loving, hurting, falling.

I left my house in a huff determined to tell Miles face to face exactly how I felt about this whole love shit. Determined once and for all to clear the air. *Fuck* what he thought—this was *my* life and I did not want his ass in it fucking it up!

But as I stood outside his door—my heart a tortured mess—my confidence waned. For that reason, I could not bring myself to knock. I just stood there, like an asshole, pacing back and forth until after much hesitation, I decided to forget the whole thing. I hurried down the hall to the elevator. Once there I decided a note would be better. Yes, a note. I would go home, pen a note then have my assistant messenger it over in the morning. While standing there lost in thought, the down arrow on the far-left elevator shaft lit up, indicating my destination. I hurried to catch it and quite to my surprise, Miles stepped off.

"Dio!" He said startled. "What a surprise, I was just thinking about you!"

Taken aback, all I could offer was a weak smile.

He noticed my stance. "Are you okay?" He asked gripping my shoulder.

I flinched, then nodded yes, still not able to meet his gaze.

His eyes narrowed in concern. "Are you sure? It looks like you've been crying. Your eyes are all bloodshot. What's wrong man?" He questioned me. I stood motionless, unable to speak. "Dio—"

Despite my attempt to hold them back, the tears resurfaced.

"Baby! What's wrong? Why are you crying? Please!" He cried pulling me into his arms. "Tell me what's wrong…"

I couldn't speak. It hurt too much. He hugged me tighter, somehow hoping, I imagine to smother whatever ailed me. When he finally released me, I noticed his eyes were just as wet as mine.

"Come baby." He whispered softly. "Let's go."

He grabbed my hand and led me back to his room. Once inside he removed his coat and mine then pulled me into an embrace. Still I said nothing. Hours passed, and my silence never wavered. We just sat there, he staring into the night, and I the ceiling. Eventually the alcohol took its toll and I drifted off to sleep. When I awoke I found myself wrapped in his arms spoon fashioned, and immediately, as if on cue, the tears returned. I shook violently in his arms, causing him to hold me closer. I could feel the warmth of his breath on my neck, and the beat of his heart penetrating my soul. And although distraught, it provided a comfort I had never known. A warm tender feeling filled my heart as I cried. Yet before I could fully bask in the beauty of this warm, awkward, strangely comfortable feeling, fear returned. I jumped up suddenly and moved to the edge of the bed. Miles, clearly troubled, pleaded with me to explain to him what was wrong. If he only knew I wondered the same thing. I too wanted an explanation as to what was wrong me. And then, after nearly three hours of silence, I spoke.

"Miles, I'm still scared."

"Of what baby?" He asked tenderly. "What are you afraid of?"

"Of us." I said gazing at him for the first time. Dejected, he leaned over, cupped his face, and rocked slowly back and forth. I knew my words hurt him. And yes, I knew it was the last thing he wanted to hear it, but it was the truth. It was how I felt.

"Miles, I still remember the day we broke up." I continued, twiddling my thumbs. "I remember it as if it were yesterday, but it wasn't. Six years have passed since that day. Six very long years—can you believe it? Six years and I can still hear you saying goodbye. I never thought, in my wildest dreams, that I'd ever hear you say those words. Never, and it hurt like hell. Do you know how many times I've replayed that day in my head—*in my dreams*? Do you know how many times I've cursed you for leaving me like you did? Do you?" I said raising my voice. "Do you know how many times I prayed to God for him to take my love for you away?"

The tears grew.

"So many nights I spent crying alone, wondering what happened. Trying to pinpoint exactly where we went wrong. Because I thought for sure, we were going to make it—*why?*" I shrugged. "I don't know, maybe it was because at that time, through you, I was beginning to believe in love. Or, maybe it was because I thought we were different—or better yet, *you*

91

were different. I don't know, but when you confirmed what that little voice in the back of my head warned me of all along, I lost it. Because you left me Miles, just like he said you fuckin' would."

I left the bed and stood near the oversized windows and peered out into the night.

"Dio," he whispered. "I was young then—I didn't know what I wanted! I was so afraid of falling in love with you! I was so afraid of what might happen to us if we," he paused, "if we went too far."

"Miles!" I screamed spinning to face him with my hands flying wildly in the air. "You don't think I was afraid? You don't think I was just a little bit afraid of what might happen if we went too far?!"

"I guess Dio, but I wasn't thinking about that then—but I see now! I see how selfish I was! I see how inconsiderate I was!"

"Do you Miles? Do you? Do you *really* see how this shit is killing me—turning me inside out—still, after all these years?! Do you really see it, or are you still thinking about yourself?!"

"Of course I see what this doing to you Dio! I love you man!" He said crying uncontrollably. "And I'm *so* sorry I hurt you! You gotta believe me. I never meant to do that, never!"

"I wish I could believe you Miles, I really do. But I can't, because I do not trust you. And because I cannot trust you, I cannot love you! Not now, not ever!"

The words cut deep. His face revealed all sorts of pain and suffering. I watched as he tried to hold back the tears, as he tried unsuccessfully to pull himself together. I watched feeling both saddened and pleased. One part of me felt he deserved this pain after what he had done to me. He deserved to experience what I went through when he told me: *love was not enough* that fateful summer night six years earlier. Yes, he deserved the pain that filled his eyes, and traced his face. He deserved every last bit of it.

But then, the other part of me wanted to reach out to him and hug him, rub his back and comfort him. That part of me loved him deeply, and yearned to ease his pain, but fear was too strong. He was in control, and basked in his power to annihilate all those that stood in his way. Fear laughed as Miles cried, and in the back of my mind whispered, *"That's what he gets for fucking with you!"*

Fear reveled in his ability to crush the one who tried desperately to destroy him, love. Fear knew how much Miles loved me. And he knew that if I gave into my hearts desire to love Miles completely, he would once again lose all power over me, and I would fall.

Unaware of fear's hidden agenda, I continued angrily.

"I'm sorry if that hurts you Miles," I said with little emotion, "but that's just the way it is."

"Dio I'm," he paused, choking back his tears, "I'm sorry that you feel this way. I really am. Like I said, I never meant to hurt you. But, now that I see just how much I have hurt you, I want you to know from the bottom of my heart, that I'm sorry. I was young. I know to you that may be an excuse, but it's the truth. I was young, and foolish, and, I made a mistake. I just hope one day you can find it in your heart to forgive me. Because if you don't, it won't be me you'll be hurting, it'll be yourself."

"Myself?" I barked. "What's that supposed to mean?"

"It means I'm free. I've forgiven myself for what I've done to you, and in doing so, I have asked for your forgiveness. I've done my part. But if you continue to harbor all these negative feelings about me, about what happened, or about, what should *not* have happened, then you're the one that's stuck. You're the one still living in the past. And the only way you're going to be able to move on with your life, is to forgive me; but most importantly, forgive yourself."

I scratched my head in confusion. *What the fuck was this guy talking about—forgive myself? Why the hell did I need to forgive myself? I didn't hurt me, he did!*

"Yeah well, whatever Miles." I said snatching my coat from the bed. "I'm out of here."

He stood and outstretched his arms. "Come on Dio, don't leave like this. I love you man."

I gripped the doorknob unmoved. "Yeah well, like you said six years ago: it's just not enough."

As I rode the elevator down to the lobby, instead of feeling relieved, I felt empty. And it didn't help that something deep inside of me, kept hinting that I had just made the biggest mistake of my life.

NINE

Jared

THE NEXT MORNING FOUND ME AT AN ALL TIME LOW. The night before, after straightening the mess my friends and I made, and trying to decipher what the hell was wrong with Dio, I longed for a peaceful night's rest. But as soon as my head touched the pillow, the telephone rang. I laid there irritated, pondering whether or not I should answer. It was after eleven and if I planned to make it into work the following day, I needed at a minimum nine full hours of sleep. By the fourth ring however, curiosity set in. "Maybe it's Michael," I said aloud reaching for the cordless. I had almost forgotten he had said he would call. But, after mumbling hello, my enthusiasm vanished. It was Jason. We had not spoken since our spat earlier that morning. Regrettably, I entered the conversation.

"What's up Jason..." I asked dryly.

"Nothing much, how about you? Are you feeling better?"

"I'm feeling okay. I was just about to go to sleep, but, I'm cool."

"Well, you sound a whole lot better than you did earlier. For a minute, I thought you were about to slice my throat or something."

I smiled. "Maybe I was..."

"Easy killer," he laughed, "remember, you've met my family, and uh, they know where you live!"

"Shit. They'll never know it was me, and, if they figured it out, well then, I'd have to get rid of them too!"

"Hot damn!" He chuckled. "I see you're feeling a lot better than this morning! It's good hearing you in good spirits man. How was the rest of your day?"

"My day was pretty good for the most part. I just lounged around the house all day."

"Wow that must be great."

"What?"

"Lounging around." He said softly. "Sometimes I wish I could take some time off just so I can lounge around. It sounds so relaxing."

"It is. I am a firm believer that everyone should take some time out for themselves. Working oneself to death ought to be a sin."

He let out a heavy sigh. "I agree one hundred percent. But I also believe, that if I work real hard now, that one day, I'll have enough time to

95

do everything I want to do"—he laughed—"and everything I don't want to do!"

"I guess that is something to look forward to." I smirked. "So what else is up?"

"Besides being excited about tomorrow? Nothing. Oh yeah, I spoke to my mom's today."

"Yeah? How's she doing?"

"Fine, but stressing herself out as usual about things completely out of her control."

"Like what?"

"Like her job, my brother, my pop's. I keep telling her to leave them grown ass negro's alone and let them live their life, so she can live hers. But she never listens. I don't understand why she puts herself through so much to take care of them knuckle heads."

"My mother does the same shit. She's always complaining about what she can't do, or hasn't been able to do all because of her commitment to others. Personally I don't get it but, I guess you have to be a mother to understand all the things they give up for their families. Sometimes I wish I could give back a little of what she thinks she's lost, but I know I can't. And that bothers me because she's given me so much—you know?"

"I do." He said thoughtfully. "And you're right. I do think you have to be a mother to understand how they operate. Take my brother for example, he's a grown man and she's still worrying about him as if he's still a child. I keep telling her someday, at some point, he's got to realize he's a man and grow up! But, he's never going to do that as long as she's taking care of him."

"I hear you man..." I said realizing how awkward those words seemed coming from his mouth—especially since he was so willing to take care of Herman's grown ass. "Hopefully they'll both realize one day that life is too short to be worrying about somebody else's problems."

"Yeah, I hope so..." He replied.

"So," I said changing the subject, "have you guys finished planning everything for this weekend?"

"Yeah for the most part this end is covered. My cousin is taking care of everything on the other."

"That's right he goes to school down there right?"

"Yeah." He chuckled. "He's afraid he's gonna run into some of his classmates while we're hanging out."

"Well that's definitely going to happen."

"I know. I told him already."

"So I take it you guys aren't staying with him?"

"Nah. We decided to rent a room. It's easier."

"Cool." I said quietly, as a long unnerving silence filled the lines. No amount of words can describe the amount of anxiety I felt during that long extended moment. But, if I had to sum it up, I guess you could say it was then that I finally realized I'd lost him, completely. But what hurt most is that he had absolutely no fucking clue. I swallowed hard, and once again changed the subject. "So look, what time do you think you can meet me tomorrow?"

"The show starts at eight right?"

"Yup…"

"Then, I can meet you by at least, seven-thirty."

"Cool, seven-thirty it is. And Jason," I said seriously, "please be on time."

"I will." He promised.

"Good, so I'll see you then."

I was about to hang up when…

"Jared…" He said suddenly. "Are you okay?"

I considered his question for a long while. *Was* I okay? Or, was accepting the truth about him, causing me to doubt myself? Or, had I simply, after all of this time, finally come to grips with reality? The reality I had long tried to ignore. The reality that spoke the truth: Jason and I would never be anything close to what I had imagined. This reality, this truth, this…epiphany, brought everything into perspective. We would *never* get it right, because *we* were never right. For each other that is. Our love had ended long before it ever began. I knew this. But, I wondered if he did? I started to tell him, just for the hell of it, but instead, I inhaled deeply, and released the words I knew he wanted to hear. "Yes Jason, I'm fine."

"Alright then knuckle head…" He said happily, completely unaware of the sadness surrounding my voice, "I'll see you tomorrow."

Afterwards I laid there with my eyes shut hoping the closure would somehow stop the tears from falling; silently praying that time would heal the wound that once was my heart.

Alone, angry, and fed up I vowed once again never to compromise my happiness for that of a man.

At the office still feeling miserable, I worked with little to no conversation, which in a way was a good thing. My absence the day before had yielded an unbelievable amount of phone calls to return, and about twelve urgent e-mails that needed a reply ASAP. I needed to get as much done as quickly as possible to avoid harassment from my boss. But by nine thirty, *(an hour and a half into what was shaping up to be one of my most trying days in years,)* I was cursing like a madman. Nothing in that goddamn office worked. The fax machine, as soon as I pressed the start button malfunctioned, and ended up chewing up a weeks worth of spreadsheets. The copier kept jamming, and no matter how many doors I opened, and closed, refused to indicate where the hell this mysterious piece of paper was trapped. The server, which allowed me to access my e-mail crashed and froze up my system. Then, after searching my desk for what seemed like an eternity, and still not locating the goddamn stapler, I cupped my face and laid my head on the desk, defeated.

"What's your problem JC?"

I looked up to see Lisa leaning against my cubicle with both arms folded neatly against her chest. "Nothing." I replied somberly. "I just hate my life."

"Yeah, what else is new..." She asked, taking a seat.

As usual she was looking good, but today for some reason there was a glow about her. I wasn't sure if it was the rich red turtleneck she wore that accentuated her cocoa skin, and breast perfectly, or, whether she had done something different to her hair. But something had definitely changed.

"You look nice today." I mumbled, ignoring her sarcasm.

She sucked her teeth. "JC don't try and change the subject this ain't about me, it's about you. When you left here Monday, you damn near floated out of here, then you took off yesterday. Now today you come in here acting all antisocial! So what is it, couldn't get in contact with none of your chicken heads last night?"

"As a matter of fact I couldn't. For some strange reason, your phone was off the hook all night long!"

Jordan stood up and laughed. "Now that was a good one Covington!"

"Who asked you?" Lisa barked. "You need to sit down and mind your business sometimes."

"My mind is my business." Jordan replied.

"Well then sit down and mind it." She spit.

Jordan raised her hand to Lisa's face and laughed. "Girl *please*!"

"What's up black people!" Steve called out as he passed by.

I threw up the peace sign. "What' up brother-man! Make sure you stop by here after you clock in."

"You still didn't answer my question JC." Lisa said indignantly.

I ignored her as both Steve and Jordan made their way to my cubical.

"Could you step aside so I could give my brother some dap." Steve said trying to get pass Lisa. She moved a half an inch, allowing him just enough room to reach in and give me a pound. "What's up brother man? I was worried about you? What happened yesterday?"

98

I shook my head. "Man, too much to drink…"

"Good for you." Lisa said with an, *I know what you've been up to*, expression all over her face. "You know you shouldn't mess with poultry during the week. You know how much they *love* their forties…"

Steve stared at her. "Now Lisa." He began slowly, "Why do you always refer to sisters as poultry—especially, since *you're* a woman? Shouldn't you find that term offensive?"

"Steve you know good and well that what *I* am, and what *he* deals with, is two different species all together. Now granted, it is a derogatory term, but that doesn't stop them from being what they are—chickens! Now," she paused uncrossing, then re-crossing her legs, "when a lady conducts herself as a lady then—"

Before she could finish her long drawn out monologue on 'The State of Chicken Heads In the Twenty-First Century', Stephen and I burst out laughing.

"Sister it ain't that serious!" He cried in between breaths. "Take it down a thousand!"

"Serious or not," she replied. "It's the truth. Ain't that right Jordan?"

"Excuse me?" Jordan recoiled placing both hands on her curvaceous hips. "Don't include me in your madness. Personally, I don't deal with those creatures—*never mind* analyze them! Ain't that right *Stevie-wevie!*" She said reaching for his cheeks.

"Woman cut that out! Damn'!" He yelled barely avoiding her cheek pinching ritual.

Lisa rolled her eyes in disgust. "Anyway, back to you JC. Are you going to tell me what's up with you, or am I going to have to sit here staring at you all day until you do?"

"Hold up—brother-man, why is she all up in your business?" Steve asked.

"Man I have no idea. It's always like this—*what can I say*—it's hard being the man!"

"Child *please!*" Jordan laughed. "You're too short to be *a* man, nevertheless *the* man!"

With that they all exploded into a chorus of laughter. My boss overheard us and in no uncertain terms suggested we all get back to work before we're each applying to: Walker and Kick-stone.

"Ah-ight people" Stephen said preparing to leave, "I'm going to hit my desk. I'll hollah at ya'll later."

Assuming they were all leaving, I turned back to my monitor. But low and behold Detective Lisa Marshall was just getting started.

"JC, I'm not moving until you tell me what's going on." She sat back and folded her arms, dead serious.

"Are you still on that?" I asked in disbelief.

"Yes I'm still on that. And I won't be off that until you tell me what *that* is!"

I looked at her in amazement. "You are one persistent sister! I hope to God you don't pester your man like this."

"I do, so out with it."

I stared at her for a long time, and from her relaxed disposition gathered she had no intention on leaving without some kind of info. I had to give her something.

"Okay! Okay!" I relented. "I've got a date tonight…"

"Oh really? What is she like?"

I hated that statement. What is *she* like? Why does it always have to be a she? Why do people automatically assume because I'm a man that as soon as I say I have a date, it has to be someone of the opposite sex? I hate that shit! Next thing you know she'll be asking me what's *her* name.

I huffed. "She's cool…" I lied.

I hated using that pronoun! It made me feel like such a liar…

"But," I continued. "I don't think we're going to be seeing much of each other after tonight."

She adjusted herself in the chair. "Why?"

"Because we're from two different worlds, and, I'm not happy."

"Not happy!" She gasped, as if I had just spoken an immortal sin. "Who is happy?"

"Huh? What do you mean?"

"I mean—who do you know, that's really happy?"

"Plenty of people!"

"Name them!"

"What?!"

"Name them." She repeated. "You say you know plenty of people that are happy, so, name them!"

"I don't have to name—"

"Ah ha!" She yelled. "You don't know anyone—do you?"

"I guess not since you're telling me I don't!" I snapped angrily.

"Ahhh, poor baby, don't get upset now that you're busted."

"Look Lisa please, don't patronize me ah-ight." I said annoyed.

"My point is JC, is that everyone is running around looking for this thing called happiness, and none of them have the slightest idea what they're actually looking for."

"I do." I answered matter-of-factly.

She seemed surprised, and as usual questioned my certainty. "You do?" She scoffed.

"Yes-I-do!" I answered defensively. Having a conversation with her was like having one with God! She swore up and down, she was the only one with a goddamn grip on life!

"So tell me then Mr. Covington, what are *you* looking for?"

"I'm looking for piece of mind, self-acceptance, and love."

She nodded her head, as if somehow my answer needed her approval. "And, what about in a mate?"

"That's easy." I replied. "Simplicity. Internal beauty, not necessarily external beau—"

"Bullshit!" She barked.

"What?" I asked annoyed. "You didn't let me finish!"

"I don't have to!" She said pointing her finger. "Men say they want internal beauty—they claim to want a down-to-earth woman, but you know damn' well they don't! They want trophy wives! They want slaves! They want—"

"Well," I interjected, "I'm not like every other man! And I wish you'd stop comparing me! I'd pick someone who was mentally and spiritually beautiful before I would someone who was just pleasing to the eye!"

She smiled wickedly. "Now Jared..."

I raised my hand to stop her. "Don't Jared me, I *hate* dumb people! Granted, some of them are good for a nut, but after that, what the hell are we supposed to do?"

"Wait, excuse me?" She asked visibly appalled. "A nut?"

"Yes, a nut!"

"Gross!" She shivered then shook her head. "So anyway, let me get this straight. You want someone who's internally beautiful, intelligent, *and* someone you can talk to?" She said holding up three fingers.

I nodded.

"Well then you're right!" She said laughing hysterically. "You're not like every other man!"

"Seriously though Lisa, not every man is interested in tits and ass, some—and I admit there are few—still believe in, and *want* love!"

"Alright Romeo, point noted. But back to this chick you're going out with tonight. What does she do that makes you so unhappy?"

I sighed. "Well, that's a difficult question."

"What's so difficult about it?"

"Well because, it's not just her, some of it is me—I mean, I don't think she's ready to settle down and I am. But for her it's like..." I paused searching for the right analogy, "she has this huge Ryder truck filled with

101

unpacked luggage that she's been carrying around forever. She wants to unload it but, she's afraid that as soon as she does and turns her back, someone's gonna take all of her shit."

"Okay…" she nodded, "I can see that. A lot of women have unresolved issues…but, what about you? What about your luggage?"

I nodded my head in thoughtfulness. "I'll admit, I do have some luggage but," she started to interrupt me but I held up my hand, and with my eyes begged her to let me finish, "mine is more like, I don't know, an overnight bag."

She threw her hands wildly into the air. "Amazing! Just Amazing! When are men gonna wake up?! My boyfriend is always talking about how women carry around "so much" shit with them—please, and men don't?! All the men I know—with the exception of my father of course—are full of shit! Tons of shit—stank ass shit!"

I stopped her. "Lisa, have you ever noticed how many blanket statements you make? All men are not full of shit! Like I said earlier, some are, and some aren't."

She paused for a long time staring at me. "So again," she finally huffed, "let me get *this* straight, because you feel she has a truck load of luggage, you're dumping her?"

"Yes."

"That's funny." She scoffed.

"What's so funny about it?"

"Well honestly speaking, it's usually the woman trying to tie the man down, not the other way around. I guess you can say this is Boomerang at its best…"

I wanted to burst her pretty little assuming bubble, but I knew if I told her the truth—that it was actually a *man* I was trying to tied down—she'd gag momentarily, then proceed to point out her case had been proven after all: Men were full of shit—tons of shit—stank ass shit! Instead I nodded my head and said, "Interesting analogy."

"So you break up with her tonight, and then what?"

I shrugged. "Then nothing. I move on."

She shifted. "That's it? And you're not at all troubled about breaking up with her? It's that easy for you?"

"No. I wouldn't say it's easy. It's actually taken me some time to reach this point."

"Why?"

"Because," I sighed, "I kinda got used to having her around. And actually," I paused not wanting to admit what would come next, "I was kinda hoping she was the one."

She sat quietly. "The one? Really? Wow…so then why end it?"

"Because Lisa, I don't want to be the second—third—fourth thought in someone's mind! I don't necessarily want to be the first thought either—shit, I don't know!" I said exasperated. "Actually, I do know. I'm tired of waiting for her to decide whether or not I am the one for her. I'm tired of waiting by the phone night after night hoping she'll call. And I'm tired of waking up the next morning disappointed she didn't." I said staring blankly at my monitor. "I'm just tired…"

She sat stunned. "I didn't think it was that deep…."

"Me either," I admitted solemnly, "that is until just now. What I really want is someone in my life who's going to love me—not my job, or my clothes, or my money, or my body—me." I lowered my head. "The sad thing about it is, I don't think it's ever going to happen."

"It will JC, believe me, it will. You just have to be patient. Before I met Emanuel, I was exactly where you are. And then, when I least expected it, I fell in love. And you know what?"

I shrugged. "What?"

"The same things gonna happen to you. So, maybe what you're doing tonight is the right thing because, it seems like she's dragging you down, and the last thing a positive young brother like yourself needs is another weight around your neck."

I smiled. "Yeah, you're right…"

"I know I'm right because I've been there before, but still I must warn you, breaking up with someone is never an easy thing to do, *especially* if you still have feelings for them. But then at the same time, you can't stay in a relationship that's suffocating you. It may not seem like it now, but honestly, life does go on."

And go on it does. I had been there before too. Lost. Empty. Confused. And I thought I'd never bounce back. But I had; with the help of my friends, and family I looked failure in the face and kept on reaching, kept on striving, until I got it right. That's when I learned: love is love, is love is love—good or bad. And no matter how hard you try to change it, change it you cannot.

Looking back now I can clearly say that I was acting selfishly. Sometimes you can want something or someone so bad, you forget or neglect to acknowledge what the other individual wants for themselves. I wanted Jason to want me, the way *I* wanted him. I wanted him to fulfill *my* dreams. I understand now, in retrospect, that my dreams of the future may not be that of another's. And as a result I cannot force those dreams, needs or wants on another. For example, I had convinced myself that I was the best person for Jason, and that he would never find anyone like me. But the truth was I *wasn't* the best person for him. He had to find his own truth, in his own way, just as I was still discovering mine.

Lisa had placed so many thoughts in my head about the night to come, that I had no idea how to proceed. But I knew I couldn't continue down this road. I had to end it. So I decided to call Kevin for some brotherly advice. After all, he had dumped many a date before…

"Accounting…" He answered.

"Is that the way you guys answer the phones over there?"

"Bitch, what are you talking about now?" He huffed.

"You answered the phone like, *Accounting…*, what happened to your name and may I help you?"

"Oh bitch please…this is not Miss Corporate America girl where you have to recite a damn' paragraph just to answer the damn' phone! Girls over here are direct and to the point! Okay honey? Now, what's up Ms. Hot Pussy-Mama Girl?"

"Nothing, just calling to see if you had any advice—"

"Advice? Advice on what honey? You know mother *always* knows best!" He said, as I envisioned him perched at his desk anxious to find out the tea, so he could point me in the best possible direction.

"How do you think I should handle this whole Jason situation?"

"What do you mean?"

"I mean I've made up my mind. I'm going to end it tonight."

"But aren't you guys suppose to go to that play tonight?"

"Yeah—and, we're still going."

"All right honey for dumping Cinderella *after* the ball! So what you gonna say bitch," he said with a mouth full of laughter, "It's been real nice knowing you girl—but sorry honey—the shoe doesn't fit!"

"It's not like that Kevin and you know it." I laughed. "I just can't keep going on like this, wondering whether or not we're going to get this shit together. I mean it's killing me. We hardly speak, we hardly see each other, and when we do, Herman's broke ass is almost always tagging along. I just can't deal with it any longer."

"I hear you." Kevin sighed. "But if you already know what you're going to do, why are you calling me?"

"I'm calling to figure out how I should go about it. Should I tell him why I'm doing it, I mean it's not like he's gonna care anyway. I probably should just lie, and make up some lame excuse, and save what little dignity I have left."

"No, just be direct. Direct, and honest. That always comes across best. Plus, it'll give you a chance to let him know just how fucked up he really is."

"How do you think he's gonna handle it?"

"I don't know. It's hard to tell with Jason. But it serves his ass right. If he had concentrated on what he was supposed to, then this shit wouldn't be happening."

"I know…"

"No you don't, because this shit really pisses me off. The only reason I hooked you two up, was because he said he wanted a relationship! Then he gets one and starts acting a fool! Trust, I'm going to let his ass have it about this!"

I sighed. "So you really think direct is better huh?"

"Yeah Jared, just be direct."

"Okay Kev, thanks."

"Don't mention it honey, but, uh, just so you'll know, my invoice will be in the mail shortly. I accept checks, master cards, visa's, Gucci—"

"Shut up stupid!" I said laughing. "You're so damn' silly."

"Yeah I know; it's all part of my charm. Anyhoooo," he said changing the subject, "what's up with you and Michael, now that Jason's finally going to be out of the picture?"

"Man honestly, I think I'm getting closer to figuring out whether or not he's down. Check this, I called him yesterday about the tattoo when I got off the phone with you. I told him how I had spoken to the artist and hooked everything up, and that he could go down there whenever he was ready. But then, right as I was about to give him directions to the shop, he says: *you're not taking me?* Kevin, my mouth hit the floor!"

"Get out!"

"Seriously I—"

"No get out! Your mouth really hit the floor bitch? How did that feel?"

"Ha ha ha—anyway jackass—after that he asked for my number and said he would call me later but, I guess maybe he was busy or something because he didn't call. But it turned out to be a good thing because Sean and Dio stopped by anyway."

"So why didn't you call him?"

"Because I told you, I don't want to read too much into this and get burnt."

"Bitch please, you've barely got the stove on and you're already talking about getting burnt! Stop worrying and call the man! Why do you think he gave you his number? Believe me, what's supposed to happen will happen. You guys met for a reason, trust me."

He was right. I was worrying too much. If it was going to happen, it was going to happen, and there would be nothing I could do to stop it.

"Yeah, maybe you're right Kevin, but first things first. I've got to get Jason out of my life, and out of my head. Once that's done, then maybe

I can focus on Michael without worrying so much. Besides, if Michael is down and we do hook up it's only right he has my undivided attention."

"Good point." He replied. "So get to it."

Later that afternoon, I grabbed lunch from the cafeteria and ate at my desk. My life was changing. At first up close, I didn't notice it. But when I stepped back and looked deeper, the change was radiating. Through sorrow, I had somehow managed to find joy.

While eating, I reminisced on my past and pondered my future. I enjoyed the change, although it came at such a hard expense. I was probably more confused today than I was yesterday. Yet somehow, it all made sense: Life *was* truly what you made it.

I remember once my moms told me to keep both eyes open at all times when dealing with people. When she first said it I was like—are you *sure* you don't drink? What the hell was she talking about: I had to keep *both* eyes open? How else would I see them?!

But now, fully aware of what she meant, it was probably the best advice I'd ever received.

Growing up, it seemed I never really spent much time with my parents, but somehow, the lessons they taught me about life seemed to sink in. Now, as an adult, I often look back and comment on what they could have or should have done, but honestly, they were good parents. They did their best to raise three children in the heart of Brooklyn. They both worked; my pops, seven in the morning until six in the evening; and my moms, twelve at night to eight in the morning. Come to think of it, they hardly spent time together except for the rare times they passed each other in the night. Not my idea of the perfect marriage, but hey, to each their own.

The times I remember most with my family are the holidays. The holidays at the Covington's were always joyous occasions—especially Christmas! My mom and sisters would stay up all night Christmas Eve wrapping last minute presents, creating individual fruit bowls, and planning the next day's events. Christmas morning would find everyone smiling, basking in the gifts they received.

One Christmas, I didn't get what I wanted. And being spoiled *(I can admit this now!)*, I threw a tantrum. Man…I went on and on about how everyone else got what they wanted and I didn't! The next thing I knew, my mother had slapped the spit out of my mouth! When I regained consciousness, and the room stopped spinning, I looked up, and to my surprise, she was crying. And to this day, I've yet to forget what she said…

"Boy you better count your blessings. Look at all these gifts you just opened! Look at them! Do you know how many kids wish they could be in your shoes right now?! Huh—do you?!" She screamed as heartfelt tears fell from her eyes.

Embarrassed, all I could do was shake my head. I didn't dare look at her.

"Well you better appreciate what you got!" She continued. "I worked too long and too hard to buy you the things you opened today—so don't you *dare* disrespect my gifts—look at me when I'm talking to you boy!"

I raised my head in shame.

"The one lesson you will learn over and over again, is that you won't always get what you want, but you be *thankful* for what you have!"

At the time I didn't understand what she was talking about. All I wanted was that gift. Now in retrospect, I completely understand where she was coming from, and I appreciate the lesson. My moms. My rock. It took some time, but the lesson is finally being learned. I will not always get what I want. Such was the case with Jason. And I was fine with that. Finally, I was growing up.

Later that evening as I prepared for my date I recalled my conversations with Lisa and Kevin. Two statements in particular stood out. *"Breaking up with someone is never an easy thing to do especially if you still have feelings for them."* And, *"be direct, honesty always comes across best."* I admit I was nervous because part of me really didn't want to end my relationship with Jason. That part of me wanted us to work it out, and give it one more shot. I mean, sure I thought Michael was hot! Who wouldn't? The niggah was fine as shit! But, if Jason said, *"No Jared, I don't want to end this, I really want to work things out…"* Then I would ask no questions. I loved him, and besides, he already had my heart.

But then, there was that part of me that knew better. The part that knew Jason would never utter those words. By believing he would change I was only setting myself up for disappointment. I had no choice but to be honest with him and myself, and stick to the plan.

When I reached the city, the sky whirled with snow. People nonetheless loitered Times Square posing for pictures, window shopping, and watching the assorted entertainers spread out along the sidewalk. By the time I made my way through the throngs of tourist and peddlers to the theatre, it was 7:15; too early as usual. I checked my wallet and after realizing I had only fifteen dollars on me, decided to find a cash machine. I stopped a passing officer and asked him if there was one nearby.

"Sure…" He said looking around. "You see that Information Center right there," he pointed up the street, "there should be some in there."

I thanked him and headed in that direction.

When I entered the building for the first time since its conception, I was completely impressed with the Times Square renovation project. A few years prior, you could barely find a legitimate business in Times Square, never mind an Information Center! Inside there were several booths with information on movie theatres, Broadway shows and local places to eat. Various souvenir shops, with miniature versions of the Statue of Liberty and Empire State Building were set up everywhere. And to my surprise, there were quite a few people inside. As I walked further into the center I noticed a row of about six cash machines on the left. I went to the first available one and withdrew sixty dollars. Afterwards I walked slowly back to the theatre in hopes Jason would be there when I returned, but just as I expected, he wasn't. He was late. I checked my watch, 7:35. 'Okay...' I reasoned, 'maybe it's the weather.' It's difficult as hell to get around New York City on a good day, but when it snowed, forget about it! It was as if everything and everyone stood still.

By 7:45 I had called him everything—*as my mother would say*—but a child of God! This motherfucker did this shit all the fucking time! If I miss even the first *five seconds* of Toni's performance, he'll never hear the end of it!

After fuming for another five minutes or so I decided to get the tickets from the window.

"Last name please..." The lady behind the bullet proofed glass barked in a monotone voice. She reminded me a lot of my fourth grade teacher Mrs. Cox. Half of her hair was pulled back in a bun, with a big clip of some sort barely holding it together, while the other half flew wild and free. Her glasses, which were attached to a long gold-silverish chain, hung down by her huge sagging breasts. And her eyes, like that of a hawk, stared menacingly at me. I spoke cautiously.

"*Covington.* C-O-V—"

"I know how to spell it!" She snapped, raising her large bifocals to her nose. I grunted, but knew she was not the root of my frustration and thus, chose not to attack. She flipped through a stack of envelopes then peered suspiciously over her glasses. "Jared?" She hissed.

I offered a smirked and nodded.

"Do you have the credit card used to purchase these tickets?" She barked. "Sure...here you go." I handed her my VISA.

She took my card examined the numbers, glanced up at me, rolled her eyes and returned them to the card. "Okay...here are your tickets. Enjoy the show. NEXT!" She yelled violently.

"Excuse me..." I said staring at her in disbelief, "but I wasn't finished." It was obvious I was annoying her by the huge sigh she released.

I ignored her and asked my question anyway. "Does the show usually start promptly at eight?"

Her eyes rolled about in her head in an exasperated mock. "Yes, promptly at eight. Is there anything else, or are you going to stand here all night asking questions? Other people are waiting."

I stood there speechless, trying to figure out what the fuck was her problem. And, even though initially she wasn't the root of my frustration, slowly she was beginning to seem like the likely candidate on which to release some heated tension.

I began formulating reads in my head. I smiled to myself thinking of the tongue-lashing this old bitch was about to receive. But before I had a chance to say any-*fucking*-thing, this bitched bellowed: "NEXT!"

Aggravated as all hell, I yelled, "THANK YOU, *bitch*," with all the sarcasm I could muster up. What the fuck did I care; I had my tickets.

"Your mama!" She retaliated.

Instead of continuing this childish feud, or bothering to get her boss, I flashed her the finger and walked away. I had more important things to worry about. I checked my watch, it was five minutes to eight, and Jason was nowhere in sight.

"If that motherfucker ain't here in two minutes," I mumbled aloud, "I'm gonna—"

"Jared!" He yelled out. "Hey! Sorry I'm late..." He said running up to me, completely out of breath. "I couldn't catch a cab so I had to walk all the way here!"

"Yeah, well, you were about to be watching the show from out here." I said, and then noticed his hair was full of snow. "Yo, where's your hat?"

"Come on Jay, you know I don't wear hats. It messes up my style!"

"Style my ass. Come on supermodel, we'd better get in here before they start without us. Here's your ticket."

"Thank you." He took the ticket and followed me inside.

An usher greeted us at the door. "May I help you gentlemen to your seat, the show is just about to start."

"Sure, here you go." Both Jason and I handed over our tickets.

"Alright let's see here." He paused reading. "Orchestra section. Okay gentlemen, right this way."

Until then I had never realized just how close front row seats were until we kept going further and further down the aisle. A tinge of cockiness flowed through my body as we walked the distance. *This* was the life, front row seats, at a top notched Broadway play, in the center of the most popular city in the world—who the hell was I to complain about my life?

When the usher finally stopped and pointed to our seats, my face lit up! We were about five feet from the stage. Close enough to see every zit on Toni's face!

As soon as we were seated, the house lights were brought down and the show began. From beginning to end, I was impressed. The lighting, the choreography, the music, everything was on point. A few times I swore Toni was looking directly at me as she ran off her lines.

Up close for the very first time I was really able to absorb her beauty. She was magnificently beautiful. Her skin appeared soft and supple—and her wig, although I knew it was a part of the costume, almost looked real.

After the show, Jason and I grabbed a bite to eat from the pizza restaurant across the street from the theater.

"What are you going to have?" He asked studying the menu.

"Probably a slice. Oh, and a piece of this carrot cake—what about you?"

"Ah—I guess I'm gonna have a slice too." He said somewhat disappointed. "I wish they had some hot wings at this joint…"

"You want to go someplace else?" I said with no enthusiasm whatsoever.

"Nah, this is fine."

Once we had gotten everything, we headed to the register where quite to my surprise, Jason paid. The four months we had been dating, I had always paid for our meals. So you can imagine my surprise when he told me he had it.

"Thanks man—whew!" I teased wiping my brow. "I thought I was going to have to steal this meal! Times are hard…"

"I know." He laughed. "I saw it in your eyes. And you know I couldn't be responsible for sending another black man to the big house, especially," he smiled, "one as cute as you!"

I smiled, but at the same time realized ending it, with comments like that, would make it much harder than I imagined.

We searched the restaurant for a booth and located one near the window.

"So, did you like the show?" I asked as soon as we were settled in our seats.

"Yeah, it was real good—especially the guy who played the beast—damn', what a voice!"

"I know, he was excellent but, you didn't like Toni?" I asked taking a bite of my slice.

"She was good, but, you could tell they had her mike turned up."

"True, but at least she didn't forget any of her lines."

"I know right! That would have been so embarrassing!" He laughed. He was doing it, that laugh, and that smile I had come to love him for, he was doing it—on purpose I bet, trying to make it harder for me to end it. But it wouldn't work.

"Hey Jared…let me ask you something," he said as his mood changed drastically. "Do you ever wonder what's your purpose here on earth?"

"All the time." I whispered.

"And? What do you think it is—I mean, if you know…"

Without hesitating I said, "To enlighten. My primary purpose is to enlighten. People always seem to come to me for advice on this or that, and it's cool. I like to talk, but more so, I enjoy sharing my many life lessons." I paused wondering whether or not I was bullshitting him or myself. I had been trying to figure out my purpose for years, *now* all of a sudden *I* had an answer? "Why do you ask?" I said sipping my drink.

"Because, I've been trying to figure out my purpose for a while now, and it's like I can't seem to put my finger on it." He said, placing both arms on the table. "It's like I feel once I figure it out, I'll have some clue as to what's going on in my life—you know?"

I considered his plight in silence while he waited patiently for a response. "Well, maybe it's not your time to figure it out…it takes some people years to figure out who they are. Discovering one's purpose is another lesson entirely. But let's just say for arguments sake, you discover what it is, do you think you're ready for it?"

He hesitated. "I don't know…I think I am…"

"Well, you have to know Jason. When God calls his soldiers into battle, you have to be ready."

"I know, I know…" He said drifting. "I just wish I knew what it was first…"

We finished the rest of our meal in silence, both pondering our futures. A couple of times it looked like he wanted to say something but he kept it to himself. Normally I would have tried to pull it out of him, but not that night. I was determined to stick to the plan; despite my hearts resistance. At one point Michael popped into my head. And I wondered if he and I ever did manage to get together would it actually work? The thought alone of him and I together caused me to smile.

"What are you smiling about?" Jason asked destroying the vision.

"Nothing, just imaging…."

"The way you were smiling it must be something good."

I shifted. "You can say that."

"So, are you gonna tell me what it is?"

I shook my head. "Nah…it's not that important."

111

"I bet." He grinned. "So listen, I was thinking of calling a car, do you want a lift home?"

"Sure, anything's better than the iron horse."

"Cool..." He said whipping out his cell phone.

This was good. I would talk about us in the car. I would tell him it was over, and that I was sorry; I had thought about it for a while, and realized it was best thing for the both of us. Then I would suggest we remain friends. After all, maybe that's what we were supposed to be all along.

"All set." He said, and placed the phone on the table. "There's just one thing though..." He whispered seductively.

For some reason, my heart started beating rapidly. Maybe he had planned an after-theatre-party at his place. Shit, I was down, even if the sex was whack. A nut is a nut, and besides, it had been a minute since I'd nutted. I leaned forward meeting his gaze, and anticipated my answer: a resounding, YES!

"I uh," he began quietly, "I uh, asked them to drop me off first. I hope that's alright? I really need to get up early tomorrow."

I sat back dejected. I don't know why I was surprised. There was absolutely no romance in this relationship. None whatsoever. I had to end it, for my dick's sake!

"Hey no problem." I said, the aggravation showing heavily on my face. In the back of my mind I mumbled, "The sooner you're out of my face, the better."

"Is everything alright Jared?"

Surprise number two of the night! Not *only* did he pay for dinner, but he actually noticed there was something wrong with someone other than himself!

"Things could be better, but then again they could be worse." I said playing with my juice avoiding his stare.

He leaned forward trying to engage my attention. "You seem, I don't know, *distant* tonight. As a matter of fact, you've seemed distant for about a week or two. Did I do something to you?"

Good question, I thought to myself. Unknowingly, he was heading directly down the road I planned to travel later.

"It's not what you did Jason," I said making eye contact, "it's what you didn't do."

"What do you mean?" He asked defensively.

I sucked my teeth. "Jason you know what I mean. It's been like four months and I still have no idea where we're going with this—this *thing* we've got, and I'm tired of traveling aimlessly."

He sat back from the table. "Wow, I didn't think we were traveling aimlessly. I thought we were chilling—you know—getting to know each other."

"Yeah we were. But how much do you really know about me Jason?"

"Now what's *that* supposed to mean?" He huffed.

I paused staring at him in disbelief. Did he really want to go there? I shrugged, and decided to play along.

"What's my favorite color Jason?"

"Blue."

"No. Cream. What's my favorite movie?"

He thought for a moment, then replied confidently: "Crooklyn."

"No. Love Jones. What do I do every Wednesday?"

"I don't know Jared—but I'm sure you're going to tell me!" He snapped, then turned and stared blankly out the window."

I shook my head. "No Jason. I'm not. If I have to tell you, then it defeats the purpose of getting to know someone, doesn't it?"

"Jared, just because I don't know those things doesn't mean I haven't been getting to know you!"

"You're right, but it's a clear indication that you haven't been paying attention!"

For the next few minutes we sat in silence, trying desperately to avoid eye contact with the other. Lisa was right this was not going to be easy. It was going to be harder than I ever imagined.

"So why you never said anything?"

"About what?"

"About how you felt!"

"Jason why should I have to say something? If you were interested, then you should have asked, or at least paid attention."

"Look Jared, I'm not perfect, nor do I pretend to know all the things to say or not to say in a relationship. But come on, if these things were so important to you, why didn't you say anything about them? Why didn't you come to me and say, *"Hey look Jason, pay attention to this, this is important to me!"* Why wait until the last minute to corner me with this bullshit?!"

"I'm not cornering you! I can only be responsible for one person in this relationship, and that's me! I did my part! I paid attention to you! I comforted you when you needed it! I was there, but where were you, when I needed you?"

He stood suddenly and grabbed his coat. "Look Jared, I don't have time for this, the car's outside. Are you coming or not?"

"Maybe I should catch my own cab."

He stopped fixing his coat and looked down at me. "You know good and well you're not going to catch one in this weather, so just come on."

I grabbed my coat reluctantly and headed towards the door. The frigid winter air caused us to walk a little faster to the car than expected. Once inside, Jason gave the driver instructions to his house and asked to hear WBLS. For the first few minutes we rode in silence. But I had shit on my chest I had to get off.

"Jason, you ever think about being in a relationship?"

"I do." He said quickly. "It just has to be with the right person."

I flinched. "Do you think you'll ever find him?"

"No, I don't." He replied coolly.

I swallowed hard. "Why not?"

"Because," he spit, "the quote unquote one doesn't exist in this lifestyle. If I were straight then maybe yeah, I'd find the one, but not in this lifestyle." He turned toward me for the first time. "Why? Do you think *you're* going to find him?"

I thought for a moment then answered: "Yeah, I am. I'm going to find him. And when I do, I'm going to appreciate him everyday I have him in my life."

"That's a nice thought." He said his gaze somewhere far, far away.

"Thoughts are all I have left. I've run out of faces and names to place on him. But yeah, no doubt; I'm going to find him."

For the next few minutes, the silence returned as we rode up the FDR caught up in the passing traffic, each wanting desperately to escape the inevitable.

"Does this mean we're breaking up?" He asked quietly, "Because if we are, I need to know for sure. I don't need any loose strings."

"Believe it or not Jason, we broke up a long time ago. I guess you can say its public knowledge now."

"So does this mean we can't be friends?"

I faced him. "No. We can still be friends…"

"What about sex? Can we still have sex?"

I shifted in my seat not knowing exactly what to say. "I don't know. My new shorty may not like that…"

"Shit! You didn't waste any time, you've already got one lined up?"

"No I don't." I said quickly. At least, I wasn't sure if I did or didn't.

He sucked his teeth. "Jared, can I ask you something?"

I nodded.

"Does this breakup have anything to do with my trip to Atlanta this weekend?"

I nodded. "A little."

"God! You're really upset about that aren't you?"

"Yeah, I am."

"Why? It's just a simple trip!"

I stared at him in disbelief. Was he serious? Did he think I actually believed that bullshit? No trip was simple when it came to Jason. The reason he and Herman went shopping last weekend was because of this trip! And I knew without a shadow of a doubt that he had paid for their tickets down there, the hotel they planned to stay in, and the car they rented! A simple trip my ass! Who the fuck did he think he was talking to?

"Okay then cancel it!" I demanded.

"You know I can't do that!"

"Then it's not so simple then is it?"

"Jared..." He said rubbing his temples, "Herman is depending on me. My cousin—"

I snapped. Enough was enough.

"Jason and I'm not!" I spit through clenched teeth. "I'm not depending on you? Why would you even take it there?! Why?!"

"I don't know!" He yelled. "If I knew this trip was going to cause so much tension between us I wouldn't have planned it."

Another lie.

"Hey, it's too late now right? I mean especially since you have all these people *depending* on you, right?"

"Jared please, the last thing I need now is your sarcasm."

"Sorry." I mocked. *Fuck* him!

"Look," he huffed, "you don't have to apologize, it's not your fault—it's not anybody's fault. I'm going on this trip because I've never gone before. I want to do this, and I'm not apologizing to you or anybody for doing what I want to do! I made a decision, and I'm sticking with that decision!"

"You know what Jason, fuck you! No really, fuck you! You think I give a fuck whether or not you carry your ass off to Atlanta? Well I don't!" I lied. "If that's what you want to do with your fucking life, then do it! I ain't trying to stop you, and I ain't trying to stand in your fucking way! Because it's obvious we're not going anywhere in this relationship. You don't love me! You don't need me! And you damn' sure don't want me—cause if you did, you'd fuckin' act like it! But if you think I'm gonna sit around and wait for your ass while you go trekking around the country, on some fucking faggot parade, then you're wrong—cause I'm not! So my friend, go on your trip. Have the time of your life—live your dreams—find your truth! But you won't do so at the expense of my heart!"

"Is it really that deep Jared? I'm saying, is it *really* that deep?"

"Yes it is. And it's too bad you haven't realized this shit yet, but one day, trust me you will." I spit just as the car pulled up to his building. He grabbed his bag and opened the door.

"I wish we didn't have to end it like this." He said pausing momentarily.

"Me too, but I think it's the best thing for the both of us."

"Yeah well, speak for yourself," he said exiting the car, "because I would've thought otherwise. But since you've made your decision, enjoy your life."

I bit my lip, halting the tears, "And you, your trip."

I watched him walk away. I watched him enter the building. I watched him pause, drop his head, then raise it back up again. I watched as he turned slowly, made two steps then stopped. I watched him watch me, as if he had one last thing to say, something I needed to hear, something I *had* to hear. But then I watched as he sighed, raised his hand and waved goodbye.

I turned and ordered the driver to leave. He would not have my heart, and my tears.

BOOK TWO

summer soft

-Stevie Wonder

TEN

Jared

IN RETROSPECT, I don't know why I took my breakup with Jason so hard. From the beginning I knew exactly where he stood on love and relationships. I knew of his vow to *never* go there again. I even witnessed on several occasions his determination to uphold this sacred promise. Never once did he lie about how he felt, what he wanted, or for that matter, from whom he wanted it. Yet still I continued blindly; convincing myself I could change him; honestly believing I could get him to see love differently; believing I could heal his pain. I could not have been more wrong. And as a result, I couldn't sit with my heart in my hand and blame him for its pain, not when I brought the shit upon myself. No, I sabotaged my own life.

You know it's funny when you finally realize how often you've actually contributed to the chaos within your life. How time and time again you've managed to talk yourself into the same reoccurring scene, somehow believing this time regardless of what has happened in the past, things will be different. It's a foolish mistake we've all fallen victim to. In the end if you're lucky, you walk away with nothing more than a scratch, and another chance to make good on life's promises. But, if you're not so lucky, like I had been so many, many times, you walk away severely bruised; doubting and questioning everything life has thrown your way.

I was wounded. Hurt. Lost.

I cursed myself for getting involved so deeply. How, I wondered, could I have been so stupid? How?

After ripping myself apart piece by piece, I decided to take a few days off from work to get my life back on track.

I don't know what it is about exercise, but somehow it has the ability to rejuvenate not only the body, but one's mind. I worked out around the clock. I awoke every morning at five-thirty, and for at least a half-hour pounded the treadmill. Afterwards I'd do at a minimum, two, to three hundred push-ups, crunches, and squats. During the day I would read, sleep and reflect on my life and its many, many mishaps. By six, I was back to my regimen of push-ups, crunches and squats. I kept to myself. No phone calls, no visitors. I needed to get as much as I could out of my system, and solitude was the only way in which I could do it effectively.

Two days into my regimen I began to realize my problem: I had no real concept, or grasp on this thing called love. I was still baffled how in one minute, love, and all its wonder, could bring into your life all the joy this world had to offer. But then seconds later a shift in the wind could tear that very same world apart, leaving a once full vibrant spirit, gutted and alone. Realizing this, one would think I would slow down, chill, relax and figure out exactly what I wanted, and, from whom I wanted it. But for some reason, I could not bring myself to pull the switch on this automatic pilot I'd been cruising on for years. I needed love. I needed a relationship. I needed that, that feeling of completion. And I could not switch gears until that happened...

Day four while curled up on the sofa watching *Love Jones,* I received a surprised phone call from Dio. At first I stared at the caller id box mulling over whether or not I should answer, considering his actions the week before. But then, reason took over. Despite all we went through, he was still my friend so I paused the movie, and answered.

"Hello..."

"Jared," he said in a hushed tone, "please don't say anything just let me get this out. I want to apologize for coming out of my face last week. It was uncalled for, and completely misdirected..." he whispered, his voice trailing off.

"Dio," I began.

"Jared please," he begged, slightly raising his voice, "just let me finish. I've been under a lot of stress lately—at the office, family drama, and now," he paused, "drama with Miles. Still, I admit, that's no excuse to take things out on the people who mean the most to me—you and Sean. I was wrong. I shouldn't have yelled and ran out like I did. It was childish. And neither of you deserved it."

A long paused filled the lines.

"Are you finished?" I asked cautiously.

He sighed. "Yes."

"Dio, what you did was fucked up. And while, I *appreciate* your apology, I still don't understand what happened. I mean, we were talking and laughing like we always do. Why'd you trip out like that?"

"I really don't know. I guess, maybe I kind of freaked out when you kept asking questions about Miles."

"But why? You asked me questions about Michael—I mean what, you can ask about my life, but I can't ask about yours?"

"Of course you can. Its just..." he said stopping suddenly.

"It's just what Dio?"

"It's just, I'm afraid."

"Afraid? Afraid of what?"

"Afraid I'm falling in love with Miles again—but not just that. I'm afraid because, for the first time in my life I have no idea what to do next."

"Dio," I exhaled, "that's it? That's what you're afraid of? That's what has you freaking out? Come on, a little fear is normal man. Plenty of people have no idea what to do when confronted with love. You know that song by Billie Holiday, *Comes Love...*" I said humming the tune. "Well people have been trying to figure out what to do when love comes for centuries! Yet it's been proven time and time again: No one can dictate the course of love—it just happens."

"Well, what if you don't *want* it to happen?"

"Don't want it to happen? What?" I asked in disbelief.

"I mean, what if you don't want love to happen? What if you just want it to stop? How do you stop it?" He said his voice rising considerably. "It's stressing me the fuck out! I can't function at work because I'm thinking about him! I can't fall asleep at night because of him. I can't—look!" He paused exasperated. "I just don't think I can take much more of this shit Jared. It's killing me!"

I couldn't understand it. How could *this* be killing him? *How?* When this was the very feeling I was searching for—longing for—*damn near* living for!

"Dio, I'm sorry, maybe I don't understand or, maybe I'm just stupid, but, *why is this a problem?*"

He sucked his teeth annoyed. "Jared, you know I really didn't expect you to understand—*Mr. Do-What-ever-it-takes-to-hold-onto-a-man!* Like I said, I have way too much going on right now to be thinking about some man! Remember what I told you last week? About love not being an option? Well it's really not! Not at this point in my life! But it's like, he shows back up and all these feelings, I thought I'd gotten over, resurfaced. It wasn't supposed to happen like that..."

I sat both in awe and confusion.

"Dio, may I ask a question?"

"Sure, what is it?"

"Why are you so frustrated? I mean, isn't this *supposed* to be a good thing? I mean damn'! Do you know how many people would *love* to be in your shoes right now? You should be thankful this is happening! It's obvious you care about him, because this is the first time I've ever heard you go on like this—as a matter of fact—this is the first time you've ever talked to me about anyone you liked seriously!"

"I know, I know. I love him Jared, I do. I always have. But right now, I really don't need to get emotionally involved with anyone—especially if it's unpredictable."

I shook my head. "Unpredictable? Dio, what does Miles think about this whole situation?"

"Shit! He's going full speed ahead! That's what's scaring me! When we hooked up the first time, he did the same shit and where did we end up? Nowhere! I can't—*no*—I *won't* do that this time. I'm not a kid anymore! I can't just *fall* in love! There's way too much at stake at this point in my life..."

"Honestly Dio, I really think you're making this way more dramatic than it needs to be. What's at stake?"

"Everything!" He howled. "For one, I'm older and more successful than I was before, which obviously renders more responsibility—and I can't let a relationship get in the way of my business—plus, I'm settled for the most part. Miles is still carving his niche. He still doesn't know what he wants to do, today he wants to model; tomorrow he wants to act! Why just last week he told me his manager got him a part in Spike Lee's latest movie! What if—"

"Dio listen, does Miles love you?"

He paused. "Yes. I know he does."

"And, do you love him?"

He hesitated. "I think so. I mean," he sighed exasperated, "that's what I'm trying to figure out. I know for sure, no one has ever made me feel the way he does. No one..."

"Then my friend, why all the excuses? You have nothing to worry about. It seems to me you two genuinely care about each other, and that's what's beautiful man. Because in the end, that's what's gonna make this shit work. It doesn't matter if his career picks up, because if his heart and soul are with you then no matter what he's doing, or where he goes, he will take you with him and vice versa."

He remained quiet for a long time digesting my words. "You're right." He finally said. "But I still can't help being scared. I mean what if I go there this time and still end up getting hurt..."

"Listen, no one can hurt you Dio, unless you allow them." I said finding my way to the window. "Besides, from what you've told me Miles seems like a great guy. He must be if he's got you acting like this."

"He is a sweetheart. But, you know what, enough about me and all my drama, how are you *Pump-kin*? Is everything all right?"

"Dio for the first time in a long time yes, everything is fine."

"Good, good, and how's Jason?"

"Honestly, I don't know. I broke up with him last week after the show."

"Really?" He asked surprised. "Are you okay? I mean I know how much he meant to you—"

"Yeah, I'm okay."

"Are you sure? Cause if you need to talk…"

"Dio relax. I'm okay. Jason and I weren't doing nothing but wasting each other's time. We needed to end it, and get on with our lives."

"Well Jared, can I just say that I am so proud of you! You're finally growing up!"

I laughed. "Growing up? What's that suppose to mean?"

"*Sweety* you know what it means! You use to hold on to dates so tight we needed a crow bar to pry your behind away!"

"You're right," I chuckled, "but I'm learning how and when to say no."

"Well it's about time! So, I guess now you have more time for your *store*—I mean," he paused catching himself, "your new friend Michael."

"Why do you always have to go there Dio?"

"I'm sorry *Pump-kin*. At least I caught myself this time. But seriously, how are things with you two?"

"I don't know. I haven't spoken to him in a few days."

"Why? What's been going on?"

I sighed. "Nothing really. After what happened between me and Jason last week, I didn't feel like talking to anybody."

"I can understand that, but *Sweety*, do you want this man or not?"

"Yeah, you know I do it's just—"

"It's just what *Pump-kin*? You better stop playing this cat and mouse game before the mouse gets bored and moves on. Forget about Jason. He's history—finally! I never liked him for you anyway. And if Michael is as fine as you say he is *Pump-kin*, then you better get on your game before the next bitch comes along and snatches him up!"

"Wait a minute," I laughed, "let me find out you and Kevin are teaming up to get me hooked up!"

"*Pump-kin*, I don't know about that bitch, but you know I'm in your corner regardless of your decision. If this boy—excuse me—if this man Michael makes you happy, then *Sweety* I'm behind you one hundred and twenty-five percent!!!"

I smiled. "Thanks man, that means a lot to me."

"Well you're welcome. And now that you have my stamp of approval get off this phone and call that man and let him know how you feel!"

"Bet, I will. But, you've got to promise me something too."

"Anything…" he said quickly, "it's the least I can do considering my actions last week."

"Well, since you've put it that way, you've got to promise me that once I hang up you'll call Miles and tell him the same thing."

"Please! Is that all *Pump-kin*? I thought you were going to give me a challenge. I'm already two steps ahead of you."

ELEVEN

Diogenes

I MUST HAVE PACED MY CONDO a thousand times before I finally picked up the phone and called Miles. Two rings later he answered.

"Hello."

"Hey." I spoke softly.

"Dio?" He asked surprised. "Is it really you?"

"Yeah, it's me."

"Wow...I'm glad you called. I was just thinking about you."

I laughed. "I hope it was good."

"It was." He said quickly. "It always is. How are you?"

"I'm okay. I was just thinking about you too."

"You were?" He chuckled. "Now *I'm* scared!"

"Don't be. It was good..." I paused, searching for the strength. "I was wondering whether or not you were busy tonight."

"Not at all, why, what's up?"

"I was thinking maybe we could hook up and, you know, talk."

"I'd love too. Where do you wanna meet?"

"Well, since you've never been to my new place, I was kinda hoping you'd consider coming by here. I mean, if you don't want to I completely understand..."

"Dio, I'd love to come by your place. What time would you like me there?"

"As soon as possible." I whispered.

"Consider me there."

I gave him directions and hopped into the shower. Immediately my thoughts traveled back to the last time I saw Miles. I had been such an *asshole* I wondered whether or not he'd ever forgive me. And if he did, could we actually make a go of this relationship. I massaged my face with the skin purifying exfoliate I had purchased earlier from Kiehl's. Afterwards, I parted my locks, and allowed the water to caress my scalp, the whole time thinking of Miles. Minutes later, feeling fully refreshed, I stepped out of the shower, grabbed a towel, and dried my five feet nine inch caramel frame. I applied Palmer's cocoa butter to my skin, wrapped a towel around my waist, and made my way to the bedroom. As I stood in the walk-in closet sifting through the collection of clothing I had acquired over the years, a mind-blowing revelation entered my head. One I had not fully thought about until then.

If I got back with Miles, I'd have to get rid of all my pieces!

At the time, I was dating about three people, none seriously of course, just your—let's meet up, get something to eat, go back to your place and fuck type situations. None of them, by far were relationship material like Miles, but then that didn't matter, because they served a purpose. One I had gotten use to. One I didn't know if I wanted to give up. Especially Darrel! Of all my pieces, he was the one who had lasted the longest—two months and counting. He was young, handsome, intelligent, and gifted! He knew where to touch me, when to touch me and how to touch me. The thought of not seeing his sexy ass sprawled across my bed after a night of passionate sex saddened me. I leaned against the closet door and sighed. Did I really want to give up the single life? Was I really ready to be a one man, man?

Then, it hit me. Maybe I wouldn't have to get rid of Darrel so quickly. I mean there was no telling whether or not Miles and I were actually going to hit it off. If we did, then no problem, Darrel and everybody else would just have to go. But until then, there was absolutely no reason to trouble his pretty little head. Neither of them…

The telephone shattered my thoughts.

"Hello."

"Sorry to interrupt you sir but there's a Mr. Miles Coleman here to see you. Shall I allow him up?"

"Yes Reid, please do."

I hung up the phone, pulled on a pair of RL lounging pants, a matching tank top and glanced in the mirror. Stunning! About a minute later, my door rattled. I opened it and was greeted to a smile I had grown to love.

"Come in, come in. I'm glad you could make it."

"Wow Dio!" He said taking in my massive foyer. "This place is beautiful!"

"Thank you."

"How many bedrooms do you have in this place?"

"Three, including the guest suite."

"The guest suite?" He teased. "Who stays there?"

"Usually my mother when she visits."

"Cool." He said, still taking everything in.

"Would you like a tour?"

He nodded yes, and so, I took him on a tour of my midtown split level condo. The first floor consisted of a formal living room, complete with a working fireplace, a formal dining room that sat twelve, my den/study, bathroom, and, a state of the art kitchen with a small, but quaint breakfast nook.

His face glowed as we climbed the massive marble staircase covered in an antique Persian runner that led to the second floor. He peered into each bedroom like a general inspecting his troops, growing overwhelmed by each of their beauty. He took in every detail, every painting and every statue. In the master bedroom, he carefully scanned the various photos of my family that sat on the bookshelf, adjacent to the leather chaise lounge situated between the two Victorian windows.

"Dio I can't believe how well you've done for yourself. Is this all you?" He asked taking in the various appointments.

"I had a little help, but yeah for the most part this is all me."

"Well you did a hellava job. It really looks great."

I smiled. "Thanks. I dreamed about an apartment like this forever but I never thought in a million years I'd get the chance to actually *live* inside of it, but..." I shrugged, "here I am. It's a lot, I know. But the feeling of euphoria I get, every time a little old white woman realizes I live here, and not delivering, is worth every penny I pay in mortgage."

He laughed. "I know the feeling. I get it every time I check into a five-star hotel. They always assume I'm lost. It's about time our people started proving them wrong."

"My sentiments exactly. Listen, are you hungry? I could order something?"

"No not really, but, it's good to see you haven't changed all that much. You still don't cook huh?"

"With my schedule, I barely have time to eat, let alone cook!"

His head fell back and released a heart-filled laugh. "We have way too much in common Dio because I can definitely relate to that!"

"I figured you could."

He chuckled a little more, before adding: "It is *sooo* good seeing you man, you just don't know..."

A warm feeling, the same one I use to get all those years ago filled my heart, and I blushed. The man had a way with words, and my heart. And he knew it.

"I didn't mean to embarrass you." He smiled.

"Yes you did."

He laughed. "You're right."

"Aren't I always?"

"Well..."

"I'm playing. Listen, would you care for something to drink?"

"Sure."

"Will wine do?"

"Actually, wine would be great."

"Cool. I have some down stairs in the living room. Shall we?"

Downstairs, I poured two glasses of a 1966 Merlot, placed *Roberta Flack's* greatest hits in the stereo, and joined him on the sofa.

"Miles listen, I have to apologize for the way I behaved last week. It was stupid. I was confused, and scared and…well, simply rude."

"Yeah, you were, but I understand. I know you didn't mean what you were saying."

I sipped my drink. "Really? How did you know?"

"Because, I could tell by your eyes. Your mouth said one thing, but your eyes, they said another. They said you loved me."

"I do love you Miles. I just wish sometimes I wasn't so scared to show you how much."

"You know Dio, It's okay to be scared." He said caressing my hand. "I get scared too. But I've come to realize I can't continue to let my fears keep me from the things I want. And right now, I want you."

"I know you do Miles. I can see it."

"Can you feel it?"

"I can."

He moved in closer. "Then what's wrong baby? I've already told you I'm not going to hurt you."

"Miles listen, I love you—"

"Dio, I love you—"

I placed a finger over his lips. "Let me get this out Miles. I need to. I've been holding this in for far too long. Like I said, I love you. You know this. I know this. When I'm with you, I feel so at ease, and safe. I feel as if everything is right in the world. But, at the same time I can't help but feel it's because I haven't seen you in a while. And that, maybe I'm acting out feelings I locked away years ago. I listen to you, and I hear you say this time things are different but, last time I thought the same thing. And, I got hurt."

He grabbed my hand. "Baby, you don't know how sorry I am that I hurt you. I wish to God that I could go back and undo the things I did, or, unsay the things I said, but, I can't. And so I live with the shame of my wrongs everyday. And I pray that you find it in your heart to forgive me. Because, I know I was wrong. I know I messed up. But I promise you, if you do forgive me, and, if you do decide to give me a second chance, believe me, I won't let you down."

I left the sofa and began pacing the room. "I hear you Miles, but—"

Miles stood, grabbed my hands and pulled me to him, his eyes revealing the love in his heart. "Baby, listen to me, I love you," he whispered softly in my ear. "More than you know. The biggest mistake I ever made, was losing you. It never should have happened, and again, for years I lived with that guilt. I was blind not to see what you meant to me. But I made a promise to myself and to God, that if I ever got a chance with you again, I would do everything in my power to show you just how much I love you, and how much it means to me to have you in my life." He pulled me closer. "So, I'm telling you, you don't have to worry. I'm not going anywhere. Not for a long, long, time…"

I relaxed and allowed myself to be held. "You promise?" I asked, seconds later.

He released his grip from my waist and held my face in his hands. Kissing me gently he whispered, "I promise."

That night, for the first time since our breakup, I let down my guard, and let love in. The feeling it provided comforted me as Miles lay snuggled in my arms. The familiarity, the warmth and the beauty of what our union represented created a flood of emotions within me. And as I held him close, I knew there was only one thing left to do.

Tomorrow I would call Darrel and tell him it was over: *I's married now*!

TWELVE

Jared

TWO HOURS, fifteen minutes, and eighteen seconds is how long it took me to work up enough nerves to call Michael. Twenty seconds later I picked up the phone punched in his number and counted the rings.

"Hello."

"What's up Michael, this is Jared. You busy?"

"No, not at all Jay. I was on the phone but, hold on, let me get my friend off the line."

Tiny beads of sweat formed on my brow as I awaited his return. For a split second I considered backing out, but realized it was a little too late for that. Sink, or swim, I had to go through with it.

"Hello? Jared?" He asked returning to the line.

"Yeah I'm here, what's up?"

"Nothing much Mr. J, what's up with you?"

"You." I rattled off confidently; *too* confidently.

He laughed. "Me?"

"Yeah you…"

"Ummm…" he hummed, "what do *I* have to do with *you*?"

From his tone I detected blushing, which was all the ammo I needed. I went in for the kill.

"Everything, if you play your cards right."

The words rolled off my tongue like hot butter off a knife. It was by far the smoothest line I had ever spit. Pure classic. But then, it hit me. And like clock work, I panicked.

What did I just do? I wondered as I began pacing my apartment. *Did I just out myself? Shit!* It wasn't supposed to happen this way, and it definitely wasn't supposed to happen this quickly—I mean—I was *supposed* to *sneak* it in—figure his shit out, *then* move in for the kill! *Damn* I fucked up big time! And to make matters worst, he wasn't saying shit! Nothing! Nadda! Zilch! I knew this was a bad move. I should have never let Dio talk me into calling! Why had I even listened to him! I knew this guy wasn't down! Fuck! And now I—

"Wow…" he said softly, bringing my uneasy pace to a halt. "I guess I have to play my hand very carefully." He paused. I held my breath. "After all, I don't want to fuck this one up."

A smiled tugged at the corners of my face as my legs weakened. *'Could this be real?'* I thought, as I found, then sat on the edge of my bed, my mouth open and every inch of my body pulsating in total disbelief. I had watched, and desired this man in every way imaginable. If ever, there was a person to love, to want: Michael Anderson was he. Hands down no questions asked. And I had just received confirmation that I could very well get my chance.

Unnerved by the sudden silence he cleared his throat. "Hello? Jared? Are you still there?"

"Yeah, yeah I'm here." I stammered. "I um…I guess I um, I didn't expect your answer."

"Why?" He asked comfortably. "We've been talking back and forth for some time now, I thought it was obvious."

Obvious. I smiled. I liked the sound of that.

"So you're cool with this?" I asked.

"With what being gay?"

"Yeah…"

He laughed. "Sure, why not. I've been this way all my life. I have no choice but to be cool with it."

That uncomfortable silence that usually follows truth filled the lines; during which time I tried as best I could to remain calm fearing severe hyperventilation. I knew for sure, at any given moment I would just pass the fuck out.

"Damn," I said breaking the quiet, "all of a sudden it's as if I'm lost for words. I'm not sure what to say, or do…"

He laughed. "I know. I feel the same way. I'm just glad you broke the ice first. If it was left up to me, we would have been talking aimlessly about nothing for months."

"Believe me," I said relaxing some, "I had to be coerced into saying something. I couldn't figure you out."

"Me?" He boomed. "What about you! You were the one throwing a brother off talking about dating Toni Braxton! I mean I knew Kevin was down, but you, I couldn't tell."

I laughed. "How'd you peep Kevin?"

He sucked his teeth. "Come on man. He was cuttin' up the whole time you guys were in the store. You could tell he was trying to hide it, but you'd have to be pretty blind not to peep his act."

I laughed even harder knowing Kevin would be pissed if he heard this. He constantly swears he's completely "undetectable", even with me telling him every time we go somewhere he needs to stop cutting up. But no matter where we find ourselves, Kevin is going to be Kevin.

"I'm not saying he was all the way out of the closet," Michael continued almost reading my thoughts, "I mean if I wasn't down myself I probably would've never clocked him. But since I know what to look for, I peeped it immediately. Besides, at BR we get at least a hundred or so homo-thugs shoppin' every day so, that alone makes it even easier for me to pick out the kids."

"Word, a hundred?" I said a little intimidated. With options like that, what type of chance did I have? "I hope you're not as helpful with them as you were with me?"

"Helpful, with you? I almost didn't help you at all." He sneered.

"Why not?"

"*Why not*? You don't remember? All I did was ask if you needed help, and you broke: *"no thank you!"* At first I took it personally but when I really thought about it, I realized I didn't do shit so I was like—whatever!"

"My bad man, I didn't mean any harm its just, well you know how people are in stores like that. They're constantly in your face asking if you need help with this or that or even worse, most of the time they're just watching you, trying to see if you're going to steal something..."

"True," he hissed with enough contempt to start a bout of fisticuffs, "but some of us are just doing our job."

His unexpected shift in attitude did not go unnoticed, and without a doubt raised a red flag. But the truth was I had no time to waste on trivial conversation. I needed to get as much information as I could out of this man, and dissing his job would get me absolutely nowhere. Besides, I had no desire whatsoever to get into the particulars of why I couldn't *stand* sales people. He seemed to enjoy his job, so who was I to put it down?

"You're right," I replied, and immediately changed the subject. "You know you had it going on that day right..."

"What are you talking about?" He said completely thrown off guard. "Weren't we just talking about my job, and your attitude?"

"We were." I said softly. "That's what made me remember the first time I saw you, and how good you looked."

"Come on Jay enough of the bullshit!" He laughed.

"I'm serious. Would you believe me if I told you I still remember, with exact detail what you were wearing that day?"

"You're playing right?"

"No, I'm not. You had on black slacks, a black sweater—v-neck as a matter of fact, and, if I'm not mistaking, black shoes."

"Oh my God!" He said shocked. "You *do* remember!"

"Of course I do. I haven't stop thinking about you since that day."

"Wow..."

"What?"

133

"It's just," he whispered after a moment of silence. "It's been a minute since anybody said something nice to me. It feels kind of strange. Almost, like I don't deserve it."

"Really?" I asked in disbelief.

"Yeah, really."

"That's fucked up. There's no way in the world anybody should feel that way, especially, someone like you. I believe people should remind each other everyday just how special they are, and how much their presence means to them. I'm saying, think of how much happier everyone would be."

"Please. It wouldn't last. It never does, because happiness is temporary."

"Temporary? Come on Michael, you don't believe that."

"Believe it? Jared I've experienced it! And I know for a fact it's temporary. It has to be one of life's most fucked up jokes."

I shook my head in disbelief. Was he serious?

"Happiness is a decision Michael. You either choose to be happy, or you choose otherwise. But the choice is yours."

"You know what," he said, once again raising his tone, "I hear people say that shit all the time *"happiness is a decision...you gotta choose to be happy—don't worry, be happy!"* That's bullshit!" He barked. "If anything, happiness occurs when people finally realize there is *no such thing as happiness*—at least not the kind of happiness we're looking for."

I sat silent trying my best to grasp his way of thinking. "Are you serious?" I finally replied having found no logic at all to his madness.

"As a heart attack." He said with little room for exaggeration. "Listen, I'm one of those people that thought they'd found happiness. I thought I found that—that feeling everybody's always running around singing about on the radio, acting out on TV, and in the movies. But you know what, I didn't. All I found was lies, deceit and more lies. So right now Jared, I couldn't be more serious. I can't waste my time believing in that shit no more."

My head was spinning. "So what do you believe in?"

"Nothing much these days, except," he paused, "for the truth as prophesized by my pops, and that is, *"life is a bitch"*. And you know what? It really is."

"Damn'," I stammered trying my best to absorb his bitter point of view, "that doesn't seem like a hell of a lot to believe in. What about love?"

"What about it?" He asked dryly.

"Well, don't you believe in love?"

"I used to. But like life, it can fuck the shit out of you…"

"Come on Michael!" I bellowed losing my patience. "I don't believe you're *this* pessimistic about life and love! There's got to be some optimism in you somewhere!"

He laughed. "Pessimistic, I am not. If anything I'm more realistic. But," he paused, "like I said I did believe in life and love before, but it got me absolutely nowhere."

I was heated. Here I was excited as hell about getting to know him, and now the truth about who he was, was irking the shit out of me! Here again was another Jason. Were there any unscarred men left in the world?

"So now I take it, because of a few fucked up experiences, you've given up on both?"

"Given up? I wouldn't say I've given up. I mean after all I'm still here. Let's just say I'm careful about who I spend my time with and, who I choose to love."

I breathed a sigh of relief. "Now see, I don't have a problem with you being particular, as a matter of fact, I like that. We all should be a little picky when it comes to decisions that affect our lives. It definitely shows you have some respect for life—but damn—you've got some really twisted views on happiness and love my man."

"Maybe, but hey, that's me. I make no excuses for who I am."

I nodded. "Respectable; very respectable. So let me ask you something Mr. Anderson, are you single?"

"I guess you can say that."

"You guess? There's no guessing. Either you are, or you aren't. There are no in betweens."

He chuckled at my straightforwardness. "I am."

"Why?"

"Why not, is there something wrong with being single?"

"Nah, not at all. I'm just trying to figure out why some one as good-looking as you is single? I'm sure, with what, the hundred or so *homo-thugs* you got running through your job on a regular basis you have no problem getting a date."

He laughed, and then fell quiet.

"Well? Are you going to answer my question?"

"Jared," he said after an extended pause, "what do you want from me?"

"Nothing, except a little of your time."

"That's it?" He asked suspiciously. "Just time?"

"Pretty much. Why, would that be a problem?"

"No, but I want you to know, that right now that's all I have to give. Nothing more."

"Hey," I said masking my disappointment, "I'll take whatever I'm given. Beggars can't be choosey. Can they?"

"It depends."

"On what?"

"On what they're begging for." He said quietly.

"What if it was the answer to a question?"

"Let me guess…" he sighed, "Why am I single, right?"

"Bingo."

"It's a long, long story. Are you sure you're up for it?"

I flopped onto the sofa and got comfortable. "I'm positive."

"Then," he paused, "let's make a night of it. There's a nice little Italian restaurant down by the Brooklyn Promenade I like to eat at. It's small and cozy but best of all, private. Let's meet there in let's say," he paused, "an hour, and I'll tell you everything you need to know."

CASRALDI'S WAS ON MONTAGUE a few blocks down from Court Street in Brooklyn Heights. Quite to my surprise Michael was at the restaurant on time, waiting for me when I arrived. I smiled thinking of all the times I had waited for Jason to arrive fashionably late. I was happy those days were long behind me. We greeted each other with warm hugs and chatted about nothing in particular until the hostess arrived. Moments later we slipped into a padded booth and began perusing the menu. When our waitress arrived we ordered our meal then immediately fell into conversation.

"You look good." I said, as a brilliant smile found his face.

"Thanks. You too."

I blushed, unused to such accolades.

"You do." He said sincerely. "I love your eyes."

I thought of Dio and his vibrant eyes. "Why? They're not colored or anything. They're just brown."

He shrugged. "So, they're still beautiful. They say so much about you."

"Like what?"

"Like," he said studying me, "you love to smile. You love good food. And you love, love."

"Damn'! My eyes say all of that?"

"They do. You'd be surprised how much you can learn about a person just by looking in their eyes. For example look in mine, and tell me what you see."

I studied him carefully. And for a moment could not believe I was sitting across from him studying him, about to tell him exactly what I saw in his big brown eyes. A warm sensation filled me because not only did I know what I saw, I felt it.

"I see, a man with honest intentions. A man who wants to be loved honestly and completely; a man who, not only wants to be loved, but also wants to be understood, because he knows being loved just isn't enough. I see a fighter; a man who refuses to give up no matter how hard things may be. But I also see a man that's been hurt, very, very badly, and he's afraid of what might happen if he falls in love again..."

He blinked suddenly and lowered his head. "You've seen more than I thought you would on your first try. I guess I'm not good at hiding things am I?"

"No it's not that, its just well, you're right. The eyes *are* the windows to the soul."

"I know. That's why I'm afraid of you."

"I don't want you to be afraid."

"I don't either but I can't help it. Like you said I've been hurt before and well, let's just say I'm not in a rush to experience it again."

I held up my hand, as if to take an oath. "I promise I won't hurt you."

He laughed and began playing with his utensils. "So do you still want to know why I'm single?"

I nodded. "If it's not too much trouble, I understand if it's personal."

"No. It's not that it's personal, it's just difficult to talk about at times."

"Then, we won't. I don't want to force—"

He shook his head. "No, I think we should. I think it'll help you understand exactly where I am right now in my life, and why my views on love and happiness seem so strange to you. But first," he said noticing the waitress returning with our food, "let's eat."

We ate in silence. During which time the couple adjacent to us finished their meal and left. I thought about all the meals I had had with Jason, and how each one had been an experience within an experience. I never knew ordering food was an actual science until I hooked up with him. He counted every calorie, and as a result demanded the waitress or waiter provide him with a list of the nutritional facts for every course he planned to consume. The first time he requested it, I thought he was playing so I laughed along with the waiter; little did we know just how serious he was. He actually refused to dine unless they provided his request. That little quirk, along with a host of others, I would not miss.

Once we were done the waitress cleared the table and returned with coffee and dessert. Michael sipped his slowly then sighed heavily. From

137

his distant troubled gaze I gathered whatever he was about to share caused him a great deal of pain. Part of me sensing the drama, wanted to stop him before he even began. The last thing I needed or wanted was someone else's shit clouding my life. But for some reason I didn't stop him. I let him speak.

"Me and my boyfriend broke up about a month ago," he said staring into his mug, "and it still feels like yesterday. It's like," he paused meeting my gaze, "I can't seem to figure out when or where we went wrong. In a way that still bothers me."

"How'd you guys meet?"

"Through a mutual friend at a party about a year and a half ago…"

"So it was a good meeting." I said rather optimistically.

"Yeah, you can say that. When we first started out everything was great. We had a lot in common. We enjoyed the same type of movies, music, restaurants. We clicked. Before we knew it six weeks had passed and we were like: *Damn, I'm feeling you.* And we were. We did everything there was to do together. It was great.

"But then one day four months into our relationship things started to change. At first, I thought it was me, because at times I know I can be extremely overwhelming." He glanced up. "I like attention," he said apologetically, "and I've been told at times I require too much of it."

"There's nothing wrong with that…" I responded quietly.

He managed a smile then continued. "So anyway, one day I asked him if I had said or done anything to spark the change, but he was like: *Nah, it's not you. It's just I've got a lot of shit on my mind right now, that's all. I just need some time to work things out.*

"By then I was completely in love with this man, so I vowed to give him all the time he needed and then some. Because more than anything, I wanted things to get better; but, they didn't. They only got worse.

"There were times Jared we would talk the whole night away, not giving a fuck about work or anything else, just each other. But then it was like all of a sudden it stopped. We talked less and less and I eventually found myself begging for his time. He didn't want to talk anymore; he was tired. He didn't want to have sex anymore; he had a headache. He didn't want to go out anymore; he was broke. I remember this one time—" He said stopping suddenly.

"This is hard for you isn't it?" I probed watching him.

"Yeah. Kind of. I've never really talked about it before."

"Then don't—"

He raised his hand silencing me. "No, I need to do this man. Believe it or not it hurts more when I hold onto it." He sipped his coffee and after a brief pause, continued. "Like I was saying, I remember this one time, I called him and asked if he wanted to go with me to see Tyler Perry's new play. He said yeah so I purchased the tickets. The night of the play after not hearing from him all that day, I called to ask him what time were we hooking up. To this day, I have never forgotten what he said.

"My bad yo, I was supposed to call you earlier...but, uh...I forgot. Anyway, I changed my mind. I'm not going."

Up until that point I didn't realize how important going to that play was for me. But, the thought of him not going however, quickly let me know.

"What?" I asked in disbelief. "What do you mean you're not going?"

"I just don't feel up to it." He said nonchalantly.

"Jeff..." I said trying to maintain control, "I've already purchased the tickets. We've been talking about this play all week! I mean come on man, why didn't you call me earlier and let me know how you felt? Who the hell am I suppose to get to go with me now on such short notice?"

"Look Michael." He spit. "I don't know—and I don't like your fucking tone either! If I don't *wanna* go, I don't wannna go! And your getting upset ain't gonna change shit! And as far as who you gonna take? Right now that's really not my problem!"

All attempts at self-restraint failed. My lungs exploded. "Not your problem? Then who the fuck problem is it then? Mine? You told me you were going—and now two hours before the show you tell me you're not?! And somehow this shit is my fault!?"

"I'm not saying it's your fault but I gotta right to change my mind, and I just did. I'm not going."

I lost it. "You fucking *self-centered* bastard! You don't *give a fuck* about anybody but your fucking self—*do you*? I'm sick of this shit! I'm sick of you and—"

"Wait a minute," he interrupted, "all I—"

"Fuck you! You fucking asshole! Fuck you!" I yelled, and slammed down the phone.

I went to the show anyway that night, alone. I sat in the audience and I laughed at the humorous scenes, and cried at the sad ones. By night's end I had convinced myself there was no way in hell he could make this shit up to me. No way. Because this time he'd gone too far and I wasn't going to take his shit anymore...

When I turned the key to my building, I was surprised to find him sitting on my stairs. Before I could tell him to leave, he spoke...

"I've been waiting here all night for you. Where've you been?"

I turned my head. *Where had I been?* I couldn't believe this fucking guy. "Jeff...you know what," I said completely disgusted, "right now I don't have time for this. I've had a long hard day and I'm sure whatever you have to fucking say can wait until tomorrow. Peace." I opened the door and motioned for him to leave.

"Michael wait," he begged, "at least hear me out first."

I stared at him. He knew I didn't want to kick him out, he knew. Just like he knew how hard it had been for me, to go to that fucking play alone. But as usual he was playing me for the fool. And of course I fell for it.

"Alright Jeff talk. You have five minutes." I closed the door and folded my arms.

"Mike look I know sometimes I can be an asshole. I won't deny that. But you know how I feel about you. You know I would never do anything to hurt you, at least not on purpose. Look, I didn't know how much that show meant to you. Had I known, I would have come with you, and you *know* that." He paused, his eyes fixed on mine. "And right now even though I know you're pissed, I hope you believe me when I say I'm sorry, and I love you, and it won't happen again."

Un-expectant tears filled my eyes, and for the first time verbally I questioned his love.

"What about last week?" I asked as I watched him divert his eyes to the floor. His silence angered me. "Oh so you have nothing to say now?"

"What do you want me to say?"

"I want you to look me in my eyes and tell me you *love me* when you hit me! I want you to tell me you don't *mean* to hurt me when you leave bruises all over my fucking body! I want you to—"

I couldn't say anymore. The tears and the pain consumed me. I cried Jared with my whole heart. I cried because I didn't know what else to do. I cried because my whole world was falling apart. And as I cried he comforted me. He whispered over and over in my ear, *"I'm sorry baby, I'm sorry."*

Standing there holding each other in the middle of my lobby, I knew it wasn't over. I knew it wouldn't end like this—it couldn't end like this. I loved him too much. He wasn't perfect and neither was I, but together, maybe we still had a chance. Together, we could do anything be anything, as long as we believed. That night our bond was strengthened. And Jared, for the first time in a long time, I felt happiness; pure untainted happiness."

"So what happened?" I asked, my voice falling to a whisper. "Things got better right?"

"Yeah for a while. And believe it or not that night was wonderful, considering all the shit that led up to it. We spent the rest of the evening together hand in hand talking about what had happened, and what we could do to make our relationship better. And for a while yeah, everything was great. Until the day I found my friend's watch in his apartment."

"What?" I asked in disbelief, "You found what?"

"My best-friend's watch." He said calmly. "It was lying face up on his nightstand. I spotted it as soon as Jeff went into the bathroom to shower. At first I denied it—*'Nah...this couldn't be Angel's watch.'*—but sure enough, it was. I remembered clearly complimenting him on the same exact watch just two days earlier. It was a metal David Yurman watch, with a blue crystal face that had only been released in Europe. So naturally none of my friends had ever seen it. Angel as stuck-up as ever, went on and on about how a *friend* of his, translation: one of the many guys he was fucking, purchased it for him while vacationing in gay *Parie*, Milan and Amsterdam. So you can imagine the pain I felt when I saw that watch on my lover's nightstand! My stomach curled. All I kept thinking is: this isn't happening! There's no way in the world Jeff would stoop that low. Sleep with Angel? Nah he wouldn't, not one of *my* friends?

"He startled me when he walked into the room fresh from showering. *'Hey Mike,'* he said slipping into his briefs, *'you got any idea what you wanna do today?'*

"Nothing much," I replied, fiddling with the watch, "maybe catch a movie and then grab something to eat. Nothing too extravagant though."

"Good 'cause a niggah ain't got that much money plus—hey..." he said straining to see what was in my hand, "what's that you're playing with?"

"Oh this?" I said holding up the watch. "I was just about to ask you the same fucking thing. What *is this* I'm playing with?"

The look on his face alone revealed the truth. As I had feared, he fucked Angel.

"Uh...that's uh...that's a watch I got from uh...from—"

I threw the watch at him. "Cut the bullshit Jeff...I know whose fucking watch this is! I can't believe you would do this shit to me, you fucking asshole!"

"Baby, wait...you don't understand. It's not what you think!"

"What the fuck do you mean it's not what I fucking think?! Do I look stupid to you Jeff huh? Do I?"

"No—"

"Then what the fuck is it then? No wait," I said stopping him before he began spewing off a slew of lies, "let me think about it for a minute...I got it! He had car trouble right. And he didn't have *anybody* to call but you—right? And you being the quote unquote *Good Samaritan* that you are, rushed out to help him! And of course that little *bitch* had to pay you back for your kindness in such a *pressing* situation. So he fucking came over here and—wait I want to get this shit right. Hmmm, what would Angel do in a situation like this? Oh I know! He sat his little ass on the couch and proceeded to complain about how he can't find a *good man* with all the losers out there. And your dumb trifling ass fell right into his fucking hands. But tell me something Jeff, because I'm seriously having trouble with this part—just how long did it take before your *dick* fell into his mouth?"

"Wait a minute now Mike, I already told you it's not what you think! Let me explain—"

"You know what Jeff save it. Because it really doesn't matter anymore. As a matter of fact, I'm glad this shit happened because I'm tired. I'm tired of getting hurt! I'm tired of convincing myself over and over that you love me, when it's obvious you don't! I'm out of here." I grabbed my coat and rushed passed him.

"Wait Michael wait!" He ran after me and flung me around! "Okay, okay you're right! I did fuck him! I admit it. It was wrong! I fucked up! But believe me man, that ain't no reason to throw away everything we have! I love *you* Mike—you, not him! Do you think I give a *fuck about Angel*? Do you think I care about him, like I care about you? He has nothing on you baby—nothing!"

I pulled away from him. "It took fucking him to figure that out?"

He reached again. "Look, can't we at least talk this shit over?"

"What are we going to talk about Jeff? Huh? What? Something new? Something we've never talked about before? If so I'm all for it; but I'm not going to talk about *this* shit anymore. We've talked about shit like this over and over again! And I am not going to do it again!

"I'm saying Jeff, am I *supposed* to believe that shit about Angel? Please! I bet you *loved* his ass last night! I bet his ass *did something* for you when you were up in that shit last night! Fuck you Jeff; you can't sweet talk your way out of this one baby." I shook my head violently. "Not this time."

As I turned to leave I felt a sharp familiar stinging sensation on the left side of my face. I moved just in time to miss the second fist intended for the same spot. Instead he missed and hit the wall. At that point I'm not sure what came over me, because for the first time I fought back and kicked the black off his ass. After the dust settled he lay crying, mumbling *"I'm sorry...I'm sorry..."* I stood there, bloodied black eye and all staring at him. I could not believe I had been with him for more than a year! Thirteen months to be exact. Thirteen months of stress and aggravation, physical and mental torture. Enough was enough. I snatched my coat from the floor and headed for the door.

"Jeff, you don't know how much I hate it had to come to this." I said gripping the doorknob. "I honestly hope you find what you're looking for because it's obvious, you couldn't find it in me."

As I exited the door I heard him mumble: *"Don't go Mike, please don't go. I need you..."*

"Life is so fucking funny Jared because, for a split second I actually considered going back and comforting him. I thought about staying; trying one last time. But I knew I couldn't. Because as much as I wanted to work it out, I knew there was nothing left to work with."

For a while after he finished speaking, I sat in silence digesting his experience. I admired him. Not because he had survived an abusive relationship, but because he had the courage to talk about it. Most people find it difficult to believe gay men everyday are emotionally and physically harassed by the people who claim to love them the most, their lovers. I should know. Vince and I had been together no more than a week before our first argument; and no longer than a month before our first fight. Two and a half years later we were averaging two to three arguments a week, and a scuffle, every two to three weeks. And I still found it difficult to explain the emotions I felt every time we came to blows or, the embarrassment I felt knowing my love of self wasn't strong enough to set me free.

"You know man it takes a lot of courage to admit when something isn't working. Do you know how many people stay in relationships that aren't working all for the sake of love?"

"A lot I imagine..."

"You're right, a lot. And do you know why they stay?"

"Why?"

"Because they're afraid. Afraid to let go. Afraid of what might happen if they don't have someone in their life. Afraid the person doing them wrong will eventually find someone else, and leave them alone to suffer with their demons. But in the end, most are afraid of the unknown. So many people hold on because they've forgotten how and why it's important to let go."

He nodded. "I feel you. That was my problem initially. I was so into *being* in a relationship and having a man, I became blind to the truth. In my heart I knew it wasn't right. I could feel it. But I stayed anyway."

"But eventually you let go. You were strong despite your initial apprehension. You took care of you. A lot of people can't say that. They literally go along for the ride oblivious to everything around them. And when shit starts to crumble they look around for someone else to tell them what to do, or to blame for how they feel!"

"Interesting..."

"What, my theory?"

143

"No, how into this conversation you're getting."

I laughed. "Is that a good thing or a bad thing?"

"Oh it's definitely a good thing!" He said with a mouth full of laughter. "No question about it!"

He signaled the waitress, informed her we were done, and requested the check. Moments later she placed the bill in the center of the table. Before I could extend my arm to claim it, he reached the distance and snatched it up. For the next few minutes I insisted on paying, or at least splitting the bill, but he held his ground reminding me he had invited *me* out. I was impressed. For one he showed up on time, and two he paid for dinner. "Finally," I whispered with a smile, "a real man."

Outside we decided to take a stroll on the Promenade despite the near frigid temperature. Once there, we realized we weren't the only two willing to brave the cold for a glimpse at the most popular skyline in the world. Quite a few couples strolled hand in hand taking in the breathtaking views of Manhattan. We located an empty bench out of view and talked more about life, love, our dreams and accomplishments. At one point having just made a joke he burst into laughter revealing the smile I had come to adore.

"You know," I said softly. "I really love hearing you laugh and seeing you smile. It trips me out how warm I get whenever you do."

"Niggah…" he said laughing hysterically, "you most definitely have the gift of gab!"

"I'm serious, see look…" I smiled touching my heart. "There it goes again. I'm beginning to think you're doing this on purpose."

He stared cautiously at me as I studied his handsome face. For a split second I considered reaching across the distance, and erasing the signs of doubt and pain that troubled him. And so, I did. I allowed my hands to start along his cheek and gently trace the lines of his lips. A stillness engulfed us as we lost all knowledge of our whereabouts.

"Jared, what are you doing to me?" He whispered softly.

"I am doing exactly what I feel, as I feel it."

He closed his eyes and sighed heavily. "What do you want from me?"

I moved in closer our faces now only inches apart. "The question isn't what I want *from* you; but rather what I want *for* you. And that Michael is happiness. That's it. Now, whether that can be achieved with or without me I don't know. Only you know that answer. I can only show you what I have to offer, and hope in time you will allow me to share some of my truths with you."

He considered my words a long time before speaking.

"Who are you? No, I mean really—*who are you*? It's like, you come into my store, catch me completely off guard—and now, you tell me all the things I've always wanted to hear. Is this real? Are you for real?"

"Again Michael, only you can answer that. All I know is that I walked into your store empty, but I walked out full. And that Michael is my truth. You don't know how bad I want to spend many a night—just like this—with you: listening to you, walking with you, talking with you. God, there is so much I want to do for you, but only you know if I will be allowed to fulfill this dream. And right now that's all it is, a dream.

He sat quietly, his eyes fixed on Manhattan, his mind processing my thoughts.

"Look," I continued. "I know all of this might sound funny and maybe for you it's coming a little too soon, but its how I feel. It's how I felt since I met you; since our first phone conversation almost three weeks ago; since I found out you were down a little over four hours ago. So for me it's not all that soon; I *want* to love you, but that all depends on you.

"So," I breathed deeply, "if you say no I will leave you alone and never bother you again. I promise you that. But should you say yes, "I paused, my heart beating wildly, "I will show you a love like no other and that, I promise you also."

A cool wind passed between us as I awaited his response. Millions upon millions of thoughts invaded my mind during the course of those few cold awkward moments. Eventually I began to wonder if I had made a fool of myself by opening up so quickly. I hadn't planned on being so forward. But then there was something about him, and about the way I felt with him, that just made me want to *be* with him, like I had never wanted to be with anyone in my life. And so it made sense to tell him how I felt, to open up, to share with him my inner most feelings. But now, from his silent distant stare I wasn't so sure.

"Jared, I—I don't know what to say…"

"Please," I whispered. "You don't have to say anything right now. Just think about what I've said."

"I will." He said kindly. "But now tell me something, why are you single?"

I tilted my head. "Because I've been waiting…"

"Waiting for what?"

"For love. True love. Lasting love. Like Mary said, *real love*."

He burst into a brilliant smile and before I knew it his lips found mine and we kissed. At first I hesitated considering our location but then threw caution to the wind. I moved in closer savoring the sweet taste of his warm mouth. As we kissed a peace settled over me and I knew for sure I

145

had finally found my love. And on that cold unforgettable night in January, I let go and let love run its course once more.

The next few weeks were right out the pages of a romance novel. Michael and I were practically inseparable. For me it was like a dream come true. Finally I was spending time with someone I loved, but more importantly, someone who genuinely loved spending time with me. Our one-month anniversary found us back at Casraldi's in the same padded booth discussing everything from music to politics. I loved talking to him. It never mattered what we discussed, just as long as I felt his gentle voice penetrating my soul. I discovered a lot about him within that first month. He loved to laugh, to sing, and spend quiet time at home listening to music. Like me he enjoyed all types of music but by far his favorite artist was Diana Ross.

"Diana Ross?" I screeched one night sprawled lazily across the sofa.

"Yes. Diana Ross. What's the problem?"

"No problem. It's just I never would have thought *you* would like Diana. She's so—what's the word—*dramatic*..."

"She's a diva! She's supposed to be dramatic!"

"True, but she takes drama to a whole 'nother level. I'm saying *eight* dress changes during the Super Bowl? *Then* a helicopter lift? The bitch has issues..."

"Bitch?! Hold up, at least people know who the hell she is! What's that sad chick's name you're always listening to?"

"Who, Dianne Reeves?"

"Yeah that bitch! How many platinum albums does she have?"

"I don't know."

"Exactly. And uh, how many movies has she starred in?"

"None that I know of..."

"What about specials? How many television specials has that bitch been in?"

I shrugged. "All of that really doesn't matter when it comes to Dianne Reeves. It's her voice, her delivery, her message that her fans love. All that other superficial bullshit comes second."

He sucked his teeth. "So in other words, the bitch can't dress, has no clout when it comes to getting *real* gigs, and can't act worth shit?"

I tilted my head and laughed. "Basically."

He threw back his head and laughed like never before. We spent many nights like that together, having the time of our lives. Lost in a world filled with endless possibilities. Living a dream. Yes, in so many ways my life with Michael was like a dream. One I vowed never to jeopardize.

"I wrote a little something for you," I said once the waiter had removed our dinner plates and replaced them with dessert. "Can I read it to you?"

"Sure, go ahead."

I removed the folded piece of paper from my back pocket and cleared my throat. I had written the letter the night before shortly after we had said goodnight. I had hoped to bring in our one-month anniversary together, but as usual he had to work. BR was restocking the floor with their pre-spring line and needed at least ten associates to help arrange the store overnight. Michael said he volunteered because he needed the extra cash to take care of some overdue bills. Initially I was upset because I thought I had been more than clear when I expressed my desire to spend that night of all nights with him, but after he explained how much he desperately needed the overtime I relented. At midnight I offered up a prayer thanking God for heeding my call, and set about the task of penning my true feelings...

> *Michael,*
>
> *When I first met you, I thought it was a dream;*
> *your eyes seemed unreal, focused on my thoughts,*
> *fixed ever so carefully, understanding my feel...*
> *When I first met you, I knew love would follow;*
> *your heart was open, your words embraced me pulling me in...*
> *My eyes closed.*
> *My heart skipped.*
> *My mind dreamed of endless talks with rivers of laughter,*
> *open air, filled with honesty...*
> *a fresh scent, unfamiliar, yet comforting.*
> *It was then I realized how special you were.*
> *How special we were, together...*
> *Two people.*
> *Two hearts.*
> *One love.*
> *I know now that love is real, for I feel it in places I've never felt before.*
> *It's hard imagining my life without you,*
> *and it hurts, imagining you without me.*
> *Sometimes, I dream of you...*
> *Sometimes I wonder if you know just how much I need you...*
> *how much I want you...*
> *Michael, when I first met you, I never imagined any of this.*

147

It never entered my mind.
And so it amazes me, how God knew exactly when to share the beauty of you.

I thank him, and I thank you.

Loving you always, Jared

Later that evening he led me to his bed and together we made the most passionate love imaginable. From that night forward, our relationship deepened. We spent even more time together becoming the couple we both dreamed of, visiting museums, restaurants and traveling.

Our third month anniversary found us in Paris, the city of love. On a whim I purchased the two all-inclusive tickets on the Internet and surprised him with them while dining at our now customary spot, Casraldi's.

"We're going where?" He bellowed causing a few patrons to turn to see what was going on.

"Paris. We leave in a week. Think you could get the time off?"

"Hell yeah! And if they say I can't, I'll quit!"

He had never been out of the country before so we had to go through the long painstaking task of getting a rushed passport from the State Department. After a long fussy day of proving he was actually a United States citizen born and raised we were all set, and ready to go.

Paris is most beautiful in spring. I had heard the stories, and managed to do my own research but never in my wildest dreams did I expect them all to be true. Paris is probably one of the most rousing cities in the world. It assaults all the senses, demanding to be seen, heard, touched, tasted and smelled. From its quiet tree lined blocks, to its thriving nightlife, Paris had it all, and we were determined to see it all. Each day we visited as many museums, shops, markets and restaurants as we could: *Notre Dame*, the city's greatest Gothic architectural achievement. *The Eiffel Tower*, the towering edifice built for the World Fair in 1889. *Avenue des Champs-Elysees*, the popular one-mile promenade, once reserved for the upper crust Parisians now served as the ideal stretch for romantic evening walks and overpriced restaurants. And of course my personal favorite, *The Arc de Triomphe*, which when translated into English meant *The Triumphal Arch*. It stood gracefully at the very tip of the Champs Elysees. Napoleon, the French emperor who conquered most of Europe at the beginning of the 19th century, ordered the arch to be built as a symbol of glory for his French Armies. Construction began in 1806 and was completed in 1836. It stood as a memorial for the many soldiers killed in World War I, and also served as the final resting-place for the Unknown Soldier, who was buried just below the center of the arch. Upon his grave burned an eternal flame.

Ever since I was a little kid and I ventured upon an identical arch on Eastern Parkway in Brooklyn, and later another in Washington Square Park in Manhattan, I longed to see the original. And as I stood their critiquing the images of famous names and happenings engraved in the monument with the man I loved, an overwhelming sense of completion came over me. Finally I knew happiness. But not only did I know it, I understood it. For so long I had searched for the keys to unlock the well of love stored deep inside my heart, not knowing when my chance to love openly and freely would come. But there, underneath the most powerful arch in the world, I realized he had finally come to save me—to show me the way—to provide to me everything I ever really needed and wanted. I loved him more *that* moment, than any other moment we had shared. Vince was not the one, nor Jason. No, they were just preludes, fiction, samples, mirages of love. Michael however, *was* the real deal. The one I could trust to lead me safely through the Matrix. The one I could trust with my most valuable possession, my heart.

"I want to thank you for bringing me here." He said, as we strolled along The Avenue to our hotel. We had just downed a three-course meal at one of the local restaurants, complete with two bottles of French wine.

"Growing up in the projects," he continued, "I never thought I would make it out of Brownsville, never mind New York. I wanted to, and I always dreamed I would, but I never thought it would happen. My family didn't help much either. I'm not sure if I've told you this before, but I'm the fourth generation of Anderson's to grow up in the projects. It's like, all my life all I ever thought I would amount to was a drug dealer like my cousin Raquan, or a crack-head like my Aunt Joyce. Or, if somehow my mother had her way, a transit worker like my Uncle Joe. Those were my idols, the people I looked up to. The ones I prayed every night I didn't become.

"No one in my family had gone or even thought about going to college. To them, it was a waste of time—something, white people did. So when I graduated from high school and said I wanted to go, they all laughed at me, even, my moms. She," he said with a hint of malice, "laughed the loudest. *'Where you gonna git that kinda of money?'* She asked. I shrugged. I had no idea. The majority of my friends' parents were paying for them. *'Welfare don't pay for no black man to go to no college.''* She continued bitterly. *"What you better do is git a job, and stop all this foolish talk about college. Look at your Uncle Joe, he ain't been to no college— barely got his GED—and he's doing just fine with his transit job. You need to talk to him and see if he can git you a part-time job cleanin' out the stations or sumthing. As big as this city is they always need somebody to clean it up. You never know what can happen from there. Maybe, if you show up on time, and do a good job, you can even git in the union...'*

"I didn't think it was possible to hate someone so much, but I did. I hated her for stomping on my dream, and making me feel like all I would ever amount to was a *transit worker*. To this day Jared, I have yet to figure out why she would say some dumb shit like that.

"But you know what," he continued after a moment of silence, "when I really thought about it, I finally figured it out. She came from a different era. A time when black people really couldn't do much but accept whatever shit was thrown to them. But shit had changed. Didn't she realize that? Didn't she know that black people today could dream, be and do pretty much anything they put their minds to? I tried to educate her but it was like talking to a wall. All she wanted me to do was to get a job, and help her out with some bills. So I did. But I promised myself that I would only work for a year—that way I could help her out, and hopefully make enough to pay for my books, when I enrolled the following September.

"My first job out of high school was at a lawyer's office downtown Brooklyn: Fitzgerald & Fitzgerald. I hated working there, because they treated me like shit, not the white people, but my fellow blacks. To them, I could do nothing right. I didn't dress right. I didn't speak right. My beard was too thick, my goatee too black. *Why'd you get an earring? Don't you know that's not professional? No wonder the black man can't get anywhere nowadays! We have no idea how to market ourselves?*

"No matter what I did to try to fit into the box, *they said* I needed to fit into, in the end it never really mattered because in their eyes I never would. My skin was too dark, my lips too thick, and my personality too ghetto. Soon they caused me to question, then hate every little thing about myself. People are always talking about how the white mans the one keeping us down—please that shit is a lie, if I ever did hear one. I learned right away white people could give two shits about how you look or act, just as long as you don't get in their way. Niggahs though? They gonna find some way to make sure they let you know shit ain't right with you, whether you ask them or not. I stopped talking at work because according to them, whatever came out of my mouth was broken English or, just plain useless. Soon I stopped believing I could actually be a student, never mind a graduate. Three months later, the crew managed to get me fired on account *I* didn't know how to work with others. The pure audacity of it caused me to curse every last one of them out before security personally escorted me out of the building.

"I was wounded. How was I supposed to pay for college if I had no job? How was I supposed to get into college if I was like they said: a walking, talking idiot? Then I started thinking: maybe mama was right.

Maybe I didn't belong in college. Maybe I was supposed to be some civil servant picking up trash, driving a bus, or scrubbing the insides of some dirty ass train station until I died. I hated my life, and her and my pops for bringing me into this fucking backward ass world. After that, it didn't take long for me to self-destruct.

"I snorted my first line on my twentieth birthday. At first it was just to see how it felt. Then, it was to have a good time when I went out. Then, it became a way to ease the pain; to cope with the fact that my life was turning out just like my family said it would. I never, ever intended for it to become a habit, but soon I was working just to pay for my next fix. I was high all the time, at work, at home, at the club, on dates, everywhere. I couldn't wake up and brush my teeth before doing like three or four lines. I needed it. I craved it. Because it was the only way I could make it through a day of my fucked up life...

"And then a year later, I crashed. I was out partying with this kid I was talking to and some of his friends. We had at least an ounce or more of coke—and man were we getting high. God Jared, I remember that shit as if it were yesterday." His voice cracked then, weakened. Suddenly his eyes were filled with a vacancy that frightened me.

"I woke up the next morning in the hospital." He said calmly. "I had been raped, then beaten to a pulp. Both of my eyes were blacked out, two of my left ribs fractured, and my left wrist was broke. Later I learned from one of his friends that after I passed out the kid I was dating, set off a round of fucking, with me as the fuckee. What possessed them to beat me," he shrugged, "I still don't know, but it fucked me up for a long time. After that, you couldn't drag me out of the house. I only left to go to work or to get something to eat. Every night I would watch television until I fell asleep and then repeat the same shit the very next day. After a year or so of doing this I found enough energy to face the world.

"I had done a lot of thinking and come to a lot of conclusions. It had been five years since I graduated from high school, and like my family I had never stepped foot onto a college campus. I was working a bullshit part-time job at a local video store and was a recovering drug addict. I had to do something to change my life before it was too late and I ended up old and bitter like my moms and the rest of my family. I needed an out.

"I don't know how, but I found my way to BMCC and with the help of the counselors there and New York State financial aid, I managed to enroll myself into college. You should have seen me on the first day of class walking around like whoa! It was the most amazing feeling I had ever had in my life. And in my heart I knew nothing or no one could stop me from becoming the man I knew I was supposed to be. Little did I know that in less than a month I would meet Jeff, and like an idiot, fall in love."

151

He stopped speaking and like clock work, the sounds of Paris that had been drowned out by his words instantly returned, reminding me of our whereabouts. A car passed blaring the Annie Lenox classic, *Why*. The power of this song; his eyes unblinking, staring helplessly into the past; and the humming of all those around me caused my heart to ache. An image of him and Jeff meeting, loving, entangled in a web of heat and desire, flashed before my eyes; only to be replaced by lies, deceit and distrust. And I wondered, why. Why would anyone want to subject him, or anyone to such pain? I walked beside him afraid to ask, afraid to speak, afraid of the truth. That we all, whether we believed it or not, harbored the same infectious trait that at any given moment, could be unleashed on some unsuspecting victim, destroying what little hope of happiness they held. It had been done to me, and although I chose to ignore the symptoms, I knew I could infect others.

"He changed my life." He said to the night. "He was the straw that broke the camels back. I believed in him. I believed him when he said he loved me, and me only. I believed him when he said it was all about me, nothing else. I did, and as a result I lost everything. I lost my will, and eventually I lost me. I lived for him. I loved for him and I died because of him. After that, I swore to God that I would never, ever give my heart and soul to anyone else. I swore. And now," he said facing me, "here I am, in the most beautiful city in the world, with a man who since day one, has treated me like no one ever in my life, considering doing it all over again."

Un-expectant tears filled my eyes as our steady pace slowed to a halt.

"I love you Jared, like I've loved no one ever in my life. Thank you." He whispered, tears lining his face. "Thank you for opening my eyes. Thank you for believing in me. Thank you for bringing me to this city and opening me up to a whole new world. Thank you for putting up with my stubbornness, my feisty attitude, and my fucked up job that always seem to get in the way. Thank you for coming into my store and offering me a chance to love you..." He paused as if searching for the words. "Because without you, without any of this," he said sweeping his arms through the air, "I would still be dead."

I pulled him into my arms and held him like I had never held him before. He had done more for me that night than he would ever know. He had finally cemented the fact that we would be together always, in all ways.

Y OU'RE REALLY IN LOVE aren't you?" Kevin asked as we strolled along Broadway on our way to *The Shark Bar*. Miles, Michael, Dio, and Aaron walked a few feet ahead us laughing and joking amongst themselves. May had just come in and brought with it a rush of pre-summer temperatures (one hundred degrees and climbing). New Yorkers, always two steps ahead of the times, and the seasons, were out in droves shopping, biking, roller-blading, and taking in as much of the city as they could. Women exchanged their spring sweater ensembles for mid-summer halter-tops and poom-poom shorts, while the guys headed straight for tanks and jeans.

"I am." I said quietly watching Michael ahead of me. It was something about the way his slightly bow legs looked in shorts. All hell was sure to break loose as soon as we made it back to the house. "He's the best thing that's ever happened to me."

"I see." He said dryly. "By the way *you're* acting, one would think you two have been dating for years, and not the little over four months you have."

"I know right. It's like we were made for each other. I love that about us."

"Dio mentioned something about you thinking about moving him in…"

"We've talked about it, but we haven't come to any conclusions."

"Do you think that's really a good idea?" He hesitated. "I mean, it's still kind of soon."

"We're thinking about moving in together Kevin, not buying a house."

"Listen bitch, all I'm saying is maybe you need to gauge your relationship this time and not rush into things like you always do. By the way, has he paid back the money he owes you?"

"No he hasn't, and for the record I'm not rushing. You should have heard the way he confessed his love for me in Paris. He finally opened up to me. He finally let me in. And since then he's changed. He's not afraid anymore to give himself—if anything, he gives more of himself sometimes than I give of myself. It's scary, because I never thought anyone could, never mind would, love me this much. You should see how he treats me, its unbelievable. That's why this time I know things are different."

"Really?" He said unmoved. "Isn't that what you said about Jason? And Vince? And if I'm not mistaken, you've practically said that about everyone you've dated."

"Look." I said growing impatient. "Yes, I may have said all those things and more before—but Kevin, don't I look happy? Don't I look like I'm in love?"

"Yes. But does that mean you have to pay his rent?"

"If that's what it takes to keep the man I love from being evicted, yes, I will do that and more."

"But Jared—"

I held up my hand cutting him short. "But nothing Kevin. Everything is under control. Things *are* different this time. You just have to believe me, sorta like I believed you when you swore up and down Aaron was the one."

The restaurant was packed beyond belief. The weather had truly brought everyone out of hibernation to help usher in the new season. There was eye candy galore: the guy behind the bar, his hazel eyes glowing brightly underneath the track lighting. The woman he was talking to, her shoulder length hair, muscular thighs and perfect teeth drawing stares from every corner of the bar. Even the ghetto-fab crew with their Cristal bottles raised high above their heads bouncing to Biggie's classic, *One More Chance*, managed to draw more than enough attention. But nothing compared to the response six attractive young men garnered upon entering the establishment. The men suddenly felt threatened by the competition we ignited, while the women on the other hand licked their lips in delight. One by one they checked us out, as if their odds of finding a good-looking black man had suddenly increased by six. Their curiosity shot through the roof when less than ten minutes after our arrival the hostess, who recognized Miles from a print ad he had done for Calvin, seated us immediately.

We had just received our first round of drinks, when Kevin posed the most interesting question...

"Would any of you marry a man?"

"Why?" I asked. "Are you and Aaron finally tying the knot? It has been two years."

Kevin shot me a nasty look while the rest of the table agreed in unison.

"Now bitch, you know I'm not into shit like that! So I don't know why you would even take it there!" He said glaring across the table. "For your information, one of Aaron's friends just announced that he and his lover of 10 years are getting married."

"Really?" I nodded. "He does know it's illegal for a man to marry another man in this country right? I mean it's not like you get any special tax right-offs or privileges like in a *real* marriage."

"True," Aaron agreed, "and it's not like anybody's gonna respect it anyway."

"Who cares what everybody else thinks?" Miles countered. "As long as the two people involved respect it. Isn't that what marriage is about? Two people loving and respecting each other unconditionally?"

"That's what it should be about." I answered. "But we all know marriage ain't what it use to be. Take my parents, they've been married 36 years. How many couples do you know, that's been together for that long, endured the rigorous task of learning and then *re-learning* their partner and still finding something new and interesting to love?"

"Not many I imagine," Miles answered. "Especially with the divorce rate the way it is nowadays. It seems people just aren't big on commitment anymore. Which brings me to your comment," he said eyeing Kevin, "why don't you believe in two men marrying? Afraid of commitment?"

"No," Dio cut in. "That bitch is just mad she can't wear white anymore!"

The entire table erupted into laughter.

"Funny bitch. But I really didn't think we were planning your wedding hoe! Anyhoo, to answer your question Miles, I just don't think it's right. Could you image two hairy men in long flowing silk chiffon gowns standing at the alter, confessing their undying love for each other to death do them part! Please, the thought alone makes me want to vomit!"

"Wait a minute Kevin," Michael said joining in, "so if Aaron were to ask you to marry him, in a not so girly ceremony, you mean to tell me you wouldn't."

"No, I wouldn't." He answered bluntly. "Because I know my man wouldn't ask me to do something like that." He scanned the table. "It's called *compatibility*, for all you new girls calling yourselves forming couples. You know, having *like* interests."

"Oh?" Dio said placing his drink on the table. "I didn't know Aaron liked dressing in drag too! The things you learn over a cocktail!"

"You know what bitch…" Kevin sneered.

"So Aaron," Miles interjected laughing, "you really wouldn't ask Kevin to marry you?"

"Not at all." Aaron admitted. "In the bible it plainly states marriage is only sacred when it's between a man and a woman."

"AHHHHH Shit!" I moaned. "Don't tell me we're going to bring the bible into this!"

"Why not?" Aaron asked defensively. "It's the only guide we have in this crazy mixed up world. Without it, could you imagine where we'd be?

"Probably a lot less confused." Dio asserted.

"I'll drink to that!" Miles said raising his glass.

"So wait a minute," Aaron said growing impatient. "You mean to tell me, you guys don't believe in what the bible says?"

I tilted my head. "Speaking for myself, it's not that I don't believe what it says or what it represents, it's just man has always found some reason—to do, or not to do all manners of evil based entirely on the bible! I mean think about Aaron, the bible has called your love for Kevin an

155

abomination. Then to add insult to injury it guarantees you both will be put to death. Why? Because it specifically states: God does not love you!"

"He's right...you know." Miles added. "People have always used the bible to their own advantage. If someone wants to scrutinize gay people, it's in the bible, Leviticus 20:13. If they want to condone slavery, it's in the bible, Ephesians 6:5. If they want to belittle women, and treat them with less respect than a man, guess what? It's in the bible, 1st Peter 3:1! And wait, what about this chosen people bull! If the Jews are the quote-unquote chosen children of God, why then are we even trying to gain favor in his sight?"

"But Miles," Aaron pleaded. "You know that's not true, God loves us all the same."

"I know that, and you know that," Miles pointed out, "but what about the rest of the world? Do they know that?"

"Exactly," I nodded. "Does the world know that God loves us all? Or are many of us running around thinking He only loves certain of us? Do we still believe he favors one group of people, over another? Or more specifically, thinks he loves straight people and not gay people?" I shook my head. "It trips me out how we stand in the middle of a world, built by a creator who made no two things alike—yet we as humans, try to streamline everything! We expect all *like* things to look, walk, talk even act the same. Heaven forbid a perfect creation made by God himself exhibits its uniqueness! Instead of celebrating and basking in its beauty we condemn it to hell!"

"Maybe it's just me," Aaron said, confusion riding his face, "but I don't get it. What exactly are you trying to say?"

"Aaron!" Kevin barked. "Why are you encouraging *Miss Thing* to continue? I thought we were here to have fun, laugh—joke! Not take on the laws of the universe!"

"Baby come on, I want to hear this." He replied rubbing Kevin's hand. "We'll be finished in a minute. Now what were you saying Jared?"

"All I'm saying is we live in a world where nothing is the same. God planned it that way. You may have two things that resemble each other, but when you really study them, you learn they don't. Yet as humans, we try to label everything and make them the same by applying rules and labels. We create categories where you have your normal shit, and your not so normal shit. Whenever people fall into the normal category, it's all good...Praise the Lord and pass the peas! But, let someone fall into the abnormal category, all hell breaks loose! And guess what they tell you, you're going straight to hell!"

"Ain't that the truth!" Miles chimed in.

"And the worst part of it all," I continued, "is that we start believing what everyone else thinks and says is the truth. We believe the labels they place on us. We abandon *what* we feel, and *how* we feel all because *Pastor So and So* or *Mr. White Man* said its' *supposed to be* this way or that way, when you know in your heart that God created us all, equally!"

Aaron held up his hand. "So, let me make sure I'm understanding you correctly. Are you saying *God* created gay people?"

"No Aaron, I'm not saying that at all. I'm saying God created *people*. We created the titles that separate us. I mean think about it. Did not God create the blind and the deaf? Did he not create the lame? And then—*after everything he created*—did he not say, this is good?"

Aaron nodded. "Yeah but—"

"Then why do we find fault in these people? Why do we suggest that they are *less than*? Why do we say, *'You are handicap therefore I should feel sorry for you, and grateful for my own good fortune'*? Why do we force our own labels on these people and treat them as if they are less human or apt than we are? Why do we do that? Is it because they somehow don't fit into the quote-unquote *normal* category we've created for them? For ourselves?"

"Jared I agree with you one hundred percent regarding the handicapped." Aaron offered sincerely. "But homosexuality is a total different matter all together! The bible says we were put here to be fruitful and multiply. How can two people of the same sex do that?"

"Good point." I noted considering his question. "But again, think about the thousands of people born sterile that practice heterosexual lifestyles? Are they any less in God's eyes because they cannot bring forth children to replenish the earth?"

He shook his head. "No…I don't think so."

"Then my friend, why should you be? Why should you be any less in the eyes of God? Believe me when I tell you, He loves you just the way you are. And remember too my friend, that the bible says man looks on the outside, while God studies the heart. I believe as long as you love God and your neighbor as yourself, you're halfway there, for those are the great commandments."

"Welllll!" Kevin yelled, raising his hand imitating a Baptist deacon. "Now can we order something to eat before I pass the hell out—damn'!

"Leave it to my baby to break up the party." Aaron said staring lovingly at Kevin.

"No…" Dio said signaling the waitress, "for once *Blanche* has a great idea."

Reminiscing on those days brings back a ton of emotions. There is no grander feeling in the world than that of love, friendship, trust, and

157

honesty. These are the keys to any successful relationship built on love. When we find these feelings we long to hold onto them forever. But, unfortunately, life has a will of its own. And when you least expect it, change occurs, forcing you to deal with the reality of *what is*, instead of *what was*. In the midst of this reality you learn rain is but a cloud away; and, if the foundation upon which you built friendship, trust and honesty, isn't secured in love, but rather in fear, you could very well lose everything you've worked so hard to construct.

Just one piece of advice from one friend to another: always build on love, and prepare for the rain. Always...because it's just a cloud away.

THIRTEEN

Kevin

The sound of an urgent telephone jolted me from my slumber early one June morning. The clock on the nightstand blinked 6:32 am. "Shit!" I mumbled, fumbling for the phone. "Who the hell could be calling me at this un-godly hour? Don't they know I need a full twelve hours of beauty sleep? *Hello!*" I barked into the receiver.

"Is this Kevin?" Came the voice on the other end.

"Yes! Who else would be answering my phone at this time of morning! I mean damn'." I snapped annoyed by the caller's stupidity. "I hope to God you ain't trying to sell me something, because if you are I've news for you!"

"Oh my God Kevin, I thought I would never find you!" She bellowed ignoring my sarcasm. "I've called just about every Kevin Smith in New York City!"

I sat quietly trying to place the voice. It sounded vaguely familiar, but at the same time didn't quite ring a bell. My mind began to race. "Who is this?" I said sitting up.

She chuckled. "I didn't expect you to recognize my voice considering how long it's been since we last spoke. But in a way," she paused, "I guess I was kind of hoping you would recognize the voice of your favorite aunt."

I almost dropped the phone.

Could it be? I hadn't spoken to my aunt in over fifteen years! "Aunt Bee?!" I jumped out of the bed and flicked on the light. "Wow! I haven't— oh my God is it *really* you! Where have you been—why haven't I heard from you? Oh my God I've missed you! I can't tell you how good it is to hear your voice!"

"It's good to hear yours too baby! You sound all grown up. Almost like a man."

"I am a man. As a matter of fact I'll be—" I paused suddenly. What the hell was I doing? She didn't need to know my age. Besides, everyone knows a diva never discloses such delicate information on such short notice. We'd discuss that matter later. "Anyhoo," I hummed, "that's not important. How are you?"

She sighed deeply into the phone. "Old. I'll be fifty-five in March. Can you believe it?"

159

"No. But I bet you *still* look fierce though!"

"Well, you know," she laughed lightly, "on my good days, if I wanted to, I could *still* pull them in."

"Alright now!" I key-keyed. "So Aunt Bee please, tell me everything! I want to know it all. What have you been up to? What new countries have you hit up? But more importantly, when are you coming to New York so that we can hit it to the stores—honey I tell you, you haven't been shopping unless you've done Ms. Fifth Avenue! Trust and believe she serves you fashion galore! And oh, we can't forget the spas—you know they have the best one's here in New York, and the *food* Aunt Bee—"

"Slow down boy! One thing at a time! I can clearly see time has not changed you one bit! You're just as energetic as you've always been, if not more!"

I laughed. "I'm sorry Aunt Bee. It's just…it's been so long since I've spoken to anyone in the family and, well—"

"I know baby." She said softly. "That's why I called. Every now and again, we all need to hear from the people who matter the most, even if they get on our damn' nerves!"

"Ain't that the truth!"

"I know it is baby. Trust me when I tell you, I've dealt with the Smith's a lot longer than you and I know first hand how *ig'nant* they can be!"

We both broke into a chorus of laughter. It was hard for me to believe I was actually talking to the first person I had spoken to openly about my sexuality. The same woman who when I told her, encouraged me to always be myself no matter what anyone else thought or said, because in the end, I would be better for it. I would always love her for that.

"You know…" she sighed, her voice settling into that comfortable tone I knew so well as a child, "I've had a good life so far Kevin. The last few years I've been fortunate enough to travel the world with the man I love, and experience some of the wonders others only dream about. I've been to the top of the Eiffel Tower, sailed along the Nile, seen the great Pyramids of Egypt up close, and I've even touched the leaning tower of Pisa. Sometimes I wonder if one woman should be so blessed considering the thousands out there suffering daily. But I know God has his reasons. This time around I am living the life. Next time, who knows, I may not be so fortunate.

"But Kevin, no matter how big, or how small, I am thankful for every little thing I have experienced in my life. Even," she paused, "the people who have caused me great pain, because through them I have learned the power of forgiveness."

I sat in silence for a while digesting her words. I knew exactly what she was hinting at, and grew hot instantly. How *dare* she call after all these years to give me a lecture!

"You're talking about my mother right?" I asked strained, my voice low and distant.

"Yes. But I'm also talking about you. It's time you two talk."

"About what?" I spit, my anger growing by the second. "I've washed my hands of her and her ignorance, and have nothing more to say."

"Her ignorance? What about your own?" She said gently. "Aren't you ready to free your soul? Haven't you held onto this *hatred* for far too long?"

"Aunt Bee, listen, I know what you're doing and believe me, I appreciate it. But I've tried on countless occasions to reach out to that woman but it's like talking to a brick wall. She just won't budge. And I cannot spend the rest of my life trying to convince her to love me."

"Kevin, I understand. And you have a point. But, just because someone doesn't love you, the way you want them to love you doesn't mean they don't love you with all they have. You've got to move beyond your mother's behavior and recognize the underlying love she has for you. Take me for example. Do you remember your Uncle Robert?"

"Do I?! He used to take me to McDonalds every time you two came to visit! Of course I remember Uncle R!"

"Well…" She sighed heavily. "Your grandmother, my mother, had a fit when I brought him home. She threatened to cut me out of her will and the family if I didn't stop seeing him."

"Why? Because he's white?"

"That, and because she was a stubborn old woman who wanted to control her life and all those around her! I can't begin to tell you how many arguments we had over Robert. No matter how much I tried to convince her that I loved him, and he loved me, she wouldn't hear of it. She kept saying it wasn't right for me to marry the man whose forefathers had raped my ancestors of their freedom and self-respect. And although I understood where she was coming from, she never once tried to see my side. She didn't want to hear how much he respected me, and pushed me to succeed. Why if it weren't for Robert I would not hold the PHD I have today. But it was because of his love and understanding that I made something out of my life. And it never once mattered to me that he was white. What mattered was that he loved me like no one had ever loved me before.

"Then one day, after pouring my heart out to her about not being able to get pregnant, she spoke the unspeakable. She told me the reason I couldn't get pregnant was because God had punished me for marrying outside of my race. Kevin I swear, you cannot even begin to believe the amount of pain I felt. I said things to my mother that day no child should ever say aloud. Things that to this day, I am still ashamed of. But at the time, in my heart I convinced myself she deserved every last bitter word, and I went five years without speaking to her. Not once did she ever try to reach out to apologize. Not, even on her deathbed. With her last breath, instead of telling me she loved me, she warned me to *repent*, before it was too late.

"I left my mother's bedside and never looked back. A week later, when the rest of the family gathered to bury her, my husband and I were on a plane hand in hand headed to Rio de Janeiro."

"I always wondered why you two weren't there." I said remembering that dark rainy day. "No one ever did say why you guys didn't show up."

She sighed. "It was my way of punishing her. I wanted her to be looking from wherever she was and see I was not mourning her death. In fact, I wanted everyone to know I could care less about her, and her thoughts of me. But that was far from the truth. Outside, I put up a good front. But on the inside, I was falling apart. For the life of me I could not accept the fact that the woman who was supposed to love me, no matter what I did, said, or became, turned her back on me. And no matter how hard I tried to get over it, or how many different ways I tried to look at it, I could not solve the puzzle.

"Then one day while walking along the white sands of Jamaica, I let go of all the pain. And for the first time in twelve years I cried for my mother. On that day I lifted my head to the heavens and screamed to the top of my lungs, *"I love you anyway!"* And the most amazing thing happened...from that moment on, I was free.

"The point is Kevin, your mother loves you with all her heart as all mothers love their children. It's just sometimes they don't know how to show it. You can't punish her for that. Love her anyway."

When she finished my face sat drenched in tears. The last time I reached out to my mother she asked me never to do so again, and verbally disowned me as her son. Now my aunt wanted me to overturn her decision—to undo *her* law. A decree I had no say in whatsoever.

"Aunt Bee, I don't think that's a good idea. I mean the last time I..."

"Listen to me!" She snapped cutting me short. "There isn't much time left! Your mother is dying, and whether she knows it or not, she needs you!"

The room seemed to darken with the utterance of those words. Did she just say what I thought she said?

"Dy—my moth—dying? How?" I asked bracing myself.

"She has lung cancer, and I'm afraid—"

"Why didn't anyone call me sooner?!" I snapped.

"We've been trying for weeks Kevin but no one knew how to reach you." She paused suddenly. "When can you make it out here?"

I stared into the shadows of my mind remembering the days of my youth when mother would gather me in her arms and swing me lovingly around the living room. It had been years since I'd seen her; since she'd touched me; since she'd cared, and now...

"Tonight." I whispered through silent tears. "I'll be there tonight."

FOURTEEN

Jared

"S O DO YOU WANT to go or not?" Michael yelled from the bathroom. I had been giving him the run around about going to the beach for a little over a month, and had no real intention of changing my mind. I hated the beach, *especially* Reese Beach. To me there was absolutely nothing appealing in seeing men of all shapes and sizes in stuffed trunks frolicking about the beach cruising for sex. Not to mention the sun that was sure to give me a headache, or the sand I would find for weeks in places I never knew existed, or the water, infested with used needles graciously donated by the hospital less than twenty feet away. Besides, I liked my complexion, and the beach would all but change that.

"I don't know..." I answered flipping through the channels. "I thought I heard the weatherman say something about rain..."

"You know damn well he ain't say shit about rain." He said standing in the doorway, his gray boxer briefs fitting snug against his muscular thighs. From the way he was standing I could make out his print. I grew excited.

"I was right there with you," he continued, "when he said *'sunny and bright all weekend with record breaking temperatures,'* so don't even try it."

I laughed. Our relationship had indeed grown by leaps and bounds. In a little less than six months we'd become the perfect couple. We did everything together so it wasn't long before people started associating us with each other. It was odd whenever they saw one of us without the other so the question, "Where's Jared?" or "Where's Michael?" had become commonplace. I can't front, I loved it. I loved having someone to call my own. I loved knowing at the end of the day there was someone to call. Someone to catch up with. Someone to dream with. And it didn't matter that sometimes it came at such a high expense. We had our problems. Our arguments. Our disagreements. But again, at the end of day our love got us through. Our love was bigger and stronger than any *would be* problems we encountered. And that made the dream real. That alone kept us striving to reach our goal, to finish what we started, to be the ones to say ten years down the road, "We did it. We made it work..."

"Baby, you know how much I hate the beach. Why can't we do something else?"

He shifted his weight annoyed. "Like what."

"Like go to the movies or something."

"The movies!" He screeched. "Who the hell wants to sit in a boring ass theater when there's record breaking temperatures going on outside! I want to get in the water, swim, play—*damn* it's summertime Jared!"

"I know but the beach is so nasty. What about Central Park?"

"I wasn't aware they installed a beach?" He scoffed.

"They haven't, smart-ass."

"Then why bring it up?" He snapped. "I've been trying to get you to go with me to the beach for weeks now! We've been to the park. We've been to the movies. Now I want to go to the beach! The B-E-A-C-H!"

I sighed and turned off the television. He was right. I was being selfish. Whenever I wanted to do something nine times out of ten he'd do it with little to no argument. His response was always: *ah-ight whatever, let's go.* So, I had no choice but to come through on this one.

"Okay, okay," I said softly, "I promise I'll go with you next week."

"Next week?! What about today?"

"I can't make it today."

"That's what you said last week when you promised to go this week."

"No, last week I said—"

He held up his hands. "Forget it. I'm sorry I asked."

I know this may sound fucked up, but, I loved the way his lips formed a pout whenever we disagreed, and in a way, I sort of looked forward to it happening. It kind of made him even more desirable. My sex stiffened.

"Look." I said pointing to my erection. He glanced toward me then quickly turned away.

"Whatever. I'm leaving. I told Damien I'd meet him and Rick at the train station by twelve."

"Twelve? What's up, I thought we were hanging today?"

"We were when I thought we were going to the beach."

"But I thought we just decided to go next week."

"We will, but I'm still going today. I made plans based on what you told me last week, and just because you've decided not to go, doesn't mean I have to cancel."

"So it's like that." I said somewhat annoyed.

"Oh no doubt," he said bitterly, "it's exactly like that."

Twenty-two minutes later I realized just how serious he was. He left me sitting in the living room watching the *wild e. coyote* try desperately to outwit the *roadrunner*.

I sat there for a while pissed trying to figure out what the hell I was going to do with the rest of my day when I thought about Kevin. I phoned his house but he didn't answer so I located his cell phone number and dialed it. He answered on the first ring.

"What up?" I asked lazily. "Whatcha doing today?"

"Jared, I really don't have time to talk right now, can I call you later?"

He sounded hurried.

"Is everything alright Kevin?" I asked worried. "Don't tell me you and Aaron are arguing too?"

"What?" He snapped. "No we're not arguing. And why does everyone think my whole life revolves around Aaron? And why do you seem to think every time I'm upset or something's wrong with me it has something to do with Aaron? There are more important things in my life than a fucking relationship, but you wouldn't know that because all you seem to focus on is my relationship!"

"Damn' what the fuck crawled up your ass! All I said was—"

"Jared look, I already told you I don't have time for this. Yet still here you are trying your best to drag me into a long winded conversation. Is it me, or do you actually have lead between your ears?" He spit then hung up the phone.

I sat there for a while holding the receiver baffled. Just when I made up my mind to call his ass back and give him a piece of my mind the telephone rang.

"What's going on stranger?" Came the voice on the other end.

"What's up Sean?" I said still confused.

"Nadda much." He responded. "What's your day looking like?"

"I'm free, why what's up? You wanna hang or something?"

"Yeah. We need to talk."

He sounded serious and although I hadn't spoken to Sean in a while I knew what was going on. He had some shit, on somebody about something. Whenever he called and was like, "we need to talk", you knew some shit was about to go down.

"About what?"

"Some shit I think you should know about."

I clicked off the television. "What shit Sean. You've got my undivided attention."

"Nah man. We can't talk about this shit over the phone. I need to see you in person."

Annoyed, I left the sofa and gazed out the window at the passing cars. It was only eleven thirty and everybody I knew and loved was starting to get on my nerves.

"Sean. You know me." I said inhaling deeply. "So you know how I get when people set me up like this. If you have something to tell me, just tell me now. Don't make me wait."

"I hear you man, but like I said, I need to see you in person. Check it, I'm going to be in front of the Waverly Theatre in about an hour meet me there ah-ight? Peace." He said then hung up.

It took me about fifteen minutes to get ready. Before I left I decided to phone Michael and leave him a message just in case he called looking for me. Surprisingly he answered on the first ring.

"What's up? I thought you were heading to the beach."

"I am."

"Then why is your phone on? I thought you guys were taking the train?"

"We were, but Damien's friend Troy decided to drive us out there."

"Troy. Who's Troy?"

"I just said he's Damien's friend."

"He's not your friend?"

"No. Today's my first time meeting him."

"Hmm. So what time are you heading back?"

"Why?"

"Because I want to know."

He sucked his teeth. "Like you care."

"Why would you say some shit like that? Of course I care."

"If you did, then you'd be here with me now, instead of on the phone. You know how hectic my job is, and how hard it is for me to get time off—I would think that would make you want to spend some time with me, but its obvious you don't."

"That's not true Michael, and you know it."

"Then what is it Jared? I don't ask for a lot. And you know what my last relationship was like. I'm not about to sit around and wait for you to do the things I want to do."

"I'm not asking you to wait. I just don't like the beach."

"And I don't always like massaging your fucking back but I do it. Even when I'm tired I do it. I do it because I know it means something to you. But if you can't see that, then I don't know how we're going to make it."

"You know," I said growing frustrated, "I hate when you say shit like that. Just because I don't like going to the fucking beach doesn't mean all of a sudden we're not going to make it. I'm saying...you've got to have a little more faith in us than that."

"I'm trying Jared, it's just that this ain't the first time you promised me you were going."

"I know, and I'm sorry. I'm working on that. But listen," I said checking my watch. "I've got to go. I was just calling to let you know I'm meeting Sean in the city. He wants to talk to me about something. Can we finish talking about this later?"

He sighed. "I guess so."

"I miss you." I said softly.

"I miss you too. You should be here."

"I know. Next time I will, I promise. But listen I really need to go."

"Alright then go. I'll see you later."

"Cool. Oh and Michael do me a favor."

"What's that?"

"Stay away from this Troy character I don't trust him."

"Trust him, you don't even know him!"

"That's exactly my point."

Immediately upon reaching the city, I spotted Sean standing in front of the theater, eating a slice of pizza and sipping on one of those fruit flavored drinks. As usual he was thugged out with construction tims, over-sized jean shorts, stalk white tee-shirt, and a red bandana tied neatly on his head; topped with a blue and white fitted New York Yankees cap. And of course he wouldn't be Sean without the jewels. He never went anywhere without his ice: A platinum twenty-inch chain that hung midway his chest with a crucifix filled with at least five karats of bagets; a ring, the size of a fifty-cent piece completely iced out, and two princess cut diamonds weighing down both of his ears. His signature goatee was trimmed to perfection revealing the lips so many mistook for LL's. Looking at him, one would automatically guess he was a wannabe rap star and not the six-figure executive marketing them.

"You look like a teenager." I said approaching him.

"Fuck you." He said taking another bite of his slice.

"So what's up?" I said, watching a cutie stroll by. He was about five foot nine, light skin, with a short waved caesar, and the *tightest* little ass I'd ever seen—and damn was he bowlegged! *Shit*, I thought to myself, *if only I were single.*

Sean sipped his soda, wiped his mouth then said, "You got here pretty fast…"

"Whatever I'm here so what do you want to talk about?"

"Damn' son! What's the fucking hurry? Can't a niggah finish his shit first?"

"I'm saying Sean—"

169

"Just chill man. Give me a minute."

A minute turned into three, then five, then ten. By the time he finished that one slice of pizza, he had commented on every niggah that walked by: Black, White, Hispanic, even this one East Indian cat—it didn't matter, they all got the same comment: "What about that one?" He'd say pointing, purposely trying to grab their attention. "You think we'd hit it off?"

"How the fuck should I know?" I spit after he'd asked the same tired ass line four times in a row about four different men I could care less about. "Ask him, not me!"

And so he did, to this brown skin cat for about twenty minutes. They talked and talked until finally I had to go up to them and tap him on the shoulder.

"Yo Sean, let's go. I don't have all day. I've got shit to do."

"Give me a minute Jay." He whispered, turning away from the guy. "Just let me get this number."

He turned back and pulled out a pen. "Damn' pardon me son but I gotta go. Let me get your number before my boy starts tripping. You got a piece of paper?"

After getting the number they embraced. "So yo, I'ma call you tonight. You're gonna be home?"

"Yeah." The guy replied grinning from ear to ear. "I'll be there."

"Good. I'll holla at you then."

As soon as the kid walked away, I broke: "It's about time niggah! I thought you called me out here to talk about something important, not to bullshit around."

"I did. But I'm sayin' Jay, just because you've found somebody doesn't mean everybody else in the world has. In case you've forgotten, I'm still single. But anyway," he said eyeing another potential victim, "let's walk over to Washington Square Park while we talk. There's too many distractions over here."

We began the walk in silence. Partly because I was annoyed with him for dragging me to the city so he could cruise. I didn't have a problem hanging out with him—as a matter of fact since Michael had decided to hang out with his friends, that sort of gave me the go ahead to hang out with mine. Besides that I always had a good time hanging out with Sean. But you don't tell me you have something important to talk about, insist I meet you in the city so that we can talk about it, then spend the next forty some odd minutes eating a goddamn slice of pizza and talking to every goddamn niggah that passed by! It just wasn't cool.

"You know it's a small world right?" He finally said.

I nodded. "Six degrees."

"Yeah well, more like three in the life." He snorted. "Anyway, the other day I was talking to one of my boys over at Columbia and he mentioned Miles' name. Immediately my antenna went up because of course I'm curious as to how he knows my *boys'* boy. So after a little probing, I found out Miles and his best friend use to date."

"Wait a minute Sean," I said stopping abruptly, "is this why you brought me to the city? To tell me Miles use to date one of your *friends* friend?"

"Yeah and to—"

"Come on man don't you know people had lives prior to being in a relationship?"

"Yeah but—"

"So then what's the big deal? I mean so what if Miles use to date this guy. It has absolutely nothing to do with who he's involved with today."

"It does," he snapped. "And if you'd stop fucking interrupting me maybe I could tell you what fuck is going on—damn! A niggah can't fucking talk without your ass flippin' off at the fucking mouth!" He paused, shot me a nasty look then continued. "Now like I was saying, Miles and my boy's best friend use to date, and from what he told me, his best friend ain't well."

I shook my head. "So what? What the fuck does that have to do with Miles and more so, me?!"

"Trust me niggah, it has everything to do with you! That niggah is sick! He has AIDS!"

I was slowly losing my patience. I could not believe he called me all the way to the city to talk about this shit! Some niggah I don't even know—shit, twenty million people in Africa was dying of AIDS. So what if this one little *fuck* had it? I hated when Sean got like this.

"Okay Sean," I said trying to mask my anger, "I ain't fucking the guy, and uh, I don't think I fucked anyone that did fuck him—and unless you're about to tell me otherwise, what the fuck does this have to do with me?"

"Look man do I have to spell everything out to your dumb ass?! My boy says Miles has the shit too! And that he's had it for years!"

It took a while for the words to settle in. But when they did, they hit hard; and for a split second everything fluttered. Slowly, as the words took form the severity of the situation brought everything into perspective: Dio.

Our eyes met. "Get the fuck out of here!" I yelled in disbelief. "Miles can't be sick! I mean—I just saw him a few days ago and he looked healthy as ever!"

"That doesn't mean shit!" He retaliated. "Do you know how many people are running around this fucking city *sick* and shit and they don't even know it?"

I shook my head confused. "Damn'! Are you sure Sean? I mean you know how people lie about shit like—"

"Trust me niggah, this shit is for real. I heard it from a reliable source."

I paced the concrete. "Damn' does Dio know?"

He shrugged. "I don't think so."

"Well, if he doesn't," I said stopping suddenly, "this shit is going to kill him! Do you know how much he loves that boy?!" I said recalling the countless conversations I had had with him about he and Miles; and how after weeks of convincing him to give Miles and love a second chance he finally decided to date him seriously. But there was no doubt in my mind whatsoever that this shit would send him over the edge. Dio was no good at shit like this. He could deal with a lot of things—*a hell of a lot*—but this?

"How sick is his friend Sean?"

"From what I've heard, he's in his final stages. He could go any day now."

"FUCK!"

How could something like this happen? I wonder if they practiced safe sex...Michael and I don't always, but I know he's okay...or do I? Do any of us really know who's safe, or are we all just playing Russian roulette?

Somewhere in the middle of my thoughts I blurted out, "I need to contact Miles—"

"For what?!" Sean snapped. "Why the fuck do you need to talk to his ass?"

"To find out if he's really sick or if this is just some—"

"Wait, wait, wait! Shouldn't you be contacting your boy? I'm saying don't you think he needs to know what's going on first?"

"Yeah—I mean no—I mean—I don't know!"

"Well I'm going to tell him!" He turned ready to walk.

"NO—WAIT!" I said grabbing his arm. "You can't tell him yet!"

"Why not?!" He barked freeing himself.

"Because we don't know if it's true. Wait and let me speak to Miles first. True or not, I think this type of news should come from him—not us! Besides, for all we know, Miles may have already told Dio, and the last thing I want to do is get in the middle of somebody else's shit—especially Dio's! You know how he gets!"

"Well I think as friends, we owe it to Dio to tell him what he may have gotten himself into by fucking with that niggah! I'm saying Jay, ain't that what friends are for? My boy could be dying—you heard, *dying*—thanks to some fucking faggot who chose not to say anything about the shit floating around in his body. And *you* want to get in contact with *him* instead of your *boy*?!"

I swallowed hard weighing both sides. "Look Sean, I see your point. Believe me I do. And I'm just as upset as you are, if not more if this shit turns out to be true. But still, I think we should speak to Miles first. We may be overreacting. Like I said, Miles may have already explained this shit to Dio. And, if he hasn't, then, I still think that maybe this kind of news should come from him, not us. So please, if you've never trusted me before, trust me on this one. Let me speak to him first."

Sean considered my words in silence. "Ah-ight…" He finally said, meeting my gaze. "But you better do it soon."

"I will." I said embracing him. "Trust me, I will."

By the time I made it back to my apartment my nerves were shot. The entire ride home I tried as best I could to piece together the puzzle but I couldn't. For some reason I could not believe the shit Sean said about Miles. Especially since I felt I knew him. Whenever Michael and I ended up at his apartment to play cards or to simply hang with him and Dio, he always went out of his way to ensure we were comfortable. He didn't seem phony or conniving or anything like Sean described. He was always straightforward and never ever hesitated speaking his mind. If he did not like something or if he had a differing opinion, he had no qualms whatsoever expressing it. So there was no way I could picture him lying to Dio. What reason would he have to?

As soon as I walked through the door, I picked up the phone and dialed his number. We chitchatted for a few minutes about nothing in particular, which gave me ample time to work on how I was going to approach him with the news. Five minutes later he asked: "So what's up? To what do I owe the pleasure of this call?"

It was a perfect lead-in to my intended discussion.

"Miles," I began nervously. "Actually I was kind of hoping maybe you could clear something up for me."

He hesitated. "Clear something up? I'm sorry I don't understand."

"Well, I heard some unsettling news today."

"News? News about what?"

"Miles listen, before I tell you what it is, let me first say how much I hate interfering in other people's lives. Especially since it seems I have such a hard enough time dealing with my own. But the news I received today was

173

well, like I said unsettling. And to be honest with you it took me a little by surprise."

"I see." He said quietly. "So what is it?"

"Well, it concerns your health—"

"My health? Why would someone be discussing my health with you, and not me?"

"Miles I hope you understand this is very uncomfortable for me."

"Well I'm not so sure about that Jared." He spat, his tone surprising me. "After all, you did make the call, so how uncomfortable can it really be? If *anyone* should feel uncomfortable right now, it's me. Because, correct me if I'm wrong, they're not talking about you. So please just get to the point."

I heeded his advice.

"Well, a friend of mine told me today that your ex is dying of AIDS; and well, he says that you have it too."

"What! Who told you this?" He demanded. "It's nobody's fucking business what my ex is going through! This is the main reason why I don't deal with you faggots!"

"Wait a minute now Miles! I know you're upset but let's not start calling names!"

"Upset? You cannot begin to believe how upset I am right now Jared—trust me!" He hissed. "Now, who told you this?"

"That's not important right now Miles. My only concern is whether or not Dio is okay."

"What do you mean if Dio's okay?! Of course he's okay! Why wouldn't he be?! What kind of person do you think I am Jared? Do you think I would put his life in jeopardy?! Huh? Do you? You—of all people should know how much I love that man!"

"Yes I do know how much you love him and believe me I'm not trying to pass judgment on you. But as a friend I hope you understand I'm only looking out for Dio's best interest! And well, if someone he's dating isn't being honest with him, then I feel he should know about it!"

"Wait a minute." He said heatedly. "Are you calling me dishonest Jared? Mister—*My-Shit-Don't-Stink?* Please tell me that's not what you're doing!"

"Look Miles, all I'm trying to do—"

"Is stick your nose where the shit don't belong." He hissed.

"No I'm not. I'm looking out for my friend."

"How—by alarming him with some bullshit?!"

I remained silent, not knowing what else to say.

"That's right Jared, bullshit! Whoever told you this shit is a damn liar. I am not sick! Tony, my ex is sick, but I'm not! And of all people

Jared you were the last person I imagined would believe some stupid shit like that. Friend." He scoffed making the word seem ugly. "You're nobody's friend. You have absolutely no idea what friendship is."

His words cut deep.

"What the hell is that supposed to mean?" I protested. "I know what friendship is!"

"Oh you think so?" He howled. "Well I'm sorry to disappoint you *friend*, but you still have a lot to learn! Friends don't accuse other friends of being dishonest! Friends don't take hearsay and turn it into truths! Friends understand that unless you've seen it with your own eyes, or heard it with your own ears, it's subjective and therefore should never be construed as anything other than what it is, GOSSIP! So thank you Jared, but no thank you, I do not wish to entertain *friends* like you!"

And with that, he slammed down the phone.

You can't begin to imagine how small I felt. He was right. I should have never taken what Sean told me as truths. I knew firsthand how people started rumors purely for the joy of it. But for some reason, when Sean was going on about it, it didn't seem like a rumor. It seemed real. Almost like Miles was somehow trying to hurt Dio. But, he wasn't. He was fine. Or so I hoped.

In any event, all I had to do now was call Sean and let him know what I had found out. But before I could dial his number, the telephone rang. I answered without checking the caller Id box.

"Jared, we need to talk!" Dio said right away. His voice seemed harried.

"About what?"

Had he heard the rumor? Or, had Miles lied to me?

"Look are you busy or not?!" He demanded.

"I'm not. Why, what's up?"

"I just got off the phone with Sean and he claims Miles has AIDS!"

"WHAT!" I yelled in disbelief. *Sean wouldn't*—not after I'd asked him not to!

"My sentiments exactly!" He replied bitterly. "I don't believe this shit. I mean, here I am talking to this bastard for months now! You would think maybe—just maybe he might have mentioned something like *AIDS* to me?"

"Dio listen, calm down..."

"Calm down?" He shrieked. *"Calm down?!* How the hell do you expect me to calm down in a situation like this? Put yourself in my damn' shoes and try to imagine how you would feel if you found out Michael had fucking AIDS! How calm would you be?!"

175

"First of all, you don't know if Miles has AIDS so don't go jumping to conclusions!   Second, I'm doing the best I can under the current circumstances!   I know you're upset, but we're not going to accomplish anything like this.   So let's just relax, and think about all of this rationally.   Okay?"

Silence.

"Dio?"

"What."

"Can we talk about this rationally?"

"Jared, listen, I can't promise you anything.   Right now I'm pissed. The man I love—the one I gave my heart to is dying of AIDS, and for all I know I could be too."

"But Dio, you don't know that.   So let's not get carried away. Okay?"

"I guess…" He mumbled.

"So what did Sean tell you?"

I listened closely as Dio painfully recalled his conversation with Sean.   Apparently Sean's friend Ron, best friend Tony, use to date Miles. Miles and Tony were extremely close, practically inseparable.   The only reason they broke up was because Tony couldn't control his anger, or his dick.   On more than one occasion, Miles had come home to find Tony in bed with another man, which, ultimately lead to them fighting.   So after two and a half years of this behavior, Miles left.   Ron told Sean, that Tony was still in love with Miles when they split, and still, to this day, he couldn't get over the fact that they were no longer together.   But, even more than that, he hated the fact that he ruined Miles' life, by well, you know…

"He said all that?"   I asked dumbfounded by all the details Sean had withheld.

"Yes." He said defeated; I could tell he was crying.   "Jared, I don't know what to do. I mean I never saw this coming. It's like you always hear about people being sick, but never in a million years, do you think you're going to be one of the ones it happens to…"   He paused.   "Jared, what if Miles *is* sick?   Or even worse, what if I'm sick?   I—"

I wanted to tell him everything was okay.   That I had spoken to Miles and he assured me he had nothing to worry about because they both were just the center of some cruel rumor—but something urged me not to go any deeper.   I had overstepped my boundaries enough already.   Now it was up to Miles to clear the air.

"Dio relax man." I said trying to comfort him.   "You don't know if you're sick.   I mean you haven't even spoken to Miles yet.   This could all be hearsay.   Lies.   Bullshit.   You know how people like to start shit."

"You think so?"

I wanted to tell him I was just as nervous as he was, and that I had no definitive answer, and I hoped to God Miles wasn't lying. But, for his sake, I lied.

"Of course. That's why you can't jump to conclusions. Right now what you need to do is call Miles, and talk to him. I'm sure once you two speak, you'll feel much better. Then just to be on the safe side, go get tested. Both of you."

"Yeah, maybe you're right." He whispered softly.

"I know I'm right, I have faith. So stop stressing yourself out. Everything is going to be just fine. Remember, God never gives you more than you can handle—and if *anyone* can handle a crisis, it's you!"

"You really think so?"

I crossed my fingers. "I know so."

He let out a huge sigh then said, "Thanks man, I feel a little better. I guess I'd better give Miles a call and get to the bottom of this."

"Do that."

"I will."

Why the hell would Sean do something like that?"

"I have no idea Michael, but believe me, I'm pissed."

"Are you *sure* you asked him not to say anything?"

"Of course I'm sure!"

He stopped massaging my shoulders. "You don't have to yell Jared. I'm just asking."

"I know, I know. I'm sorry. It's just—I can't believe he would do some shit like that. I asked him not to tell Dio. He promised he wouldn't, but then he did. I don't understand what the fuck is his problem?"

"Jared, people do dumb shit like that all the time. I don't know why they do it, I just know they do. A friend of mine did the exact same thing to me once."

"Really?"

"Yeah. He liked one of my co-workers, and although we both had our suspicions about him being gay, the guy still gave off man. I told my boy not to say anything to him because you could tell that if he was down, he didn't want to be called out—besides, at the time I wasn't sure if I wanted him to know about me. But Marlon was having a fit to talk to this boy. He kept saying how he *knew* they were soul mates, and that my selfishness was keeping them from being together. Still I held my ground, because me and Rob were cool and I didn't want anything to fuck that up." He paused. "Babe, am I squeezing your shoulders too hard?"

177

"Nah. Not at all. It feels good. But go on, finish what you were saying."

"Yeah well," he said gripping my shoulders. "Low and behold Marlon ran into him one night at a bar in the Village. I can't remember if it was the east side, or the west—but according to him, when he saw him, he couldn't resist kicking it to him. But," he said re-applying a small amount of heating lotion to my lower back, "here's the kicker. Come to find out Rob—his quote unquote *soul* mate—the love I was *preventing* him from having—wasn't even gay! And when Rob put two and two together, he automatically associated Marlon's actions—and the fact that Marlon and I were friends, to my friendliness with him. In his head, I was only being cool with him, so that I could *get* with him, sorta like what Marlon was doing."

"Why do straight men do that?" I hissed. "I hate that! Why do every last one of them, think every gay man in the world wants to sleep with them! Damn that shit kills me!"

"Me too, but hey that's life…"

I shook my head. "Yeah, I know but anyway what happened between you and your boy Marlon?"

"Oh we remained friends for a little while after that but eventually I stopped calling him, and he stopped calling me and we just sort of lost contact. But, friendships are like that. One day everything is tight, and it seems like it will be that way forever, but then something happens and you start wondering: damn', why were we even friends in the first place?"

"You know, that's exactly what I'm wondering now. I never thought in a million years Sean would do some shit like this to me. I mean we've been cool for like forever, and I just thought we'd always be friends—I mean, yeah we've had problems in the past, but it's like now I don't know if I can trust him. Ever."

He ran his fingers across my back one last time before lying beside me in the bed.

"Jared, let me ask you something?" He said softly. "And I don't want you to think I'm taking his side or, that I think what he did was right, but—don't you think you're being a little too hard on him? I mean he was just as worried about Dio as you were, so, it kinda makes sense that he told him."

I nodded. "Kind of, but, if he was going to tell Dio anyway, why get me involved? I'm saying, he could have just told Dio, then told me—or had Dio tell me. But it seems to me, he told me because he wanted to know what he should do—what *we* should do."

"True, but maybe he changed his mind. Maybe after talking to you, he realized that he should have talked to Dio first and then—"

"Well he should have called me and told me what he was going to do."

"Why?"

"Because I was involved—and because he knew I was going to talk to Miles, that's why!"

"I know Jared, but—"

I sat up. "But nothing Michael. Sean fucked up, period. He shouldn't have told me he was going to wait if he wasn't. And if he changed his mind he should have told me. That's the way I would have done it."

He laughed. "That's just it. He's not you, so you can't expect him to do things the way you would."

"It's not about doing things the way I would Michael, it's about doing them the right way."

"Your way," he scoffed, "or the right way? I know sometimes you can get the two confused."

I stared at him. "I don't get them confused. And I resent the fact that you think I do."

Silence. Then, a sigh.

"All I'm saying Jared, is that maybe you should talk to Sean about what happened. Maybe he has a good explanation. I mean if you guys are as good of friends as you say, then don't you think it's worth saving?"

"No I don't. I don't think its worth saving. He fucked up. I would have never done anything like that to him. Never. And if that's the kind of friendship he wants, then he can have it without me. But what I want to know is why you think I get shit confused?"

He rolled his eyes and just sort of looked at me, as if I was the one with the problem.

"Are you still on that?"

"Are you going to explain yourself?"

Silence.

"Are you?" I repeated.

"No. It was just a comment."

"A comment?" I hissed, feeling my anger quicken. "A comment is: you look nice today, or, that's a real nice hat—but when you start talking about me being self centered—or worse, confused about shit going on in my life, then there's no way in hell you're making a comment as much as you're making an accusation."

"It was a comment."

"Really?"

"Yes, really."

179

Christopher David

"Then you know what," I said snatching the sheet from under him, "I think you should leave."

"What?!" He asked in disbelief.

"If you can't explain what the fuck you meant by that bullshit you just spit then, I think you should get the fuck out. I'm already upset and I don't need any extra bullshit clouding my mind."

His eyes narrowed. "Are you serious?"

I turned, threw the sheet over my head, and covered my ears.

Hell yeah I was serious.

FIFTEEN

Kevin

RAW TERROR GRIPPED MY HEART as the DC-747 ripped through the clouds, revealing the City of Angels resting peacefully below. Heavy beads of sweat formed on my brow as the once distant city of my past came sparkling into view. I clasped my hands together in an effort to remain calm, but to no avail. The thought of seeing my mother after eight years of exile tore at the seams of my stitched heart. What if my aunt was wrong and she rejected me again? What then? Do I remain by her bedside and demand she accept me? Or do I go, and let her die in peace? The weight of indecision burdened me as the plane began its final descent. I peered nervously out the window searching for an answer—a sign—or some possible way out of my predicament. I did not want to face my mother.

I floated off the plane, and through the sea of commuters hurrying throughout the terminal. It took some time but eventually I found baggage claim. It seemed an eternity passed as I stood waiting for my luggage to appear. Soon I began worrying if by some chance someone had picked up the wrong suitcase in haste. *"It shouldn't take this long."* I mumbled frantically searching the belt. I was just about to locate an attendant when I saw my leather bag slowly making its round along the conveyor belt. When it reached me, I checked the lock to see if it had been tampered with. Much to my delight everything appeared intact. *"Good,"* I mumbled, just as I felt a gentle tap on my left shoulder. I turned and came face to face with a beautiful middle-aged woman, dressed to perfection in a dark blue pants suit, with a silk floral wrap draped neatly across her slender shoulders. I smiled pulling her into my arms.

"Aunt Bee!" I gasped, flooding her with kisses. "It's so good to see you."

"Ahh, and you will never know how good it is to see you Kevin." She said gripping my broad shoulders.

We held each other for a long while despite the hustle and bustle encircling us throughout the terminal. It felt good holding her. It felt even better being held. I closed my eyes and remembered the last time my mother held me like this. I remembered how good it felt. How warm it felt. And secretly, I longed to have her hold me like this again. Just like this.

"How is she?" I asked finally releasing her from my grasp.

She removed her sunglasses and dabbed the corners of her eyes with a handkerchief.

"Not well I'm afraid Kevin. It seems this disease is getting the best of her. It's not like Clara to give up, but, she's been fighting this battle for months now, and well, she's tired. It's written all over her face." She paused, studying me with tearful eyes. "I'm just glad you were able to make it here on such short notice. And," she smiled lovingly, "I'm sure your mother will be as well."

I released a heavy sigh. "I hope you're right Aunt Bee. I hope you're right."

We left the airport and drove straight to the hospital. During the ride my aunt took the liberty of educating me on lung cancer, and the havoc it had reaped on my mother. For as far back as I could remember my mother had always been a smoker. When I was younger she tried to hide it but it never did any good, I always smelled the faint scent of nicotine lingering in our home. The day I finally caught her in the act she admitted her addiction, warned me of its dangers, and vowed to whip my *black ass* if she ever caught me with one dangling from my lips. I promised; but later that evening after pondering *her* stand on cigarettes, I questioned her: *"If it's so bad Ma, then, why do you do it?"* She placed both hands on her curvaceous hips and spit matter-of-factly: *"Because I'm grown, and I can do what I want to! Besides that, I'm strong. And when you're strong, can't nothing hurt you."*

Twenty-four years later it seemed her pack and a half a day habit had finally caught up with her. I guess she wasn't as strong as she thought.

"When they first diagnosed your mother with lung cancer," my aunt says flying down the Santa Monica Freeway in her brand new convertible Mercedes Benz, "her doctors urged her to quit. But you know how stubborn Clara is. She kept right on smoking until eventually, the tumor spread from her lungs to her breast, then from her breast to her stomach. Had she quit, the scheduled surgery to remove a portion of her lung might have saved her life."

I stare out the window listening, but not listening. I really don't want to hear what I'm hearing. I don't want to consider the truth. I don't want to hear about death, and my mother, and her cancer, and her smoking, and her doctors or any other shit that has me speeding down the 405 wishing I were back home. Wishing I could wake up from this nightmare and have Aaron whisper, *"It's alright baby. It was only a dream, a terrible, terrible dream…"*

But it's not. The truth is: I'm in a car with my aunt whom I've not seen or spoken to in years rushing to the hospital to visit my dying mother who long abandoned me, because of my lifestyle. And I have no idea what

I'm going to say to her—what she's gonna say to me—or if she'll be able to say anything at all!

My aunt is still talking. She doesn't realize I'm not listening. She doesn't realize how much pain I'm in, and that my heart has not stopped pounding since she called earlier this morning. She doesn't know I haven't eaten in hours. Or that I feel like vomiting, or that my hands won't stop sweating, or that my head is about to implode, then explode. She doesn't know I'm scared to death to come face to face with the one woman who for so many years meant everything to me. The very woman who rubbed Vicks Vapor Rub across my chest when I was sick, the woman who taught me how to drive, how to sew, how to love.

I'm hurting, and believe it or not, I never thought I could hurt like this. I never thought I could house this much pain. I didn't think my heart—any heart—was deep enough to house this amount of pain!

I can't stop the tears from flowing. I want to, but I can't. I begin rocking back and forth, my hands covering my face, my mouth open but no sound escaping. My aunt finally notices and immediately pulls to the side of the freeway. She gathers me in her arms and whisper, *"It's okay baby...it's okay..."* a million times over. I stay there in her arms for a long time crying into her warm flesh, wishing it were my mother's. Praying, she won't turn me away. Again...

The hospital is cold. The walls. The floors. The people. All cold. No one looks like they want to be there. Everyone seems as if they'd rather be anywhere, except there. I know how they feel. I would give anything to be someplace else. Any place, but here.

My Aunt knows the routine. She holds my hand as we hurry pass the information desk and head straight for the elevators. She hasn't stopped holding it since the car. She knows now that I need her. She knows. Once inside she presses eight. I smile. My mother's favorite number; what a coincidence.

As the elevator begins to travel the height she grips my hand firmly.

"Kevin..." she says softly. "Be strong. Your mother needs you now. If she sees you're upset, it may upset her. Okay?"

I nod.

"If at anytime you feel overwhelmed just tell her you need to go to the bathroom and leave the room. Okay?"

I nod.

"Good. Now, when we get there I'm going to go in first and talk to her, because I don't want to surprise her too much. I want to make sure she can handle this. Once she knows you're here, I'll come out and get you. Okay?"

I nod once more.

When we exit the elevator we turn left and begin the trek down a long corridor. I count the steps. I count my breaths. I count anything that will keep me calm. I don't want to think about what's happening. I need to remain calm.

One hundred and forty-two steps later we land in front of her door, 838. I commit it to memory. I don't ever want to forget 838. I don't ever want to forget it.

My aunt points to a seat and instructs me to wait there for her. I do so without question. I feel weird. Almost like a child who has lost his way home...and I'm scared. Scared my family has moved on without me. Scared they've forgotten who I am. Scared I'm no longer welcomed.

And then, I remember.

Is there something you want to tell me Kevin?" My mother asked just after I had walked into her house eight years prior. She was sitting at the kitchen table reading the Daily Globe. As usual the place was spotless, not a dust ball or finger print anywhere to be found. She wore her regular house lounging wear: A floral housedress that snapped up the front, with matching headscarf and slippers. I leaned over to kiss her on the forehead, but she pulled away.

"Why'd you do that?" I asked, angrily and somewhat embarrassed. She had never turned down a kiss before; at least not from me.

"Because you're ignoring my question. Is there something you want to tell me?" She repeated.

"No." I answered taking a seat.

"Are you sure?"

"Yes mother I'm sure."

"Well then, get up and leave this house."

"Leave? Why?"

"Because, I will not have a faggot and a liar sitting in my home!"

The blow came hard, and before I could catch my breath, or figure out where it came from, she had closed the paper and started out of the room.

"Ma!" I yelled frantically jumping up from the table. "What did you say?!"

She stopped and faced me, her eyes revealing her true feelings, hurt. "I said get out! I did not raise you to be *what* you are. It ain't right. And I will not have it in *my* house."

"Ma, what I *am* has nothing to do with the way you raised me." I cried. "I am *still* Kevin. I have not changed. I *still* wake up every Saturday morning and clean my house. I *still* respect and adhere to my elders. I *still* wash my hands before I sit at anybody's table. I still—"

"Read the bible?" She hissed. "Do you Kevin? Do you read it?"

I sat back down. I knew she would go there, that's why I had never told her. I knew for certain, *her* God would not approve. I knew he would forever cast me into the fire and brimstone of hell. And I knew *she* would approve.

"Yes mother, I read the bible."

"Well then you must have skipped the part that plainly said, if a man also lie with mankind, as he lieth with a woman, both of them have committed an abomination: and they shall surely be put to death; and their blood shall be upon them."

"Everything we do in this damn' world is punishable by death mother so tell me what's the point of living?" I hissed.

Her eyes widened. "Did you just cuss in my house?" She ran across the room and slapped me in the mouth. "Don't you ever use that language in my house! Ever! I don't know what's gotten into you Kevin!" She yelled tears flooding her face. "First this gay mess, then you lie to me, and now you cuss! I know I raised you better than this! I know I did! What's wrong with you!"

"Nothing!" I said crying. "Nothing."

"Then why are you purposely trying to hurt me?"

"Mother what are you talking about? I'm not trying to hurt you!"

"You are! Living like you are is hurting me! I didn't raise you to chase no men—to be no sissy! No wonder you ain't brought a girl home in years! Did you think I wouldn't find out? Did you think nobody would tell me? Well they did! They told me all about your little secret life. They told me they seen you hanging out with some man that's about to get married. They said that whenever he ain't with her, he's with you! They said ya'll be sleeping together, goin' out, and everything. God knows if he don't want that woman, he needs to go on and let her be! It don't make no sense to bring her into ya'll mess. It's sick Kevin! You hear me—sick! And I don't want no parts of it. None whatsoever. And what makes it even worse, is that you know what your father did to me! You saw how he ran around with all those women and flaunted it in my face! You saw how he hurt me, and now you're doing the same thing to somebody else?! You're going to destroy somebody else's home—somebody else's life?! It ain't right Kevin and you know it! So when you walk through that door today, don't come back. Forget you ever had a mother, because as of today, I no longer have a son."

"But Ma—" I screamed hysterically, "please listen to me, I'm not trying to hurt anybody! I'm not trying to do anything to hurt anybody! I'm not! All I'm trying to do is live. Is that so wrong?"

"When you leave here today Kevin..." she spit, her voice low and bitter, her eyes narrowed into tiny slits, "don't *ever* come back."

She turned and left the room.

I heard her mount the steps.

I heard her slam her door.

I heard her cry out to the Lord.

She never came back down.

She never said goodbye.

She never once said she loved me.

I sat at that table for a long time before I finally drummed up enough energy to go. Two months, later I left for New York.

K evin..." My aunt says startling me, "she's ready to see you now."
She repeats her earlier instructions, and warns me that today has not been a good one for her. She can barely speak, so I'm not to make her. I listen intently and nod my head to the instructions. When she's done, I take several deep breaths before I stand. When I do, my legs feel weak, and I fear they will not support my weight. I grasp the wall and pull myself together. *"Be strong Kevin."* I hear my aunt mumble, *"Be strong..."*

Slowly I move towards the door. I take one step, then another. Before I know it my hand is gripping the doorknob, and every nerve in my body is on high alert, fearing what lies on the other side. I consider backing out. I consider boating passed my aunt, pass security and through the glass sliding doors that brought me to this God-awful place. Instead, I inhale one last time before turning the knob.

When I enter the room, it's dark except for a pale green table lamp in the far-left corner of the room with no more than a twenty-watt bulb. The table upon which it sits holds several cards and flowers arranged neatly in size order. The blinds and neutral curtains are pulled shut concealing the vibrant sun filling the June sky. I somehow manage to take everything in except for the bed upon which she lays: the oversized wall clock that reads ten minutes after five, the radio alarm clock softly playing Walter Hawkins, the royal blue and white checkered patterned floors polished to perfection, even the bathroom with its pale blue tile less than ten feet away from her. I take it all in piece by piece, every color, every pattern, every imperfection...because I know once I see the bed, once I see her lying in that bed, suffering, dying, all of this will disappear and only her and I will fill this room. And I need to remember. I need to remember it all.

I stare at the clock for a long time watching the seconds tick, tock, tick, tock. I know I have to look eventually. I know at some point I'm going to have to look at that bed, and acknowledge the woman lying within it. I know it, but I'm afraid. I continue staring at the clock watching the seconds tick into minutes, listening to her breathing, rather, the respirator breathing for her. It's a frightening, cold, distant, hollow sound. One I'm not used to. One I'm not sure I want to remember, but I know I will. I will remember it all.

And then I hear movement.

"Kev—in..." The voice calls weakly. I turn and suddenly come face to face with my mother; only, it's not her. And as I walk towards her, I realize she's much thinner than I ever remember, and her hair—the long, beautiful shoulder length hair she was once so proud of—is short and thinning. Her skin is pale and lifeless, and her eyes, sad and distant. I want to cry, but then instantly remember my aunt's stern warnings. So instead I choke back the tears and force a smile.

"Hey Ma..." I whisper gripping her frail hand. "How you feeling?"

"Not—" She coughs violently, and I watch in horror as her whole body responds. She squeezes my hand with all her might until finally the attack subsides. She takes several deep breaths before trying to continue. "Not well..." She finally manages, her voice scratchy and weak, "Not well at all..."

"You look well..." I lie trying to ease the tension. She sucks her teeth and we both laugh. I stare at her for a long while, until all the fears that proceeded this moment dissipate, and a warm feeling fills my heart.

"Ma, there is so much I have to tell you. So much I want to share..." I say gripping her hand firmly. "But first, I want you to know I never meant to hurt you. I never meant to cause you any type of pain. I love you too much. And," I paused, tears filling my eyes, "I never intended for you to find out about my life the way you did. I wanted to tell you, but I just didn't know how. I guess I thought I was protecting you somehow by not telling you. The truth is I didn't want to disappoint you. I didn't want you to judge me, or think I was any less of a man. I wanted your respect, but more so, your love. And I knew for sure, once I uttered the words, *"Ma, I'm gay..."* I would lose it all.

"I knew how you felt about homosexuals. I knew. That's why I kept it from you. Why do you think I moved out of the house as soon as I turned eighteen? I knew it would become more and more difficult to hide my lifestyle from you. So I ran. I ran as fast as I could from you and God and friends and anyone that didn't promote my way of life—from anyone that sought to destroy me with their words, or with their God.

Christopher David

"Ma, people honestly believe gay people choose their lifestyle like one chooses their socks, and that is so far from the truth. As far back as I can remember I've been attracted to men—and no, not just sexually—physically, mentally, emotionally and spiritually attracted to someone who looks, walks and talks like me. I can't explain it, just as I can't explain why I was born black, or why you and daddy were my birth parents. All I know, is this is who I am…and I am not ashamed, not anymore.

"That day, in the kitchen…when you told me you no longer had a son…" I pause trying to collect myself. I feel the anger rising and once again remember my aunts warnings. I try breathing. I try counting. I try thinking of something else, but I can't. I'm already there, I'm already angry, and there's no way out. And although the right thing to do would be to leave out of this room before I say something I might regret, or worse yet, something that might hurt her, I remain. Because what I have to say matters, and she needs to know how I feel before it's too late.

"That day in the kitchen was the worse day of my life. I could not believe the woman I had loved since birth threw me out of her life. Not because I killed a dozen people, or because I raped small children, or because I committed some other heinous crime—no—she threw me out of her life because I fell in love with a man! Because I loved someone she didn't approve of! And I hated you for a long time because of that. I hated you because you forgot who I was. You forgot you birthed a son who looked up to you, who depended on you—who thought the world of you! A son who defined hero as "my moms"!"

Tears begin filling her eyes, so I stop and walk to the window. I pull back the curtains and open the blinds. I stare out into the valley for a long time half-listening to her sobs. I know she's hurting, because I am. I'm hurting all over. Only for me it's been this way for years. I want a hug. I need a hug. I wish Aaron were here…he would hug me. He would tell me everything was going to be all right—*God* I miss him. I wish he had come. I really wish he had come…

I remain at the window afraid to turn back to the bed, afraid to face her again. But I must…there's still so much more that needs to be said.

"When Aunt Bee called me this morning," I said returning to her side, "I didn't know what to do or to think. I was afraid to face you. And for a moment, I thought about staying in New York. I thought seriously about letting you die without the son you disowned eight years ago. I thought about it, and I almost did…" I said drifting, "I almost stayed. But then something moved in me. Something caused me to remember all the good times we shared together. Something or someone touched my heart and chipped away all the anger and hatred and frustration I held against you, and despite all my resistance I boarded that plane. I boarded it because I

188

knew deep in my heart—no matter what—I still loved you. And I prayed you still loved me, your long lost prodigal son.

"So, I'm here, whether you like it or not. And we're going to get through this, you and me, together."

I lean forward and kiss her gently on the forehead and whisper "I love you." She tries to speak but her voice fails her, and for a few scary minutes she lets out a series of dry choking coughs. When she relaxes, tears stream her face. I grab her hand, and without uttering a single word, her eyes reveal the words pouring from her heart. They tell me she loves me, and that she's missed me, and that she's sorry she let me go. I nod and with a gracious smile let her know I understand. I sit in the chair next to her bed and rest my head gently on her bosom. I lay there, a bundle of emotions staring off into the darkness, knowing precious little time lay ahead.

And so, I begin unraveling the chapters of my life, one by one while my mother lay attentive, listening.

SIXTEEN

Diogenes

MORE THAN AN HOUR HAD PASSED since my conversation with Jared. I sat quietly in my bedroom counting the times Miles and I had had unprotected sex. My head ached with each new recollection. I stopped at twenty-six. Twenty-six times, with no condom and penetration, maybe more, maybe less. I couldn't be for certain because our sex life, much like our relationship was often spontaneous. But not once, in all those times had I considered AIDS. I thought of everything else, his eyes, his smell, his touch, his compassion—everything, but the unthinkable.

And why would I think of that? Why? He didn't look sick—there were no visible marks or signs that could have tipped me off. He didn't cough excessively or take an unusual amount of pills, or suddenly begin losing weight. He was normal, as normal as any normal person could be, so why—how could I ever suspect him? I believed in him. I trusted him. But now, as a result of that trust I was going to die.

Suddenly my skin began to crawl. It was as if I could feel the virus snaking its way through my flesh one cell at a time. I felt its intentions. I felt its growth. I ran to the bathroom, stripped from my clothes and frantically began searching for lesions, weight loss or any other sign of the dreaded disease that would soon destroy my life. I screamed as I clawed at my flesh wishing I could rip it from my bones and rid myself of the shame lying below its surface, but to no avail. The damage had been done. All there was left for me to do now was sit, and wait.

So are you going to take the part?" I asked him the night before. We had just returned from a painstaking fashion disaster masqueraded as a *show* hosted by an up and coming designer, who unfortunately, my magazine was doing an exclusive. Halfway through the event, Miles leaned over and informed me the audition he'd gone on for John Singleton's new film had come through. It was a small part with about thirty lines in five critical scenes which would all but make or break the movie. Filming was scheduled to begin sometime in July.

"I don't know." He said fixing a drink at the bar. "It would mean living in LA for about a month and a half give-or-take, and I don't think I really want to do that."

"Why not? This is a chance of a lifetime."

"I know. But I'm not sure if this fits into my life right now. I have a few photo shoots scheduled during that time for some pretty big ad campaigns and I don't think legally I can get out of them, or, if I want to get out of them. Besides that," he said joining me on the sofa, "I don't think I could stand being away from you for more than a day."

"Please." I asserted. "Don't let me or anybody for that matter stop you from pursuing your dreams. You've worked too damn' hard to get an opportunity like this to just up and let it pass you by. Think about it Miles, this could very well be your ticket to a new life."

"But what if I don't want a new life?" He asked, catching me off guard. "What if I'm happy with the one I have here, now, with you?"

"Miles...that's nice—real nice but..." I stammered searching for the appropriate words. "What I'm trying to say is...um...um..." I stopped frustrated, paused then breathed. "Listen. I know you're happy here, I am too. But your dreams are so much more important. I've heard you talk about acting, and how exciting it would be if you actually had the chance to live out that dream. And now you have that chance. Please don't give that up for me, or anybody. This is your chance to do what you've always wanted to do. Be what you've always wanted to be. Do it, because if you don't, you'll regret it for the rest of your life."

"But what about us? The last time we put our careers before each other we ended up apart. I don't want that to happen again."

"We were a lot younger then, and we went about things all the wrong way. Believe me when I tell you I'm here for you, and I'm not going anywhere, anytime soon. I promise you that."

His eyes watered as he pulled me to him, and pressed my head against his chest. "You see," he whispered, holding me tight, "this is exactly why being away from you will all but kill me..."

Moments later we would engage in the most tantalizing sex imaginable, unprotected.

The problem with relationships is that you put your trust in people. You trust them, and they lie to you. They trick you. They deceive you.

How could he do this me? How could he not tell me! I screamed, as the overwhelming reality of what was really happening to me—to my life— came hurdling into view.

I trusted him! I believed in him—I believed in us—and this is the thanks I get! This is how I'm rewarded! I could kill him! I could—I swear I could!

I'm not doing this again. I swear I'm never doing this again. I'll never give my heart to *anyone* again. I swear never, again…

I cried straight for two days, two days and two nights. I reached out to no one. I let no one in. I didn't bathe or eat or at times breathe. I just wanted to die. I wanted to just disappear. That's all I wanted to do.

By day three my voice mail had filled with messages. Some from friends wondering how I was holding up, others from my assistant wondering why hadn't I shown up to work. And oh yes, dozens from Miles wondering why I had not reached out to him; why I was ignoring him; why all of a sudden had I shut him out? I listened intently to each message then pressed erase.

Later that evening a white envelope was slipped underneath my door. I stared at it for more than an hour before picking it up and reading its contents.

Dear Diogenes,

Let me first say this, you are not alone. I too feel and understand your pain. About a year ago I received a mystery phone call warning me I should get tested for HIV. When I hung up the telephone I couldn't stop the tears from falling. I kept wondering how? Why? Who? All of a sudden the one thing I thought I could always avoid came knocking.

The next few days were hard. There were so many emotions: anger, fear, confusion, followed by numbness, frustration, and depression. But it wasn't until my test came back positive did my life really begin spiraling out of control. Oh God Dio I tell you I completely lost it. How could I have HIV! How? When I had been in a committed relationship for years…when my partner swore I was the only person he was sleeping with! Nothing prepares you for that moment. Nothing. One day you're planning your big bright future, and the next, your wake. I kept telling myself: "You have to be strong. You have to be strong. You can get through this. You can get through this." But no matter how many times I said it, in the back of my mind I knew my days were numbered. Because once you know you have it, you can never not know again.

But as a person living with HIV I will tell you this, even though your life may feel like it's over, in truth its no. Unless you decide it is. Believe me, I have my hard days. Days when I feel like my life is in the hands of my

193

doctors, insurance company and symptoms...and if by some chance one of them slips, I'm gone. And then there are the days when grief and sadness swallows me up and spits me out whole. But I maintain...I'm still here. I'm still breathing. I'm still living. And I refuse to go out with a whimper.

I know you have flipped to the end of this letter to find out exactly who this is, and I'm sure you were very disappointment to find no name there. But, I will tell you this, I am someone who loves you dearly. And when the time is right, and you need me most I will reveal myself to you. Until then, reach out to those who love you because they need you now, just as much as you need them. Your outcome doesn't just affect you, it affects us all.

Signed,

A friend indeed.

I placed the letter on the coffee table and began to cry. I wasn't alone after all. Somebody somewhere understood.

About an hour later I phoned Miles. At first the conversation was strained. I blamed him, he blamed me until it became painfully obvious neither one of us really wanted to talk to the other. We ended the conversation shortly after deciding the place and time we would take our test. I hung up the phone and went straight to bed.

That night I had the strangest dream. I dreamed I was in a room full of people, all types of people, young, old, black, white, short, and tall. They were all sitting in white wing backed chairs encircling me. I had on a black suit, I know because they all had on white robes and I thought to myself, "Am I dead?"

The first one spoke.

"Welcome."

His full deep voice startled me.

"Don't be afraid," he whispered, "we're not here to harm you."

"Who are you?" I asked taking them all in.

A short pudgy woman answered. "To some we're death. To others we're a cure."

"A cure? A cure for what?"

"It all depends on what ails them." Another answered.

"What if it's fear?" I asked.

"Ahh, there is nothing to fear but fear itself." A white haired man who looked to be about fifty replied. "I do believe one of your leaders spoke those words. Now what was his name?"

"Franklin D. Roosevelt." A young man said. "The thirty-second president of the United States."

"Yes, yes." The old man nodded. "Mr. Roosevelt...wise words from a wise man. Tell me young man," he said, focusing his attention on me. "What is it you fear?"

"Death." I said loudly.

"Death?" A young child laughed. "Surely you jest! What is there to be afraid of, everyone must die!"

"Now, now child," the old man motioned, "many men fear the unknown. You would know this had you lived a bit longer."

"How did he die?" I asked studying the child who looked to be all of ten years old.

"AIDS." The old man answered quickly. "The same disease that now threatens your life. His mother gave him the disease at birth. Poor lad...he never really had much of a chance. From the very beginning his days were numbered."

Suddenly tears appeared out of nowhere and began filling my eyes.

"There's no need to cry." A woman spoke. "He suffers no more."

"But he's dead!" I screamed. "Dead! And I don't want to die! I don't want to die, not like this—I'm too young! I have too much to live for! It's not fair I tell you! It's not fair!"

"Fair!" The eldest of the men bellowed, sending his voice echoing throughout the expanse. "I know nothing of this fairness you speak! Is it not fair that the old should perish after having gained a working knowledge of life? Is it not fair that the blind should walk the earth wondering what those who have sight fail to see? Is it not fair that the few who choose to seek the meaning of life and all its wonder often suffer greatly, while those who sit idly by criticizing their findings flourish?"

I shook my head not knowing what else to say.

"Then speak not to us of fairness my son, for we know it not. And yet, if you must speak, do so only in truth, the language of love."

I held my breath. "I am afraid." I said through tears. "I don't want to be, but I am. I am afraid to die."

"The child was right you know." A woman responded. "All men must die."

"Yes, but when it's their turn, not before. We shouldn't die before."

"Who gives you the right to determine one's time?" She asked, her voice rising slightly.

195

"I can only speak for myself." I answered quietly, not wanting to anger her, or the old man. "I know for me I'm not ready. My life is just beginning."

"Just beginning?" Another queried. "Then why have you been so careless with it?"

"Careless?" I asked confused.

"Yes." Another answered. "On numerous occasions you have engaged in sexual activities with people carelessly. It seems at times you've found great pleasure in casual meaningless sex, all the while knowing the dangers it held."

"I was looking for the one."

A few of them laughed. "The one...tell me my son, *who* is the one? And if by some chance, while on your search you stumbled upon this great omnipotent being, would he, the *one*, have the power to alter the habits you have created during your hunt? Is he or she that powerful?"

"I doubt it seriously." Another answered before I had a chance to respond. "Humanity thrives on fiction. Fictitious lives, living out fictitious truths. The *one* is merely an excuse to sample the multitude."

"Is it really?" Another spoke. "No wonder so many are dying at such an alarming rate."

"They're dying because they have no self-control. Isn't that right young man?"

"No!" I answered defiantly.

"No?" He repeated. "Then what other reason could there be? Surely you do not expect me to believe many of the diseases that plague man-kind are a result of self-control?"

"Some..." I answered, "but not all. Humans care about their lives, they care whether they live or die even if sometimes their actions prove otherwise."

"I see." He nodded. "So are you saying you care?"

"I do care. I didn't realize how much I cared until..."

"You felt you would lose it." The child answered.

"Exactly. I love my life. I love my family—my friends. And if I were to lose them I'd—"

I shut my eyes and began to cry once more. The thought of not being able to do the things I so often took for granted unnerved me.

"Son, we are not here to condemn or set free. We are but a memory of what's to come."

"I'm going to die aren't I?"

"Goodbye my son..." He whispered, as they all stood to leave.

"Answer me! I'm going to die aren't I?"

"Peace be unto you..."

196

"Answer me god-dammit! I'm going to die aren't I! I'M GONNA DIE!!!! I'M GONNA DIE!!!!"

I awoke screaming, drenched in sweat and for the next few hours could not find the courage to close my eyes. Instead I laid awake wondering how this awful disease had come to roost in my life.

O ur appointment was for ten the next morning. I was surprised to find so many people present when we arrived. Like my dream all types were represented: straight, gay, black, white, young, old, preps, thugs—you name them they were there. A few looked comfortable, as if this wasn't their first or last trip.

I made my way to the back of the room trying my best not to gain anyone's attention, which in a way would have been surprising. Miles and I had agreed to forgo appointments with our respective doctors and instead visit one of the city's many free clinics. Initially the thought was confidentiality; both of our doctors were in the life and as such, our friends. The last thing we wanted to do was set off alarms, and the gossip mill. But having graced the city's finest, and I say that with heavy over-dramatic sarcasm, I was beginning to wonder if we had indeed made a mistake. In a word, the place was hideous. The waiting room, *(if that's what you want to call that roach motel)* was bathed in a sea foam green, accented in a flamingo pink. There was a metal desk, the kind teachers must have used in the seventies, in the front with a pen and a pad with a sign that read: Please Sign in & Take a Seat. Someone Will Be With You Directly. A small television hung from the ceiling showing shorts on how to protect yourself and others from contracting STDs that looked as if it were filmed the weekend before my mother's conception. Above the desk, hung a big ass industrial clock that took me a while to realize it wasn't even working. Nothing about the place was warm and inviting. Not the waiting room, the people waiting, or the clerk that burst into the room every few minutes to count how many people were waiting.

After Miles signed in, he sat down next to me and began perusing a wildlife magazine, oblivious of his surroundings. It completely incensed me. How could he be so calm when in less than an hour, we would be taking a test that could forever change our future? Wasn't he worried? Didn't he care? Or had he resigned to just deal with whatever laid ahead? His passiveness angered me to no end.

"You could have picked a better clinic." I spit through clenched teeth.

"It was the closest one." He responded, unbothered.

197

"Fuck closest one, this shit is disgusting! If I *don't* have anything, I probably will by the time I leave this shit hole!"

He sighed heavily and continued scanning the periodical.

"Did you hear what I said?!" I spit, raising my voice. A young girl, who looked to be all of seventeen turned to see who I was talking to. Met with silence, she turned back around.

"I heard you." Miles answered.

"Then why didn't you say anything?"

He closed the magazine. "What do you want me to say?"

"Anything! Just don't sit there and ignore me!"

"Alright." He said eyeing me from head to toe. "When are you going to take off those shades?"

"When I get home." I spit.

"But there's no sun in here."

"So?"

"So, take them off!"

"No."

"Well, at least take off that trench coat. I know you have to be burning up. It's at least eighty degrees outside!"

"I know how hot it is Miles." I snapped. "I don't need you to remind me."

"So you're just gonna sit there, with your coat on, those shades, and that big ass hat pulled down over your face."

"Yes! And if you have a problem with it, then take it up with someone who cares."

My voice raised an octave too high. Both the girl and a couple two rows ahead turned around to see what was going on.

Miles chuckled. "Do you see now why I haven't said anything? *You* want to go there, but I'm not going to."

"Miles you know what, fuck you! In case you've forgotten, I'm sitting in a room full of *low lives* waiting to take a test to see if I'm going to live to see my thirty-third birthday. At the same time wondering how the hell I'm going to explain this shit to my mother, how I'm going to continue running my business, or for that matter remain in this fucking relationship if my test turns out positive! So please, spare me the little speech about *your* not wanting to go there!" A group of people turned around and stared at me. "And I wish you people would turn around and mind your business! This doesn't concern you!"

The young girl sucked her teeth just as Miles began to speak. "What did I tell you last night Dio?" He spit, trying hard to contain his budding anger. "Didn't I tell you how your over dramatic bullshit can turn me the fuck off?! Look at you! You're sitting up here trying not to bring attention to yourself when that's all you're doing! You don't think people are wondering why the hell you're wearing a coat, shades and that big ass hat in the middle of the summer! Is this what you call inconspicuous?"

"No—" I spit feeling my anger quicken, "it's what I call protection! Something you *should have used* in your last relationship!"

The words hit him hard. I wanted to take them back. I wanted to say I didn't mean it, that I was sorry. But it was too late. The damaged had been done. Fuck it...

After a few heated minutes he spoke, "You know what Dio that was a low blow. Sometimes I wonder if you know the effect you have on people. Sometimes I wonder if you know that the poison that spews from your mouth hurts them, and at times, kills them. And I can't help but wonder if I had said the same shit to you, would you *still* be sitting here? Or, would you have done a classic Dio—flip your collar and leave? But thankfully, I'm not like you Dio." He spit, as if the thought alone caused him great discomfort. "I'm not about being a *super*star. I'm not about putting others down just so I can build myself up. I'm not about fame and fortune. I'm about life and love, two things I see you can't get a grip on."

I sat there staring at him, not believing what I had just heard, a part of me wanting to slap the taste out of his mouth for daring to speak to me like that. How dare he! How fucking dare he come for me—when I was the one suffering—when my nerves were a fucking wreck! Did he not understand that my life was spiraling out of control and I had no idea how to fix it? That for the very first time I realized no amount of money in the world could solve my problems? Could he not he see that? Could he not see the pain in my eyes? Or hear the hurt in my voice? What, did he think, this was easy for me? I had never—ever—been summoned to take a fucking test to see if I had some goddamn disease! This shit was eating me alive, and he was coming for me?!

Unexpected tears filled my eyes and lined the edges of my face. Miles noticed, and discreetly—despite his anger—reached out and began rubbing my hand, unknowingly soothing my pain. My first impulse was to snatch it away and move as far away from him as I could, but it felt good. He felt good. And I knew in that brief moment when his hand and mine were one, that he would never leave me, or hurt me, or do anything intentionally to destroy the bond we shared. And I loved him for that.

"Excuse me gentleman," a health aide whispered, "but the doctor will see you now."

We faced each other for a long while hoping to prolong the moment. In his eyes I saw something I never wanted him to reveal: Fear; followed by a stream of tears. Immediately my whole body began to shake.

"I'm sorry..." He whispered through tears. "I'm so sorry..."

I sighed deeply, and with courage I never knew I possessed, I tugged at his arm and pulled him to his feet. Then slowly, with my heart lunged in my throat, and Miles by my side, I unwillingly began the next chapter of my all too dramatic life.

SEVENTEEN

Jared

THE NEXT FEW DAYS were spent playing counselor to my friends. Kevin was in California worried sick about his mother, whiles Miles and Dio anxiously awaited the results of their test. After the dust settled and Miles calmed down, I telephoned him and apologized for infringing on his privacy. It took some time and a little effort on his part, but he eventually gave in. *"I'll forgive you this time Jared,"* he warned minus the finger, *"but this time only. Just remember, everyone who feeds you information, ain't your friend, and it doesn't mean they're looking out for your best interest."*

I thanked him for the advice and assured him there would be no second time. I had learned my lesson.

Afterwards, surprisingly, dealing with Miles was a piece of cake. Dio on the other hand was a whole different story entirely. Afraid his life was coming to an end he began taking drastic steps. First, he met with his lawyer and revamped his will. Then he cleared his calendar for the next three months and appointed his Managing Editor, Vivian Sattire, Acting Editor-In-Chief of WARES, which completely took everyone by surprise. Vivian and Dio had never quite seen eye to eye on the creative direction of the magazine. She with her political science, women liberation background always insisted the magazine go left, while Dio with his I don't give a fuck, its my magazine and if you don't like it get your own, temperament always insisted they go right. Needless to say, the magazine always went right.

But, as shocking as his leave of absence was, he took over dramatic to a whole 'nother level completely when he asked me to meet him at Our Lady of Greater Mount Zion Non-Denomination Church of New Jerusalem Cemetery and Mausoleum.

"What?!" I yelled in disbelief. "Why? Dio don't you think you're taking this all just a little too far? I mean you haven't even gotten your results back yet!"

"Look. I don't have time to argue with you Jared. It's my life and I'm calling the shots. I promised Mr. Manginelli that I'd meet him at his office at 2:30. You have about an hour to meet me there. So you need to decide rather quickly if you're coming."

I wanted to tell to him to kiss my ass, but then he'd only hang up without allowing me time to talk some sense into his thick ass head. Instead I relented and promised to meet at the church in exactly one hour.

I reached the church at 2:25, and spotted him out front pacing back and forth.

"Dio," I asked as I walked up to him, "what are we doing here? This is foolish. You're not dying."

"How do you know?" He whispered embracing me. "For all we know, this could be it. The end of a great life gone all too soon, and if it is *Sweety*—trust—I want it done right! The last thing I want is for you girls to fuck up my last rites. My plan is to make sure I go out the very same way I can in *Pump-kin*, sparkling!"

I laughed in mock disbelief. "You're serious, aren't you?"

"As a heart attack." He replied. "So let's go. We mustn't keep Mr. Manginelli waiting."

Salvatore Manginelli was a tall lean man about forty-five years old with a head full of reddish-brown hair. He wore a dark suit with a bluish-greenish paisley tie, and matching handkerchief. His office was decorated tastefully with a traditional wooden desk and a maroon high-back leather chair. Behind his desk hung a huge painting of a sunrise with rich full colors. There were two large windows with ivory colored vertical blinds slightly opened on the left wall of the office, allowing warm rays of sunlight to penetrate the room. On his desk and the wooden bookshelves throughout his office were several pictures of what I assumed were his wife, two sons and daughter. All of this took me a bit by surprise. For some reason, I had expected him to be a cold dull man, similar, if you will, to Egor from the cult classic Frankenstein; and his surroundings to be dark and dismal. But quite to my surprise he was warm and pleasant.

"So Diogenes," he said taking a seat behind his massive desk. "You're here to begin planning your final services."

"Yes," he nodded, "and I was hoping you could give me some guidance as to how to go about it."

He nodded. "Well I must say you're making a wise decision, planning ahead." He adjusted himself in his chair and glanced my way. "Is this your life partner here with you?"

"Oh God no!" Dio shrieked shaking his head violently. "No, no, no! This here is my good friend and confidant Jared Covington. My boyfriend,"—he paused—"excuse me; my life partner couldn't make it today. So I asked Mr. Covington here to join me." He leaned forward. "His presence here is fine though isn't it?"

He smiled. "Oh sure. Here at Greater Mount Zion we applaud all walks of life. Mr. Covington is more than welcomed to stay. Maybe by watching you plan your services, you will somehow encourage him to begin planning his."

"I don't think so." I said dryly. "I still have a lot of living to do, unlike some parties here in the room."

He laughed. "I'm sure we all do Mr. Covington, but it's never too late to begin planning because death *is* inevitable. And yet it's so unfortunate many people don't see the need to pre-plan their final services. But, here at Greater Mount Zion, we encourage everyone when possible to pre-plan. We find it's the best way."

"Why?" I asked sitting up. "Doesn't that somehow take the fun out of living?"

"No." He smiled warmly, and then went straight into his sales pitch. "It actually creates a type of security, certainty, and in some ways we like to think of it more like a gift of love for the people we leave behind. Think about it. When a loved one dies, someone has to take the time to gather all of his or her vital statistics and historical information, which is necessary to receive a death certificate. Then they must arrange and pay for the funeral services and, the final resting-place. These things alone can often take days to complete! Which in turn prolongs the burial process, and, increases the stress levels of the bereaved.

"Because of situation like this," he reasoned, "thousands of families are beginning to pre-plan their funerals." He paused, then clasped his well manicured hands together. "The bottom line is this Mr. Covington, if you want to avoid the haste, worry, stress, and emotional overspending so many families experience upon a loved one's demise, then pre-planning is the way to go."

"I'm sold!" Dio said enthusiastically, almost leaping out of his chair. "Where do we begin?"

Mr. Manginelli smiled. "Well first, the basics. He reached and removed a manila folder from his desk and handed it to Dio. "I'll need to know things like your full name, social security number, date of birth, your profession, and so on. Then we can dive right into planning the specifics. For example, have you ever given any consideration as to whether you'd like to be buried or cremated?"

"Actually…" He paused. "I never really gave it much thought." He leaned back against the chair and crossed his legs. "What do you think Jared?"

"What do I think?" I replied annoyed. "Do you really want to know, or are you merely asking out of courtesy?"

"Of course I want to know…don't be silly." He said with his, *we're in front of white people bitch—so don't you dare embarrass me,* tone. "Why else would I ask?"

I considered his question carefully. "Well in that case, I think you're crazy for being here. As a matter of fact, as soon as I leave here, I'm going to talk to my friend over at Bellevue about admitting your crazy ass on a *pre*-psychotic basis!"

He mumbled something under his breath, then turned his attention back to Mr. Manginelli. "I've thought about it." He said taking on a serious tone. "I'd like to be cremated. I've never liked dead bodies much, and besides," he said his voice cracking, "there's no telling what I'm going to look like when it's all said and done. So yes Mr. Manginelli, cremation is the way to go."

"Dio—" I began.

He held up his hand and continued. "I also wanted to look into some mausoleums; a big one, with three or four pillars, and maybe some stained glass widows. Do you offer anything like that?"

"Of course we do. We actually have quite a selection of mausoleums. You can even have the interior detailed to your exact specifications."

"Really?" He said growing excited. "You mean I can have it designed inside and out?"

"You sure can."

"Oh wow, I never would have thought you could actually—"

That was it, the final straw. His growing excitement over the pure stupidity of this whole conversation had hit its peak. How could he be serious? How could he actually sit there, with a straight face and be serious—when he hadn't even gotten the results from his test back yet?!

"Dio listen!" I said interrupting his vigil with Mr. Manginelli. "This is ridiculous! You're not going to die for another forty or fifty years! For Christ's sake, you're only thirty-two years old! I'm not going to sit here and allow you to kill yourself off! It's stupid!"

"Mr. Manginelli, would you excuse us for a moment?" Dio asked rising slowly.

He nodded. "Take your time."

Six steps later we were in the hall.

"Look Jared, I asked you here for support," He spit spinning around in one swift motion, "and if for some reason you can't offer me that, then maybe you should carry your black ass home."

I went to counter but was stopped before I even began. "This is *my* life, *my* dilemma, and *my* solution. How I choose to deal with it is likewise *my* business—not yours—not Miles—not any fucking bodies! So before you open your mouth to tell me what you *think* you know but don't—think about it, then do me a favor, and shut the fuck up!"

He left me standing in the hall, fucked up and lost.

When I entered my apartment an hour later the soothing sounds of Will Downing filled the space, which meant only one thing: Michael was there.

We had not seen or spoken to each other in almost a week, since the night I, not so nicely, asked him to leave. When he reached home later that evening, he left me a lengthy message rimming me about kicking him out over what he termed: *stupid childish bullshit.* And in no uncertain terms told me: *What you need to do is grow the fuck up.*

A few times as I listened to him go on and on about how disappointed he was in me, I started to pick up and explain my behavior, but I didn't. I just laid there, staring blankly at the ceiling absorbing every ounce of his anger.

I felt stupid for what I had done, but, at the same time I felt justified. Sure I had once again allowed my emotions to run amuck—but I was hurt! And I felt—I truly believed he was trying to attack me by rubbing the way I handled the whole Sean situation in my face. He had no right to say what he said, even, if it were true. So what if I sometimes got shit confused...so what. Sean was wrong, and if I had to prove that to him, then, neither he nor Sean understood who I was. I was human, and although I hated admitting it, I did make mistakes. But if he somehow expected me to be this perfect man—with no flaws—or no mishaps—and all my shit together wrapped neatly in one big ole' sparkling box—then he was wrong, because I was not that man. And no matter how hard I tried, I could never be that man.

Listening to Will croon, *"I don't wanna lose you; I love you as you are..."* I realized the problem. Defeated, I flopped on the sofa and sank into a deep depression. I hated my life. I hated it because it was my fault. I created the image he saw. I was the one who pretended to be this guy who had it all figured out. I was the one who led people to believe I needed no help, no support, because on my worst days I still had it going on. And although I knew it was all a lie I lived it because it was the only truth I had ever known. Early on they warned me: Never let them see you sweat; never let them catch you lying down. It was our creed—our motto—our life! And so I had to live it, whether I liked it or not; whether it choked the shit out of me, or not. But not a day went by, that I did not pray the lie would somehow become the truth, and one way or another force everything out of place, into place. But it never did. The lies, the life, my life only got more complicated, and stressful and unbelievably difficult to pull off.

Why, I hear someone ask. Why do this to yourself? Why create this fictional being and try so hard to be him, when you know in your heart you will never be able to live up to the demands he will place on you? Why pretend to be perfect?   The perfect man; the perfect lover; the perfect employee; the perfect friend, the perfect son—when all you can really be, is you?

I hear you.   And believe me, I have asked myself those very same questions countless times, but the answer has always remained the same: Nobody *wanted* him. They, like me, wanted the dream.   And so, that's what I gave them.

"How long have you been here?"

"A few minutes."

Silence.

"Do you want to talk about what happened?"

"No, not really."

"Well, I think we should."

Silence, then: "If we must, we must."

"What's wrong with you?"

"What do you mean?"

"I mean what's wrong? What happened? You've changed."

"I haven't."

"You have. When I met you there was a light about you. It seemed to follow you wherever you went but now…what happened, where'd it go?"

"I don't know. I wasn't aware I had one."

He paused. "Is it me? Am I doing this to you?"

I thought for a minute. "It's not you."

"Then what is it Jared—please tell me. I'm beginning to worry…"

My eyes began to water. "It's nothing Michael really."

He lowered his head into his hands for a few minutes, then looked up.

"Then why is it so hard all of a sudden to reach you? Why does it feel like sometimes you hide from me? Like you hide from the world? I don't get you. You worked so hard to get me and us to this point…and now it's like," he paused, catching his breath, "you shut down, and lock me out. Why?"

I used my shoulder to wipe away the tears. "Because now the real challenge begins."

"Challenge? What challenge?"

"The challenge of love.   You see, its one thing to say you love someone, and yet quite another to actually admit you are in love. But, to commit to another your heart and soul with the sacred promise to love them *even though*, is often too much for many.   And as a result it sends them scurrying back to single-hood. So the challenge begins now. I have issues Michael. Plenty of them. Ones I know about, and others I have yet to discover. The question is, how long will you be around to help me get through them…"

There. I'd said it. I'd let it out. Here was his chance. If he'd ever wanted out, I had all but opened the door for him. The choice was now his.

He grabbed both my hands and held them tightly. "Jared we all have shit about us that stink sometimes. Believe me, at some point you're going to smell mine. But I promise you, if you can deal with all the bullshit that's gonna reek in mine, then there's no doubt in my mind I *can*, and *will* deal with yours."

EIGHTEEN

Kevin

MY MOTHER DIED THE MORNING OF JUNE TENTH. All of us, me, my two aunts, and my Uncle Robert, were in the room when she breathed her last breath. There were a few tears shed, but nothing more. She had given strict instructions: No Mourning. Her death should be celebrated, for she was no longer living in pain and had joined her father in Heaven.

By her beside lay a package with specific instructions on how to handle her services. She was to be buried in her favorite white silk dress. Her coffin and any flowers surrounding her were to be white, all white, with no exceptions. Her favorite spiritual, *His eye is on the Sparrow* was to be sung by her cousin Robin in her honor.

Immediately, I went about the task of ensuring everything went exactly as she had planned. Thankfully, everyone was more than willing to play his or her part in fulfilling her final dream. I was so busy running around that day preparing, it wasn't until later that night I discovered a letter with my name scrawled across the front in the package my mother had left. When I opened the envelope, my eyes filled with tears. The first line read: *Dear son.* It had been years since she called me son, and now I'd never hear those words again. I read the words once more...

Dear son,

I know when I meet my maker, I must account for many a thing I did during my life. But none will pain me more than trying to explain to him how I let my son go for so many years. I won't try to make excuses, because there are none. I only hope you can forgive me, because from the bottom of my heart, I am sorry.

I want you to know it's not your fault, but my own. When I first learned of your sexuality, I got so angry because I just knew it was my fault. I kept thinking, if only your father had stuck around long enough to help raise you, maybe things would have been different. Maybe, you would have turned out different. I blamed myself for ruining your life, and in doing so I pushed you away. I couldn't confront you everyday knowing I had failed as a mother. I just couldn't do it...

But I want you to know this: I never stopped loving you. Never. I loved you Kevin from the very first moment I laid eyes on you, and not a day went by that I didn't think of you, and offer up a word of prayer to God to look over you, and keep you safe.

But it wasn't until you walked through those hospital doors, did I realize just how much I missed you. And at that moment, I accepted you Kevin for everything you were. At that moment, what I thought mattered all those years when I was being selfish, didn't matter much at all. I was just so happy to have you back in my life again...happy, to hold you again.

Son from this day forward if you follow nothing else I've said, make sure you make better with your life, than I did with mine. Make sure you hold all those you love close to you and never let them go. And always, always remember, no matter what you're going through, you-are-loved!

I've got to go now. I'm tired. But not before I tell you, I'm proud of you son for teaching an old dog, a bunch of new tricks...

Love always, your mother,

Mrs. Clara B. Smith

That night I felt a warmth I had not felt since childhood. My mother loved me—she really loved me! Finally, all was right with the world.

Her funeral was held two days later. The grass was as green as green could get, and the sun brighter than usual. The snow-white casket and accompanying flowers, made the grass and reflecting sun appear even more vibrant. Somehow I imagined my mother looking down, cigarette in hand, approving the peaceful sight.

Although hundreds of people wanted to attend, we kept the gathering small allowing only a few close friends and relatives to attend the memorial service, as per her request. We surrounded her casket each with a single rose, told stories, read poems, and sang songs, all in her honor.

When her body was lowered into the ground, we each threw our rose atop of her casket as the minister offered a word of prayer. At one point, I felt the tears welling up in the bottom of my soul, but stopped when I remembered something she had whispered to me moments before her demise.

She exhaled, shut her eyes then smiled. "Kevin..." she spoke softly. "You be strong when I'm gone. Everyone will be depending on you...most of all me." She pushed out another breath, and closed her eyes once more. I stroked her hair and begged her not to speak. She shook her head, then continued. "I loved you Kevin..." she rasped, peering deep into my eyes, "even when you thought I didn't."

I leaned in closer and wiped the steady stream of tears flowing from her eyes, then whispered, "I know mother, I know."

I held her close to my heart for a long time, and in my arms she took one last breath, and was gone.

You know, as I look over my life at all of the mistakes I've made, and all the time I've wasted, I often wish I could go back and do it all over again. But I know this is impossible. None of us can undo or relive a moment in our past. We can however make each new moment we live rich. We can look forward to the future and make for ourselves the life we've always dreamed—the life we've always wanted. My mother did. And if I could be half the person she was, then I'll know for sure, none of my living will have been in vain.

NINETEEN

Jared

FRIDAY AFTERNOON WHEN I RETURNED FROM LUNCH I noticed yet another email from Sean. It was the seventh of the week and the second that day. He had taken to writing since I hadn't returned any of his phone calls.

The truth had been revealed: Miles did not have AIDS, or HIV, and neither did Dio. Both were fine. Come to find out, Miles' ex lover Tony lied. He had discovered through hearsay that Miles and Dio had gotten back together and were seriously pursuing their relationship. Angry that Miles had never entertained his many requests to rekindle, he sought out to do anything possible to ensure their *would*-be reconciliation failed. And it almost worked thanks to Sean, and regrettably, myself. Had we both waited, gotten the facts and *then* preceded, Dio and Miles probably would have sailed through their ordeal with little to no worries. But because we put our noses where they didn't belong, all hell broke loose.

In the end, I was thankful the foundation upon which they built their relationship was able to withstand the pressure of the storm. In time, they forgave us, each other and continued their journey, together.

I, however, was still having a hell of a time forgiving Sean. I understood his motive. I understood his position, but, the damage had been done. And as a result, our friendship had been frayed. So it didn't matter how many times he apologized, or Michael, and/or Dio begged me to speak to him, my decision was final, and I wasn't going to bend.

I opened the email and prepared myself for yet another drawn out apology that would go unanswered.

```
Jared, of all people, I expected you to understand.
    When my boy Ron called and started talking about his
friend Tony and Miles, I panicked.  You know how much I care
about you niggahs.  The last thing I'd want is for one of you
to be involved with some cat that's trying to fuck you over.
That's why I told Dio.  I had to tell him.  I couldn't risk
waiting until it was too late.  Dio needed to know what he
might have gotten himself into.
    Now, had I known Ron's boy was a fucking liar I would
have never said anything to you or Dio!  You know I don't get
down like that!  Come on black, you know that ain't my style.
```

213

But, the way you've been acting since then is fucked up
man! It's like you can't see a niggah's intentions were in
the right place. You ain't returned none of my calls, replied
to any of my emails, or even tried to reach out to me to talk
about this shit! What's up with that? I thought we were
boys? I thought we swore never to let anything come between
us? Maybe you lied about that shit, but I didn't. I meant
every fucking word of it.
     I'm saying Jay, life is already hard as hell, but to
know my best friend in the world ain't trying to talk to me,
is making this shit that much harder.
     So yo—CALL ME NIGGAH—write me—do something!   Damn'!
How long are you going to fucking avoid me? I miss you man.

     Respect. Sean.

I closed the email, leaned back into my chair and exhaled. I allowed
my attention to fall on a framed picture I had purchased years ago. It was a
cartoon rendition of two friends holding hands. On was blue, the other
white; both were smiling brightly. Underneath written freely were the
words: *Love heals all…*

All my life I had truly believed in the power of those three simple
words. And I knew with just an *ounce* of faith, it very well could. But that
afternoon for the first time ever, I doubted it ever would.

J.C. can we talk?" Lisa asked filling the seat across from me. Her voice
was low and lifeless. When I looked up I understood why. Her eyes,
normally bright and cheerful, were red and puffy.

"Is everything alright Lisa? You look troubled."

She dropped her head, and dabbed the corners of her eyes with a
napkin. "No." She said softly. "Thing's aren't okay."

This was a rare moment indeed. Never, in all my years working
with her had I seen her so vulnerable. Her exterior had always been so
strong, so together. Witnessing the opposite not only worried me, it
frightened me. "What's up?" I said quietly. "Talk to me."

She lowered her head and sighed deeply. "You know…" she began
softly, "I don't understand why people can't be honest. For once in my life,
I'd like to meet someone who knows what they want, and is honest enough
to stand up for it." She shifted her body. "And, if they can't be honest with
me, at least be honest with themselves. That's all I ask. That's all I want."
She paused and ran her fingers slowly through her hair. "That way, I can
make a decision as to where I want to place them in my life."

She stopped just as a stream of tears made its way down her cheek.
She wiped them away quickly then sat quietly staring off into the distance. I

waited patiently for her to regroup not knowing where the conversation was heading.

"I caught him Jared."

"You caught who?"

"Emanuel." She whispered.

I raised my brow carefully. "Cheating?"

She nodded painfully. "And he had the audacity to say: *It wasn't me!*"

I shook my head in disbelief. Too many times I had witnessed brothers run that same tired ass line on many an unsuspecting woman. I sighed exasperated. "How'd you catch him?"

"About a week ago," she began slowly, "I was out shopping along Fifth Avenue, looking for a pair of chocolate mules, when I spotted this beautiful cashmere sports jacket in the window of Sax's. I stood there imagining how good my man would look come fall sporting that jacket. So, I purchased it, as an early birthday gift, and spared no expense in doing so. I figured I could hold out until then, but, last night I got so pumped up about surprising him I knew I wouldn't be able to wait the two months to his birthday. So, I jumped in a cab and headed to his house."

I looked at her with that knowing look that read: *You called right?* She shook her head. I moaned.

"Ah Lisa. You know you're supposed to call first..."

"I know. I know. But I was so excited. I didn't even think about calling. Anyway, when the cab pulled up to his building, I thanked the driver and gave him a crisp twenty-dollar bill for his services. Just as I was about to step out of the cab, I saw him. He was about to enter his building, but, he wasn't alone. His hand, my hand—the one I groomed on a weekly basis—was in the hand of another woman. And the worst part about it was that they actually looked happy. Like two little school kids caught up in puppy love. I winced when he stopped suddenly, cupped her face, and lovingly brought her lips to his. He never kissed me in public! He always claimed it was in poor taste—that people who were really in love didn't have to prove it to the world!" She shook her head. "And I actually believed that shit! J.C., I was so mad, and hot, I almost lost it! My first instinct was to jump out of that cab and beat the shit out of him and that bitch! But luckily, for both of them, reason took over. And as much as I would've loved kicking both of their asses, as a lady, I vowed a long time ago never to stoop to such a level. Instead, I swallowed my tears, and headed home.

"When he called hours later, I confronted him on what I saw. He lied, said it wasn't him, and played it off as if I were just imagining things."

"What did you say?"

"I told him to go fuck himself!"

"Good." I nodded. "More men need to hear those words."

She scoffed. "He didn't seem to think so."

"Why, what did he say?"

"He called me a stuck up militant bitch! Then hung up the phone."

I laughed. "Well you know that's not too far from the truth Lisa…"

She reached over and playfully hit me on the shoulder.

I smiled. "You know I'm just playing. He was just mad because he got busted. Most men relish in there power to deceive. You pulled his card, that's why he lashed out."

"Still, I just don't understand it J.C. Everything was going fine. He didn't seem unhappy or like he was missing anything. And I'm usually good at noticing people's behavior. But, this time, I never saw it coming. You're a man, why do you think he did it?"

"Did what?" Jordan asked appearing out of nowhere. "Cheat on you?"

"Where—" Lisa stammered, doing a three-sixty. "Where the hell did you come from?!"

"Listen girl, I'm not being rude but please…I heard everything you said through these fake wanna be walls. Plus, you know there are no secrets in corporate America. Anyhow," she said sitting in the chair adjacent to Lisa, "the reason he cheated is the same reason why all men cheat—"

"And why is that?" I interjected.

"Because," she said with ease, "they're big babies that want everything under the sun, and then some. They want a wife and mother at home to take care of the children, and all of the other household nuances, and then they want,"—she raised her hands to indicate quotes—"the shorty on the side, they can hit up every freakin' chance they get. It's nothing new. This same behavior has been going on for years because women allow it. Now," she said tilting her head, "what women need to learn is independence."

"Independence?" I repeated.

"Yes." She nodded. "Independence. Women for centuries have been stepping stools for men. We have always bent over backwards to keep our family together, to keep our homes together, to keep our lives together, while all along our men are usually the ones ripping it apart! We remain with that man that ignores us, or the one that beats us believing the whole time he will change. We put everything and everyone in front of ourselves, and our happiness. We stay for our children, or our parents, or even our friends, all mind you to keep up appearances! When our spirit wants nothing more than to be free!

"Some of us," she scoffed, "will *even* go as far as to trick ourselves into believing our children will be better off with a father that's *a little* abusive, than no father at all." She shook her head. "What kind of madness is that? Instead of teaching our children to stand up for what they believe, we teach them to settle for less than they deserve. We teach them that it is okay to be put down, as long as the person doing it claims to love you. We teach them that women are passive docile followers, while men are aggressive assertive leaders. And as funny as it may seem, it's not the men in our lives teaching these lessons; it's the women.

"I watched as my mother taught me, unknowingly of course, that I will always be second to my man. I watched as she showed me first hand, that because I was a woman, my dreams, my desires, my life didn't matter— at least not after I had a family. Because, once a husband and children entered the picture my life as I knew it would end, and a whole new one would begin. It wasn't until I kicked my husband to the curb and divorced his trifling ass, did I realize I learned all the wrong lessons from my mother. On that blissful day I began learning some new lessons and affirmed with myself: Yes, I am a mother. And yes, I may be someone's wife. But before all of that, I am Jordan. And my needs do matter."

I scratched my head perplexed. "So you're saying *independence* will solve the problem of men and their promiscuity?"

She laughed. "Child please! Only castration will stop that! All I'm suggesting is for women to realize once and for all that happiness comes from within, not without. I want women to understand you do not marry happiness in a white gown, in front of 200 guests, and a cute little flower girl! Happiness is a condition, a state of mind. It is not your husband, your child or your home. Sure, these things can add to your happiness, but at any given moment, they can also take from it. Once women realize this, then damn' it—there is no stopping us! We will not settle, or for that matter, cater to the ego of a shiftless man. When he starts acting up we can say to him: *Listen, I love you, but that doesn't mean I have to take your shit.* And simply walk away. When enough women take this stand, men will have no choice *but* to respect the women in their lives, or face the consequence of being alone."

Lisa shifted then said, "That's all well and good. But, what are you doing to educate women by bringing this type of knowledge to the foreground?"

"Listen Lisa, I'm not going to pretend I can help all women, because I know I can't. Some will agree with my philosophy and some won't. Believe it or not there are still some women out there stuck in the ice ages who honestly believe they should be subservient to their man. For them," she chuckled, "prayer is needed. But, as far as one little girl is concerned, she will know that her mother is an independent woman, in control of her own destiny. She will know that she can be any and everything her little heart can dream. She will know that because she is a woman, people will limit her ability and desire to achieve all based on her gender. But, she will also know—by example—that all things are possible through Christ Jesus. The fact that she is female will mean nothing to her, because before all of that, she will know she is human."

Lisa nodded her approval. "We need more mothers like you."

"I know, but not to fear. I'm not the first, and I damn' sure ain't the last of great mothers. But," she said crossing her legs, "on to the most pressing issue of the day. What are you gonna do about Emanuel and his trifling ass?"

"Nothing!" She said harshly. "He made his bed, and now he must lay in it. I have far too much self-esteem to run behind a cheater like him. Plus, you should have seen the chick he was with! She was un-beweavable!"

We all broke into a chorus of laughter.

"That's what I don't understand..." Jordan said pulling herself together. "If a man's gonna cheat on his woman, why find the tackiest creature out there? God knows if I ever cheat on my man, you best believe he's gonna be a step above what I already got at home!"

"Okay!" Lisa laughed. "And not some hood rat!"

"Or, some cheap carbon copy of Little Kim!" Jordan said slapping her five. "Let's face it girl, most men wouldn't know a good thing if it was staring them straight in the face. But you know what, I'm not worried, because when the time is right, both you and I will meet the man of our dreams."

Lisa glanced at her watch then stood preparing to leave. "I hope you're right girl, 'cause, I'm not getting any younger, and this game is getting real tired."

Michael and I were fast approaching our tenth month anniversary, and I found myself once again racking my brain trying to think of something special to do. In the nine and a half months we had been together, we managed to do just about everything: Plays, concerts, trips, restaurants, you name it, we'd done it. So coming up with something unique and *interesting* proved to be quite a challenge.

After exhausting just about all of my options I asked Kevin if he knew of anything special I could do. But as usual, he was no help. He went on and on about how I had done *too much* already:

"What, with the weekend getaways, the top notch restaurants, and damn near paying every last one of his bills I'm surprised you have any

money left to maintain an account—never mind think of something else to buy!"

I had heard the same lecture from him about twenty times in twenty different ways, for close to six weeks. And while I appreciated his concern, I was beginning to grow frustrated by his lack of trust in my decisions, and my relationship. So again, *in detail*, I spelled out my love for Michael and insured him I knew exactly what I was doing.

And for the very first time in my life I did. Since that fateful day in January, my entire life had changed. I had received a long over due promotion, and was finally making a salary I felt complimented my level of expertise and lifestyle.

My relationship with my mother, which had been strained since the day I discovered my attraction to men, was drastically improving. At first the change took us both by surprise. Where she had come to expect one, maybe two calls a month she was now receiving three to four a week. When she questioned the sudden show of affection, I simply replied, *"I don't know. I guess, I just feel good, you know..."*

And I did. I felt as if I had been given a second chance at life. A chance to be and do all the things I was too afraid to do, or rather too ashamed. Before Michael, my choice in lifestyles had limited my dreams. Not a day went by that I didn't stop and wonder how could I ever live up to the expectations of my family, who had long begun to ask: *When* would I marry? *When* would I father children? *When* would my *real life* begin?

And they looked to me to provide them with answers to questions I knew I could never give. Questions that slowly and deliberately ate away at what little self-esteem I had managed to savage for extreme emergencies. Questions that *caused me* to *question* my very existence. Eventually, I too began wondering: How could I ever live up to the great American Dream? How would/could I ever fit into a world reserved exclusively for heterosexuals?

Michael and his understated presence changed all of that. He came into my life when I needed him most and filled a void no one but he could have filled. I had loved others before him, but none provided the amount of hope he did. Finally with him, I could dream again. I could look forward to the future with a smile knowing everything was going to be all right. It was by far the best feeling in the world, and I reveled in it. No more worries. No more questions. Only love. What *more* could one man ask for? What more could one man *want*...

I had lived far too long in the realms of doubt, and self-pity, and low self-esteem and for the first time in my life refused to walk around with a big ass VICTIM sign scrolled across my chest. I knew love. I understood its grace and was more than appreciative it had finally come to rest in my life.

So, to give thought to the negative whims of others would only prove detrimental. And I wasn't about to sacrifice the most important thing in my life because of fear, or the unsolicited concerns of others.

Kevin sat completely still listening intently as I rambled on and on. Once I had finished defiantly defending my relationship he stood quietly and headed for the door.

"You know Jared," he said stopping suddenly, "I remember how excited you were when you first purchased *Lalah Hathaway's* CD, and how you couldn't wait to share with me the wonder of *When your life was Low*. Listening to that song I recalled every time I had given my all from the depths of my soul to friends, to family, to lovers, believing all the while: *This will make them love me. This will make them stay.* But in the end, I learned life is something you can't dictate, and *it will* run its course with or without your help." His eyes softened, "Contrary to what you may believe, I've never doubted *your* love for Michael. I know that it is as deep, as the Nile is long. But I believe *Lalah* phrased it best when she crooned: *always remember my friend, the world will change again, and you may have to come back, through everywhere you've been...*"

He opened the door and looked back. "When you need me," he said softly, "I'll be there."

Clairvoyance if you will, is having the power or ability to discern things not readily available to the senses. One said to possess such a skill can usually perceive matters far beyond the range of *ordinary* perception. Kevin, my friend, my confidant, my ace—or whatever other synonym I could use to describe him—possessed this ability. And though often times he was way off the mark about his predictions, the times he was right on, more than made up for his shortcomings.

Shortly after he uttered those words the walls of my relationship, as if willed through his lips, began to crumble.

In our nine and a half months together we weathered our share of doubt. We went through the motions most couples go through. But we held fast to our promise to love each other through it all, always, in all ways. We believed in the power of love, and even more so in its healing. But the two weeks leading up to our tenth-month anniversary, saw a whole new beginning and a whole new us. One I don't think our relationship was ready for.

"I'm hanging out with some of my friends tonight." He reported.

I switched the receiver to my left ear. "Weren't we supposed to hang out tonight?"

"Yeah, but I forgot it was one of my friends birthday's, and well, a bunch of us are going out to celebrate."

"On a Thursday?"

"Yeah, why not?"

"No reason. Its just," I huffed, "you know I cook on Thursdays. I mean, should I save you some, or are you even planning on coming by afterwards?"

"Probably not. I'm not sure how late we're going to hang out. So," he paused, "most likely I'm just gonna head home."

"I see." I said reaching to turn off the oven. "Have fun."

"I will."

That's it? I huffed. No, *'I miss you'*! No, *'I'm sorry for changing our plans so suddenly'?* No, *'I'll make this up to you somehow'? What the fuck?!*

"Michael?" I called out desperately trying to mask my anger.

"Yeah?"

"You never said whose birthday it was."

He hesitated. "My friend Roy."

"Roy?" I repeated.

"Yeah Roy. Why, is there a problem?"

"No, no problem at all." I lied, sensing the battle lying beneath his tone. "I was just curious."

After hanging up I sat on the sofa trying my best to recall the names of all the friends he'd ever talked about since we got together. I came up with about ten, and not one of their names was Roy.

"So did you and *Roy* have fun last night?" I asked shortly after letting him in the following evening.

"Yeah we did." He said ignoring my sarcasm. "We all went out to dinner and talked about old times."

"Really." I said sitting on the sofa. "Who else was there?"

He dropped his bag by the door and flopped on the ottoman. "The regulars."

"Like who?"

"Does it matter?" He snapped suddenly.

"Yeah it matters. What's the big deal in telling me?"

"Because Jared, I know you, you're trying to build a case."

"A case?"

"Yes. To see if I was cheating."

"No, that's not what I'm doing. I'm just trying to see who my man was hanging out with, that's all."

"So now you're babysitting me?"

"Only if you need it. Now who's Roy?"

221

"Roy is an old friend. If that's not enough then—"

"Well it's not." I spit cutting him short. "Did you date him?"

"Why Jared? Would that make you feel better?"

"No, but it would shed some light on the matter at hand."

He sucked his teeth annoyed. "If I knew this was going to turn into a fucking interrogation I would have stayed home."

"It doesn't have to be an interrogation. If you just answer my question, this will all be over with."

He studied me for signs of trust.

"No Jared," he said seconds later, "we never dated."

I crossed my legs. "Did you sleep with him?"

"Did you sleep with Kevin?"

"Kevin is not the issue."

"Well neither is Roy!"

His heated tone revealed the truth. "You *did* sleep with him."

"Wait a minute!" he said rising to his feet. "How are you gonna speak for me?"

I matched his height. "I'm not. But, did you, or didn't you?"

He shook his head in disbelief. "I *don't* have to answer that."

"Damn' it Michael did you, or didn't you?"

You know what," he said reaching for his bag, "I don't have time for this shit. If you have a problem trusting me, fine. But I will not stand here and allow you to give me the fucking third degree for some shit that isn't even your goddamn business! Who the fuck do you think you are?"

"Who do I think I am?" I repeated in disbelief. "What, you need me to remind you? I'm the man who loves you—the one trying to figure out *who the fuck Roy is* and why all of a sudden is he coming up in *my life*—changing *my goddamn* plans and I never even *heard* of his fucking ass until last night!"

"I told you," he hissed, "Roy is a friend! I have known him for close to ten years—and *if you think* that after knowing me for only ten months you could possible know every fucking person I know—then I'm sorry to tell you, you won't!"

"*Did* you *fuck* him!"

"Yes I fucked him!" He screamed without warning. "Is that what the fuck you want to know?! Yes I fucked him! I fucked him! I fucked him!"

He left me standing alone, in the middle of the living room, with my heart split in two. Later that evening I tried several times to reach him, but to no avail. Instead, I laid awake most of the night questioning. Doubting. Crying. My thoughts everywhere. I paced until I couldn't pace anymore, and yet still I paced some more. Only one thought remained consistent, and

I silently cursed myself for dredging it up in the first place: God, I *hated* when Kevin was right...

The next morning my luck improved. He answered on the second ring.

"So why didn't you tell me about him before?"

He sighed into the phone exasperated. "Because Jared, do I have to disclose *every* nuck and cranny of my life to you? Can't I keep some things to myself?"

"Sure. But something like hanging out with a guy you *used to fuck* is a whole different story."

"We fucked once five years ago!"

"Once. Twice. What's the difference, you still hung out with him."

"He's my *friend* Jared."

"So you have no attraction to him whatsoever?"

"No—*I mean* yes, but only as a *friend*."

"And you haven't thought about sleeping with him *once* since the last time you guys slept together?"

"No Jared, not once."

"So why only once? You didn't find him attractive? He wasn't good in bed, or what?"

"No nothing like that." He paused. "You wouldn't understand."

"Try me." I insisted. "I've been known to surprise people."

Several minutes passed.

"Michael!"

"We were friends!" He huffed. "He was in a relationship at the time and I'm not sure if it was more curiosity on my part, or his, but there was always a sense of desire between us. One day, after weeks of not getting along with his lover he confided in me. We were alone at his place, and before I think we both realized what was happening, or what we were getting ourselves into, we were in bed together."

"*Even though he had a lover?*" I said with disgust.

"Yes Jared." He snapped. "Even though he had a *fucking* lover."

"Did you at least feel bad about what you did?"

"Of course I felt bad! What kind of fucking question is that?! I loved Roy, and I never, ever wanted to do anything to complicate his life."

"But you can complicate mine?"

He exhaled heavily. "You know what, I'm not going to even dignify that with an answer."

Silence filled the lines.

"So does *Roy* know about me? About us?"

"Yes Jared. He knows I'm in a relationship."

"So why didn't you tell me about him?" I shot. "Why did I have to pry information about him out of you, but, you can just tell *him* about *me*?"

"Because, you take shit to the next level. And I don't always want to go there with you."

"I go there because I love you."

"No," he replied with brutal perception, "you go there because you're paranoid."

P aranoid-*smaranoid*. My concern was genuine, and not some preconceived plot to uncover the secret world of promiscuous partners. *Why* couldn't he understand that? Was it *really* that complex, or was he just making it more difficult than it needed to be?

Stumped, I sought advice.

"*Pump-kin* please," Dio said waving his hand, "get over it. More than *half* of the children have slept with their Judy's. It's an everyday thing in the life!"

"I haven't slept with you!"

"Ha!" He scoffed. "That's because I don't *want* you!"

"Come on Dio." I said growing frustrated by his lack of seriousness regarding my plight. "Should I be worried? I mean he never even mentioned this guy until last night. If they're such good friends, then why am I just hearing about him six months later? Why now, huh? Am I really supposed to believe they're *just* friends?"

"*Sweety* listen," he said placing his cocktail on the table, "*trust* is something you question when someone gives you something *to* question. The man slept with a friend of his years ago. There's no need to start pushing the eject button until you start seeing hickey's on his neck, or worse," he smirked, "his dick."

I shifted in my chair annoyed. I knew I should not have talked to him about something as serious as this.

He noticed my vexed expression.

"*Pump-kin* listen, you've got a good man, and I know for sure Michael's not going to do anything to hurt you, or your relationship. But," he leaned in and grabbed my hand, "right now, my concern is not on whether or not he's cheating, it's whether or not you love him as much as you say you do."

"What is that supposed to mean?" I barked snatching my hand from him. "Of course I love him! I'm crazy about him!"

"Then, like you tell everyone else: *act like it*! A large part of loving someone Jared is *trusting* them. If you can't do that, then why are you even in it?" He shot crossing his legs. "And, uh, if I'm not mistaking, you were the one that gave me that advice too…"

Dio was right. I hated admitting it, but he was. I was acting like a fool, and as usual, I was blowing a simple situation way out of proportion. After all they had only gone out to dinner right?

I have something to tell you." He said a few days later. We had just finished watching the season finale of OZ and were about to retire for the night to get some much-needed rest.

"What's up?" I said carrying the remnants of our dinner to the kitchen.

"First promise me," he said following me, "you will not over-react like you always do about everything."

I heard him, I did. But at the same time I admit I wasn't really paying attention. I was more focused on putting away the leftover food, and washing the dozen or so dishes in the sink before heading off to bed. I had a long day ahead of me that began with a nine-o'clock meeting with my boss's boss, which of course meant I had to be on my *Ps* and *Qs* because that bitch was sharp. Nothing—and I do mean nothing—got passed her.

"Yeah, yeah. Go ahead baby, I'm listening."

"Well, remember last week when I told you, me and a group of friends went out?"

"Yeah," I said testing the water. *(It took forever for that shit to get hot.)* "For your friend Roy right?"

"Right. Well…remember how upset you were when you found out who Roy was?"

"Yeah. But you know what," I said just as the water began warming up. "I spoke to Dio about that, and well, I realize I did blow that situation way out of control. You said you guys were just friends and I should have left it at that instead of giving you the third degree. I need to trust you more. But," I said smiling, "it's so damn hard to do when you're dating someone so fine…"

I expected him to smile, blush, or do something to show his appreciation, but I got nothing.

"Are you okay?" I asked studying him.

"Yeah, I am. It's just well, what I need to talk about is kind of serious."

"Go ahead I'm listening…" I said somewhat embarrassed.

He leaned against the counter and folded his arms against his chest, "Roy," he paused nervously, "wasn't the only person there from my past."

My heart thumped, and for a split second I swore it had stopped. *Did he just say what I thought he said?* I reached and turned off the water. "What was that?" I asked hoping I had heard wrong.

"I said," he began slowly, "Roy was not the only person there from my past."

"That's what I thought you said." I admitted gripping the sink readying myself for the blow. "Who else was there?"

He hesitated.

I walked to the refrigerator, grabbed the dishtowel, and dried my hands.

"Who else was there Michael?" I repeated my voice unbelievably calm.

"Jeff."

"Jeff!" I screeched. "What the fuck was he doing there?"

"He and Roy are friends."

"What?! What do you mean they're friends?"

"They're friends." He whispered his eyes fixed on the floor.

"So why didn't you mention this earlier?"

He shrugged.

"You don't know why, or you don't remember why?" I demanded.

He shrugged again.

"Is that why when I asked you who else was there the other night you refused to answer me?"

He nodded.

I bit my lip halting the tears. "So what happened...what did he say to you?"

"Well, when I first got there he tried to talk to me but I pretty much ignored him. I wanted nothing to do with him. In fact, Roy had said he wasn't even going to be there, because he knew I wouldn't come if Jeff was planning to show up."

"So he lied to you."

He shook his head. "No, he didn't lie. Jeff told him he really wasn't going to be there. But then he showed up out of nowhere."

I studied him. "Are you telling me the truth?"

"Yes. Completely."

I huffed. "So what did you talk about when you did speak?"

"He just wanted to know what I was up to. He had heard I was dating someone and wanted to know if it was serious."

"And what did you say?"

"I told him yes."

"Yes you're dating someone, or yes it's serious?"

"Yes to both."

I narrowed my eyes. "And what did he say."

"He didn't say anything. He just nodded his head."

"That's it?"

"That's it." He sighed. "But..."

"But what?" I demanded.

"But," he repeated. "When I came home from work last night he was waiting for me at my apartment."

Un-expectant tears leapt into my eyes. I threw the dishtowel on the stove and stormed out of the kitchen.

I wanted to hit something.

I wanted to grab something—*anything* and strangle the fucking shit out of it, then hit it!

How fucking dare he! How fucking dare he show up at my man's house unannounced and think he has the right to just *pop up* whenever or wherever he feels as if he has it like that! As if he's still the one! As if—

"Jared. Jared! Jared!!" Michael repeated keeping my pace. "Listen calm down. I'm just as upset as you are about this. But please, listen to me!"

I stopped suddenly, my back toward him, my eyes over run with angry tears. I felt myself there again. Hurt. Alone. Stranded, in the one place no one ever wants to get ditched, love.

"What did you do?" I rasped.

"I," he hesitated, "I talked to him."

I winced. "Inside or outside of your apartment."

"First outside," he paused, "then, inside."

"Inside!" I screamed. "You let him inside of your fucking apartment?! Why the fuck would you do some *stupid* shit like that?!"

"Because, I didn't want my neighbors all in my business! What else was I supposed to do?!"

"Send his fucking ass on his fucking way! That's what the fuck you *should* have done!"

"He only wanted to talk Jared!"

"I don't give a fuck if his ass was lying in the fucking street with a gun shot wound to the fucking head—he has no business whatsoever being inside your apartment!"

His eyes widened. "So now you're going to tell me who I can and can't have in my apartment?!"

"When it comes to that motherfucker—yes!"

"Well, I don't know who the fuck you think you are, but my fucking mother lives in the Bronx—not Brooklyn! And she's about the only person that's gonna tell me what I can and can not do!"

"Well when that bitch—"

227

"Hold up! *What?*" He roared jumping in my face. "What the *fuck* did you call my moms?" He bit his lower lip. "I swear to fucking God Jared—" he spit through clenched teeth, "if I *ever* hear some shit like that out of your fucking mouth again I swear—"

He tucked and bit his lower lip again and retreated to the other side of the room. We each stood fuming, with our backs against the other, lost in thought. That's when it happened. I tried as best I could to hold it back, but I couldn't. It was too strong. For the first time ever, I hated him. And I so wanted him to just leave, or die, or something...I'm not sure what, but I know I did not want to feel the pain I was feeling. I did not want to imagine the thoughts I was imagining, or hear him admit to the unthinkable. Not when I trusted him. Not when everything I had, depended on the stability of my relationship, this relationship...

"What the fuck am I doing..." He whispered shaking his head. "What am I doing..."

"I don't know Michael. I really don't. But we're supposed to be in a relationship—an exclusive one! You don't see me waltzing all of my ex's in here *parading* them in your fucking face!"

"What *the fuck* are you talking about!" He said raising his tone. "Ain't nobody parading anyone in your fucking face!"

"Then what the fuck are you doing? Please, explain it to me. First Roy, now Jeff—"

"I told you before, Roy is not my ex!"

"That's right," I spit with all the sarcasm I could muster up, "ya'll just *fucked*, right?"

A thick silence with all sorts of possibilities sat between us. The longer it stretched, the tenser the situation became.

"You know what Jared, sometimes I can't stand you."

"You can't stand me?" I bellowed in mock disbelief. "Well if the truth be told, sometimes I can't stand your fucking ass either! You *whine* and *complain* and *cry* about how *bad* Jeff treated you, how *much* he ruined your life, and how *glad* you were when you two were over—and then you invite the bastard up to your house for *tea* and *crumpets*?! And you can't stand me! Fuck you niggah! If anybody has a right *not* to stand anyone around here tonight—it's me—not you, me!"

"Are you finished?" He asked glaring at me.

"No I'm not! I should have seen this shit coming—I should have known you weren't being honest about how you felt about me, about him. Everybody kept warning me *"take your time Jared, slow down Jared, if it is meant to be, it will be Jared,"* and what did I do?" I screamed hitting my chest. "I ignored all the fucking warnings and followed my stupid heart! What the fuck is wrong with me? Why can't I get this shit together? Why can't I get it through my thick ass fucking head that this love shit is for the fucking birds!"

"Jared listen, it's not—"

"*Fuck you* Michael!" I roared. "Fuck you…"

"But Jared—"

I held up my hand. "Just go Michael, *please*. Go."

He studied me, and after realizing I was completely serious, gathered his belongings and left.

I missed work the next morning. Something I had no intentions of doing, and probably should not have done seeing how my meeting with my boss's boss had been scheduled for well over a month. But had I gone, and tried my best to focus on their life or death issues regarding new account procedures, I would have failed miserably. So instead I rose at dawn and hit the pavement. I ran from Nostrand Avenue in Brooklyn to Central Park in Manhattan.

It felt good to run. To leave all my problems, and worries, and headaches, behind and simply concentrate on the road lain out ahead of me. Each time Michael popped into my head I pushed him out and ran harder, determined not to falter. The night before I almost gave into the loneliness and nearly compromised my own sanity once again for the sake of another, but I remained strong. And found the strength after picking up the phone nearly seven times to dial his number, to place it back on the cradle, and leave it there.

The truth was evident, and although my heart wanted to forgive and forget, my mind knew better, and reminded me constantly, over and over again why *this time* I needed to be strong…

He has no respect for you. None of them do. How could they, when each has found some type of senseless-joy in seeing you suffer? If they really loved you—I mean really loved you—wouldn't they take care of you? Nurture you? Do right by you? No, they don't love. Never have; never will. Besides, how dare he let that son-of-a-bitch into his house! The same niggah that used to beat his ass on the regular! The same niggah that caused him to put on hold the most important thing in his life, school—how could he let him back into his life never mind his home? How, could he do that to you? Why would he do that to you? It proves he has no respect for you! It proves that he could not love you! If he did, then you two wouldn't be going through this shit. He would have told that bastard Jeff to go fuck himself because he was in love, and happy and—and—free!

You don't need him Jared. You don't. Fuck him—and Jason—and—and—all of them! Fuck them all! You don't need any of them bastards in your life taking from you—hurting you over and over again. You'll be fine all by yourself. All by yourself. Yes, all by yourself. Just you and me...that's it...nobody else. Just you and me...

On and on I ran, sometimes fast, sometimes slow. But all the time determined to free myself from the past. A past that had let me down, once too often. A past that had always led me to the inevitable: nursing a badly wounded heart. No, this time things would be different. I would not go running to him with my heart in my hand desperate to make amends. I had finally had enough of the bullshit relationships harbored. Enough of people playing with my heart as if it were indeed some type of joke! I was a human being—flesh and blood—bone and fiber—and whether people *wanted to* respect it *or not*, my feelings did matter! And it was about time I let everyone know Jared Covington was not someone to be *fucked* with.

I went the entire day without calling him. Without wondering when *he* was going to call, or even caring *where* he was. It simply did not matter. When I was ready I would talk, and not a moment sooner.

Four days later, five and a half hours before our tenth month anniversary, I found him on my doorstep unshaven, wearing a pair of netted basketball shorts, and a stalk white tank top.

"Where've you been?" He whispered.

"Work."

"I know that." He said quietly. "Why haven't you called?"

"I was busy."

"Too busy to pick up the phone?"

"You'd be amazed how busy one can be when focused."

He let the comment pass. "We need to talk."

"About what?" I asked leaning against the stoop.

"About you and me and what we're gonna do about this relationship."

I sighed. "Our relationship would be just fine if you stopped inviting strange men into your apartment."

He exhaled slowly. "You're not going to let that go are you?"

"And you're not going to apologize are you?"

"For what, living my life? Making my own decisions?"

"No, for inviting the one man that could carve an ocean between us into your home!"

"I didn't realize he had that kind of power." He scoffed.

"And I didn't realize you still loved him."

"I don't love him!"

"Then act like it!"

"I thought I was!"

"How? By inviting him into your house?!"

"No," he spit, "by loving you—or at least trying to love you! Something you make so goddamn hard to do!"

His words silenced me. I had heard those same exact words once too often: once from Vince, and several times from my first love. Both claimed I became this *impossibly* difficult person to deal with once we exchanged those three little words: I love you. Of course I never saw it, or understood the reason for the assault on my character—especially since both of them had so many issues of their own. You would think they would try working on their *own* shit before they started pointing out mine. But hearing it from Michael made me wonder, maybe I did make it hard…

"What do you mean?" I said meeting his gaze.

"I mean I have been trying to do everything I know how, to do right by you. But it's like everything I've been doing the last few weeks is wrong. And I'm really starting to believe something is wrong with me— there has to be, since everything you do is perfect, and everything I do ends up *fucked* up."

I lowered my head, not knowing what else to do. "That's how you feel?"

"I do. And it's not a good feeling. It's like," he paused, "I already *know* you're too good for me. And that you're so much more intelligent than I am, but," he sighed, "I like to think sometimes we're equals or at least pretend we are…but," he looked away hiding his tears. "It's so hard to when every time I turn around, you keep reminding me of how useless and stupid I can be."

I looked up at him, my own eyes beginning to water. Those weren't his feelings; they were mine.

"You're not *stupid* Michael, or useless…"

"Then why do I feel that way when you talk to me?" He asked facing me.

I turned away. I thought of all the horrible things I had promised myself I would say to him when this moment arrived. I had rehearsed it a thousand times, at work, on the train—so much so that I knew most of it by heart. But sitting there with every opportunity in the world to finally say the things I had felt in the depth of my soul, I froze. And I could think of nothing, but how *selfish* I had been…

He reached and pulled my hands from my eyes, revealing my shame.

"Are you going to answer me?" He asked quietly. "Why do I feel that way when you talk to me?"

"Because," I rasped, my face wet with tears, "*I'm* the stupid one. And the sad thing about it is," I paused catching my breath, "I'm just realizing it now."

231

The next morning I awoke to the rhythmic sounds of light raindrops outside my window and the pleasure of Michael's warm mouth savoring my sex. I opened my eyes and traced the curves of his chocolate muscular frame secretly admiring each one. I pulled him to me, and breathed in his intoxicating scent. His smell—a mixture of his favorite cologne, and his own masculine aroma—had become an aphrodisiac. An addiction. A requirement of sex, and I craved it, like an addict his fix.

Gently his lips grazed my face, my neck and my hardened nipples, causing tiny quakes to erupt throughout my body. He knew my spots, and didn't hesitate to pleasure them all, one by one.

When finally his tongue found mine he kissed me, as if he had never done so before, sucking and pulling my tongue deeper and deeper into his mouth. Then, without the slightest warning he stopped, and stared at me. My heart raced into overdrive, and I felt things inside of my chest I just couldn't explain, things I had not felt in a long, long time. It was like, all of a sudden, everything, the rain, his eyes, his aroma, his touch, felt right. And I just wanted to kiss him again, and again, and again. And so I did.

I kept my arms wrapped tightly around his waist pulling him into me while my fingers explored his smooth sexy skin, skillfully relaying the secret messages fluttering within my heart. It amazed me how his body responded to my every touch, and how after months of being together, he still anticipated each one.

With his help I loosened my grip and allowed him to guide me on top of him and then slowly inside of him. We moved slowly at first, but our pace soon quickened as we found then mastered our rhythm.

Overcome with emotion I began to cry. Never in all my life had I been so close to another to feel such emotion. Never had I risked so much of my heart and soul in the name of love. Never had I found myself lost in a world filled with *so much* possibility. I loved this man, with every muscle, hair and pore of my body. And it didn't matter that the last few weeks had been filled with one issue after another, because in my heart I knew his love would always be there, and so too would mine.

Soon we both collapsed physically spent in the after glow of love listening to the melodic sounds of the rain.

"You know I'm crazy about you right?" I whispered, my hand stroking his belly.

He turned his head slightly. Our heads touched. "I know…"

"And you know I'm sorry about everything that's gone down in the past few weeks' right?"

"Are you?" He said softly.

"I am, and, to be honest with you, I'm somewhat embarrassed. A lot of the things I've warned my friends not to do in a relationship, I've found myself doing. And believe me, its never pleasant finding out you're not the person you always thought you were. But I realize love does that to you sometimes. It sorta clouds your vision, you know?"

He nodded.

"But," I continued, "I've had sometime to think, and I realize now more than ever, you were right. I still have a lot of work to do on Jared. And, I'm ready to start tackling those issues. I only hope I can with you by my side. I know that's asking a lot but…well, you know."

He kissed me gently on the lips, and instantly I felt a rush. "The reason I came by last night," he began, "was because I realized it was wrong of me to invite Jeff up to my apartment. I'm not sure what I was thinking, but I know I should have considered your feelings. I should have put the shoe on the other foot. I should have been more thoughtful. I know that now."

He brought his left hand up to my lips, and traced the curve. A long moment of silence passed. I closed my eyes.

"Jared," he whispered, breaking the silence, "I'm here today for many reasons. One, to apologize from the bottom of my heart, because the last thing I ever want to do is lose you. Believe me, I know how lucky I am to have you in my life, and I want to keep it that way. The second reason I came," he smiled brightly, "was to wish you a happy, happy, anniversary. And the third," he said kissing me once more, "was to let you know, I'm here, with you, for as long as you will have me…and then some."

Warm tears filled my eyes. I wrapped my arm around his waist and pulled him to me. He had once again confirmed our love was real. And that, not only was his love the love of my life; it was my anchor.

Funny, how we never intend for our past lives to take center stage in our present life, but somehow, through some will of its own, it always does. I wish I could say I put the whole Jeff situation behind me after weeks and weeks of discussing it over and over. I wish, I *could have said*, "the past is the past", and moved forward un-bothered by Jeff's mindless attempt to rekindle a relationship with the man I was so madly in love with, but *had I uttered those words*, had I fixed my mouth to say it, it would have been the biggest lie I'd ever told. More than I like to admit I am not that strong, not by a long shot.

Each morning I awoke afraid, wondering would this be the day he would show back up and take, what I *unknowingly* believed, rightfully belonged to him. As a result, all the trust and faith I had bestowed in

Michael during the eleven months we spent together went flying out of the window. And as much as I hate to admit it, I became that *timid, insecure* man I had always feared. I questioned everything: his whereabouts, his friendships, his late night phone calls even his unwillingness all of a sudden to sleep with me (which was largely due to my constant, *supposedly* inconspicuous, searches of his body).

Nothing about our relationship made sense. But then again everything did. Michael did not love me. Sure he *said* he did, and he tried in every way imaginable to *prove* he did, but in my heart of hearts I *knew* he really didn't. How could he? How could he love me, when I myself had such a hard time doing it? All the books I had read of personal stories of people who, just like me, suffered from little to no self-esteem, but had worked day-in and day-out to bring about change in their lives, did little if nothing at all to change the way I felt about myself. I hated myself. I hated the way I spoke, the way I looked, the clothes I wore, even the air I breathed—because in my mind I truly believed I did not deserve it, none of it. I was a loser—an aberration to society—an abomination in God's eyes—and a failure in my own.

No matter how many times my friends and family told me how *talented* I was, how *successful* I was—how *unique* I was, I still could not bring myself to believe the words they spoke. And so, I longed to be somebody else. To live a life less taxing than the one I had been given. To be that person everyone *thought* they saw in my eyes—to finally be free.

You may not believe me, but I promise you it is true, many a night I lay awake cursing God for having put me here in this hell. I cursed him for abandoning me, and allowing the wolves to come and gnaw at my flesh. To pick, and tear, and rip the heart and soul out of me, only to leave me lying there, lifeless, waiting patiently for time to finish me off. I cursed him because—if he was so *merciful*—so *powerful*—so *wonderful*—why then did he *make* me to suffer? Why did he choose me, and a million others like me, to be the brunt of this cruel twist on life? Why me? Why us? Why like this? I *hated him*, and silently sought to defy him. I dared him to show himself—to explain himself—to ratify these feeling buried deep in the depths of my being! Feelings that were causing me to lose faith in him; in life; and in love...

These thoughts *(I'm almost sure of it)* caused me to lose it, and Michael.

I became a madman. I probed and probed and probed to the point he stopped answering my redundant self-incriminating questions. Instead he would sit quietly, bent over, his face buried in his hands listening to me as I ranted and raved about my suspicions on his intentions to purposely and willingly break my heart. I knew, and convinced myself I had *proof* that when the opportunity presented itself, he would, *without a second thought*, leave me abandoned and alone.

Why?

I have no logical answer, but I have reached some reasonable conclusions.

Maybe it was because I grew up alone. Sure my family was there. And yes, I received all the necessities every parent must afford their children—food, clothing, and shelter. But, the one thing I needed to ensure I was ready for the harsh winters of life, I went without. Love.

Most people would argue that because my parents never allowed me to go without the obvious necessities, that they were indeed, in their own little way, expressing their love for me. But I beg to differ. Love is more than physical tangible objects given in the name of responsibility. Love is time. Love is hugs. Love is saying: *Baby, no matter what you are, or who you become, I will always love and respect you...*

They never said that to me. So it was obvious they didn't care.

Or, maybe it was simply because I really truly believed no one could ever look at me, and honestly find something decent to love.

I'm not sure which answer made more sense, or if eventually with enough time I'd discover more but, no matter what I said or did, he remained silent digesting it all. Once in a while, when I would say something completely off the cuff, he would look up, stare angrily at me as if he was about to counter my belief, but then like a sheepish dog being blasted by his master, he would return his head to his lap with no contest whatsoever. That *completely* unnerved me, and often caused me to fly further into hysterics! I needed him to yell—*scream*—or do *something* to make me believe he did indeed love me, and that he had no intentions of leaving me, or hurting me, or doing anything to jeopardize what we shared. But I got nothing from him, absolutely nothing, until one day he snapped.

"It's over Jared." He said quietly, just after I had accused him of cheating.

"What do you mean it's over?" I screamed over my pumping heart. "Just like that," I snapped my fingers, "you're going to throw everything we have away? Just like that?"

"I am not throwing away anything you haven't destroyed already."

"Now this shit is my fault?" I said jumping to my feet. "I catch you in the middle of a lie and you throw the blame in my fucking face?"

"I lied because you left me no other choice."

"You lied because you got busted! You were the one who told me you were going to be home all night!"

"Yeah, but you were the one who decided to check up on me, to see if I was lying! What kind of shit is that? I told you before, I don't need anybody babysitting me!"

"Apparently you do, you fucking liar!"

"No fuck you Jared! I'm so fucking sick of you! You always think everything is about you! You always think somebody is out to get you! Well I'm sorry to burst your bubble—you self-centered bastard—but the rest of the world could care less about what's going on in your warped little fucked up head!" He grabbed his head wildly with his hands. "You don't know how fucking tired I am of hearing about you and your shit! *Your feelings*! *Your suspicion*! *Your fears*! It's finally becoming clear to me that you could give two shits about how anybody else feels but yourself! Walking around always talking about you're depressed—I wonder if you *really* wanna know how depressed you've made me?

"I've apologized to you a million times over about inviting Jeff into my place but, I don't think you've even heard me once! And I've been trying real hard, not to let your little comments about my fidelity get to me because I figured sooner or later you would see that I'm doing everything in my power to be honest and up-front with you about how I feel. But, I'm starting to see you ain't gonna stop pointing the finger or playing the fucking victim—you're gonna *keep* riding this shit out until I *slit my fucking wrists* to prove to you just how sorry I am! But you know what—you can *suck my dick* because your fucking ass ain't worth it!"

"Hold up—what?"

"No you hold the fuck up! I thought you were different Jared!" He spit, the words slicing the already fragile air. "I thought you were so fucking on—with no little hang-ups and shit like the rest of these punk ass motherfuckers running around calling themselves men—but I see now you're not! You're just as *needy* and *selfish* and *stupid* as the rest of them—and I don't need none of this shit in my fucking life! None of it! Not now, not ever!"

"So," I rasped, my heart still slamming against my chest, "I guess now you're going back to Jeff. That's who you were with the other night...right?"

He looked at me as if I had three heads. And as cold as ice spit, "You *really are* fucked up in the head aren't you? I wasn't with Jeff the other night stupid—I was *with* somebody else—"

Huge tears burst from my eyes, as my heart found then mastered a new and faster beat. I lunged forward and grabbed his neck, and with as much pressure as I could *squeeze* from my limbs, began sucking all the air from his lungs. He struggled; his eyes—the same eyes to which only weeks ago I pledged my un-dying love—bulged from his head, as they tried desperately to come to grips with what was happening. I held fast, despite his violent squirms to set himself free. Soon the color in his face—his deep rich chocolate face that I had come to not only adore, but worship—began to fade. Tears of despair, pleading, and hopelessness fell from his eyes—and I so wanted to stop, and tell him how sorry I was for hurting him; for inflicting on him *my* pain, *my* sorrow, *my* helplessness; for not believing in him, and in his words—and oh what beautiful words he once shared with me—but I knew, I knew, if I had stopped, if I had for but one moment loosened the grip I'd placed so tightly around his neck, he would have never forgiven me. Never. And I could not face living my life without him.

For this reason alone I continued, until his eyes rolled to the back of his head. Until his arms lay barely moving along his side. Until I heard the last grunt of life seep through his near-perfect mouth; until my fingers ached of pain...

When all was done the room was dark, save for the subtle glare of a street lamp lingering silently through the living room windows. Carefully I placed him on his back on the sofa and pulled the ottoman up to where he lay. I watched him for a long time; half wondering how it had come to this, and equally appreciating how incredibly beautiful, warm and peaceful he looked. His eyes, lips, and hair though awkwardly still, still managed to excite me. Soon I abandoned the ottoman and somehow managed to snuggle up beside him. There I breathed in his hypnotic scent over and over, and wished like him I could crawl into a hole far, far away from the disaster that is my life.

I kissed him gently on the lips and whispered in his ear, "Don't worry baby, I'm on my way..."

EPILOGUE

Kevin

Jared's funeral was the saddest day of my life. I hadn't been able to cope with his death since his mother phoned and reported the news.

None of us had seen or heard from him or Michael for more than a week, and we had begun to worry. I called Dio, he hadn't heard from him. I called Sean, he hadn't heard from him. I called his mother, and although his calling pattern had improved for about two months straight, she hadn't received a single call from him in about three weeks.

Jared had always been somewhat of a loner, so he would disappear often, but never more than a day or two would pass before he would reach out and let someone know he was alright. So for *none of us* to have not heard from him in close to seven days was a bit unusual; it just wasn't like him...

We each took turns calling him around the clock but by day seven, Mrs. Covington had had enough. Worried sick, she decided to go by his apartment and have his landlords let her in.

After learning that they too had not seen or heard from Jared in a couple of days, her heart beat rampant with fear and she just knew, or rather felt, something had happened.

She mounted the stairs cautiously, not knowing what she would find. After fumbling with the keys for a few awkward moments, she finally inserted the correct one and pushed the door open. The stench that flowed from the apartment buckled her knees, but it was the sight that sent her crashing to the floor. There, lying on the sofa was her only son, and, another man weaved in an intense embrace, dead.

Beside them lay an empty medicine bottle and a piece of torn notebook paper with the words: *I'm sorry...but there was no other way...I only hope one day you'll understand, Love Jared,* scribbled on it.

She took it hard. We all did. I tell you, if it weren't for Aaron, I...I don't think I could write these words you're reading this moment. Life just doesn't seem the same without him.

I wish I could call him up and ask him to go shopping...or...

I wish I could tell him just *how much* I loved him—how much I *needed* his friendship—how much this very moment I *miss* him—how much we *all* miss him, but I can't. And, that's what hurts the most.

239

When Aaron and I arrived for the viewing at nine, we were surprised to find the church already filled to capacity. The wake wasn't scheduled to begin until ten-thirty, and the funeral eleven-thirty. I was hoping to get there early just to have a few private minutes with my best friend, but it appeared everyone else had the same idea.

Everyone was there: His mother, his father, his two sisters, and their children. A host of aunts and uncles—even his grandparents. His childhood friends. A whole section reserved exclusively for his co-workers was filled beyond belief. I recognized a few of them, Lisa, Jordan, and Steve from rare meetings at his job. I waved to them and managed to front a smile.

Sean, Dio, and Miles were all seated together. Not too far from them was Jason and Herman, and two rows behind them was my former best friend, Vince. Aaron and I greeted them all then asked Dio to save us the two seats beside him and Miles while we went to view the body.

As we walked to the front of the church, it hit me. My best friend was *dead*. Frantic tears burst from my eyes as I stared down at the lifeless box housing my best friend. *How could this be? How can he be dead?* He's but twenty-six years old! How could this happen? *If only I had done more*—if only I had been a better friend then maybe, just maybe he wouldn't be lying here in this box. Maybe we would be in DC somewhere *cruising boyz—laughing—playing*—enjoying our youth! Maybe…just maybe if…

The tears flowed one after another, and as much as I wanted to, I couldn't stop them. I felt like screaming to the top of my lungs: *Why God Why?!* First *my mother*—now *my best friend*!!! Why are you *punishing* me? Why are you *doing this* to me?! What did I do? What-did-I-do…

My knees buckled, and if it were not for Aaron, I would have surely been on the floor. "I can't take this—" I moaned holding tight to him, "it's *too much—way* too much…My best friend is not supposed to be dead! He's supposed to be alive with me! What am I gonna do?!"

I started crying louder. So loud, it seemed I set off the entire church. Everyone was crying. Everyone was mourning. Everyone was hurt.

I felt arms embracing me, words consoling me, lives changing trying desperately to accept the unexpected—wishing there was someway to invert the hands of time and bring their loved one back—back from the unknown—back from misery, back into their arms…

"It's okay baby. Let it out. Let it all out." His mother whispered while grasping me tightly. "We all know how you feel…we know."

I hugged her tighter because I knew out of all of us she was suffering the most. She lost her baby, her life, her *world*. I wanted to console her. I wanted her to know she shouldn't worry, because I was there—and if she *ever* needed me—*ever*—she could call, anytime, no matter the hour, and I'd be there. But I couldn't. I was too shaken up. So instead I prayed my hug transferred those feelings. I prayed she understood that I was there. That I'd always be there…

We stood embraced until my heartfelt tears became muted sobs and I managed to summon enough strength to walk her back to her seat. But not before I leaned over my friend and kissed him gently on the forehead. He'd never know how much I was going to miss him.

"I want you to speak Kevin." She said taking her seat. "I know how close you and my son were. I know he loved you. I want you to speak about him today, and please, don't hold back. Be honest. He will appreciate it, and so will I." She grabbed my hand. *"Will you do that for me Kevin?* Will you tell me about my son?"

I hesitated. "Mrs. Covington—I—I don't know what to say?"

"Just tell the truth about my baby. Good, or bad. Just tell the truth."

I nodded my head, praying the words would find me. "I will Mrs. Covington. I will."

An hour later with the church filled beyond belief, the minister took the pulpit draped in a black robe. The congregation settled and gave him their undivided attention. He was a handsome man who looked to be somewhere in his late fifties. His tall slender frame towered well above the podium. His presence was powerful and thus, demanded respect. He'd done this many times, so is disposition was calm. He understood the pain everyone was experiencing. He saw it in their eyes, and felt it in their souls. He spoke of the pain. He spoke of the lost. He knew it was sudden. He understood the raw emotion. He reminded us of Lazarus, and how, when he died, Christ our Lord, could not help but weep for his friend. He too knew and understood pain, so yes it was okay to release it. He encouraged us all to embrace one another, to comfort one another, but above all, love one another throughout this delicate time of bereavement. His voice was powerful and authoritative, yet soothing and comforting. Many sobs could be heard throughout the church. I looked around at all the people who loved Jared just as much, and in some cases even *more* than I did. I saw the pain in their eyes, and like the minister urged, I wanted to hug them. I wanted to encourage them to be strong, despite the loss of such a *great* spirit and an even greater man. There was so much I wanted to do to let the world know my best *friend did not* die in vain…

After the prayer and scripture, the minister opened the floor to the congregation. Mrs. Covington was the first to speak. She walked quietly to the front of the church and looked on her only son, her last born. She raised her hands to the heavens and let out a gut wrenching howl. Moments later, she took her arms and wrapped them around her body as far as she could, and rocked silently back and forth. She did this for a long while. When she finally turned and faced the audience, her face revealed the pain she'd tried so hard to hide…

"I did not *know* my son." She said in a voice full of shame. "I *thought* I did, but, I didn't. As a mother that pains me because, there is nothing worse than losing a child…but losing him to the unknown—" her voice cracked and faded. "I can't tell you exactly how I feel because I myself don't really know. Everyday since that fateful day I've awakened hoping this was all just a dream. That my son…" she turned and faced him briefly, "my *beautiful, self-sacrificing* son is alive and well. But he's not— and what makes it even worse, is that I *did not know him*. I did not *know* his pain—his *loneliness*…I wish I had. *God knows* I wish he had trusted me. I wish he had let me in…" She wiped away a steady stream of tears with her handkerchief, and sighed deeply. "But, as I stand here today in the presence of my heavenly father, I thank *God*, for the things I did know about my son, because whether he knew it or not, he made me the *proudest* mother in the world. And *I'll always* love him for that. And today," she pointed to us all, "you all will teach me the things I did not know about my son. You will share with me, and my family, the good and the bad times you've shared with Jared, because we *need* to hear it—*I* need to hear it. So don't be ashamed, and don't hold back…because I love my son, more today than any other day in his short lived life."

She wiped her face and slowly returned to her seat. One by one, people filed to the front of the church to honor Jared Covington. They laughed. They cried. They shared so much about him I had never known; his childhood; his teenaged years; his college years—even his work life. Listening to the many speakers, one would believe that the young man that lay at the front of the church had lived a full life, and not the twenty-six short years he had. He touched many. He had loved many, and in their own way, they had loved him back.

When Sean made his way to the front of the church my heart almost broke in two. He had taken Jared's death worse than Dio and I because he never got a chance to apologize to Jared face to face. He had not seen or heard from him since their meeting in the city weeks earlier. Facing the church, he could not stop crying. I had asked him if he wanted one of us to accompany him, but he declined, saying he needed to do this alone. After several minutes of silence he spoke.

"This man changed my life." He said, his voice failing him. He cleared his throat and continued. "He helped me in ways I never thought any one person could. He helped me find myself; and for that, I owe him *my life. I* should be lying in this coffin, *not* him. Many a night we spent talking on the phone with him convincing me not to give up on life. And I almost did, several times, but Jared would not hear of it. He hated the word *'quit'.* He pushed and pushed and pushed until finally now, *today,* I understand what he meant when he spoke so eloquently about life, love and the pursuit of happiness. I only wish," he paused wiping his face, "I could have been there for him in *his* time of need. I wish I could have shared a little of *his* knowledge with him, and ensured him all was not lost and that life—*despite all of its mishaps*—goes on. *He* taught me that!" He yelled pointing to the casket. "*He* taught me never to quit—*never* to stop, and to always do my best! And I'm mad because *he* gave up! *He* quit! He—" Sean stopped suddenly and cupped his face. A deep agonizing pain, from the bottom of his stomach surfaced, and he cried deep heartfelt tears. He tried desperately, to regain his composure, but after several attempts, gave up and returned to his seat, lost.

Dio and Miles went up together. As usual their appearance was impeccable. They stood side by side, both in dark suits, white shirts, and silver ties. Seeing them together warmed my heart. They were the perfect couple: two handsome independent well-groomed men making a life together. Jared would be proud.

"This man here..." Dio said pointing to the casket, "is responsible for the union you see before you today. I know standing here in the house of God *some of you* cannot or rather, *will not* accept the love I share for this man, and the love he shares for me. But nevertheless, Mrs. Covington has asked that we share all, and as I stand before you, I am not ashamed to say I love this man—but more so, I *love* my best friend Jared for helping me embrace this love. I can't begin to tell you all the late night calls, lunch dates, and *impromptu* conversations we shared devouring love and relationships. Like Sean mentioned a few moments ago, he helped me find myself. He helped me discover one of life's greatest treasures, love. And for that I am forever indebted to him." He paused, turned to Miles, and grabbed his hand. Everyone's attention fell on the two men holding hands in the middle of *Christ the King Church of our Lord and Savior Jesus Christ Tabernacle.* A few people who couldn't see stood just to ensure they didn't miss a thing. After several minutes, and much anticipation, Dio continued.

"Miles," he said staring deep into his eyes, "we owe it to my best friend to nurture the love he saw in the two of us. And as I stand here before him, this church, and you, I promise to do everything possible to ensure our love survives because, that's the way *he* would have wanted it. And what better way to honor him..." he glanced toward the casket, "than by defeating the odds?"

Miles grabbed him and pulled him into an embrace. This had been the first time Dio had ever proclaimed his love for anyone publicly. The press would eat it up, but he didn't care. His best friend and his love were all that mattered. Mrs. Covington set off the applause, and by the time Dio and Miles took their seat, the entire congregation was in accord. Everyone, including the minister could not help but feel the positive energy that filled the air. Jared had indeed touched many.

Once the church settled his mother turned and faced me, and with a nod let me know it was time. Instantly, as if on cue, I felt like crying.

"No," I whispered aloud. "I *will not* cry. I will not cry."

I stood slowly and exited the pew. As I made my way to the front of the church thought after thought filled my head. Where was I those last fleeting moments of his life? *What was going through his head?* Was he crying? Was he *waiting—praying*—someone—*anyone* would call and help him through this ordeal? *I* should have called. I *should have* been there—to console him—to talk to him—to let him know *I loved him*—that we *all* loved him—and that this was not the way! There were other choices—other means to go about healing love—other ways to go about—no, I should have been there for him, I should have, there are no excuses: I failed him.

When I turned and faced the church all eyes fell on me.

What would I say? *What could I say?* I abandoned my friend? I let him down? It's my fault he's not here right now? Had I been a better friend then none of us would be in this situation? None of us would be mourning? No, I *couldn't* say that, but I *had* to say something, but what? I *missed* him? I *loved* him? He was the best friend I *ever* had, and now that he's gone there'd never be another? No, because everyone already knew that—everyone knew there would be no replacement for Jared, he like the sun, was one of a kind.

I stood there silent, rumbling my fingers, until finally the words began to flow...

"A few months ago I buried my mother, and at the time I thought that was the hardest thing in the world to do. I didn't think I would be able to deal with that lost. I doubted whether or not I had the strength. I underestimated myself, just as now I am doing the very same thing. I'm questioning whether or not I have the right words to say to soothe your pain *Mrs. Covington*. I'm questioning whether or not I have the power to convince you *Sean*, that Jared *did indeed* love you, just as he loved us all. And I am also questioning, whether or not the love he had for every last one of us in this room, he had for himself. I mean think about it. It's so easy for us to love another, *but to love ourselves?* It is rare indeed. We spend so much time loving and comforting others that unfortunately, not enough of us take the time to truly get to know ourselves. It's no wonder it's often

244

impossible for us to see, or feel the love others shower upon us. *Look* at this room. *Look around.* Look and see how many people loved this man lying dead before us. Look at the many different faces. *Look at them all*, and tell me, *honestly*, do you think Jared had any idea he was loved this much? Do you think if but for a moment—*a split second*—he knew his death would bring about so much sadness, so much confusion, he would have done the unthinkable? Do you think he would have been so selfish? No...*not* Jared. Not the self-sacrificing son *Mrs. Covington* spoke so highly of. Not the man that would give his *last dime* to a stranger on the street, no, *not my* best friend. Believe me, Jared had *no idea* he was loved this much. He had no idea his life—his presence—his *smile* meant so much, to so many. Believe me when I tell you, he had no idea.

"You know," I paused looking over the crowd, "since I received that life changing phone call, I've thought of over a million things I could have said or done, that could've, or would've saved Jared from taking his life. I've thought of them all. Why just moments ago, walking down this aisle I thought of a thousand different possibilities. But the truth is, albeit painful, none of us could have saved Jared. Not one of us, except of course, Jared. He was the only person that could have pulled himself out of the hole he had dug for himself. The same hole, so many of us here today are digging for ourselves. And if we're not careful, we too may end up in the exact same situation—angry, lost, and alone.

"I didn't come here today to lecture anyone. As a matter of fact, I had no intentions of speaking. Had it not been for Mrs. Covington, I would be out there sitting mourning, just as you are this very moment. But standing here, I'm starting to understand the lesson...I'm starting to see.

"It has been said time and time again that everything happens for a reason, and not by chance or luck, or misfortune. Whatever the situation, it is up to us to take the time to discover the meaning of each occurrence in our lives. Jared's death is not an accident. It is a wake up call. He is in fact teaching us a valuable lesson. And that lesson is the importance of self-love and self-acceptance. He's teaching us that in order to recognize love you must know love. You must experience it *first* hand. You must be friends with yourself *first*, before you can truly be friends with another. You must accept yourself first, *without* conditions, *without* restrictions, before you will be able to accept another. Because, once you accept yourself, *as you are*, the universe will provide to you the very thing your heart desires. No questions asked.

"That's what Jared is trying to teach us. He's trying to tell us not to wrap ourselves *so tightly* to another that we lose sight of who *we are*—or, our worth! He forgot...but he left behind a message for all of us to heed. Love yourself. Want yourself. Live with truth and integrity. Do not hide who you are or mask your imperfections because of what others might think or believe. No, open yourself up for *all the world* to see the light resonating within your soul. *That's* the lesson! *That's* the purpose! That's why we're all here today—not to *mourn* Jared Covington's death, but to celebrate his experience.

"So, I *will* get through this, and so will you. Because by doing so, not only do we honor our friend, our son, and, our brother, we honor ourselves."

Author's Note

For those of you who might judge me: *God has smiled on me...he has set me free...he's been good to me...*

There was a time, not so long ago when I would have cared what you thought me. I would have let your thoughts dictate my life. I would have hid the light radiating within me for fear of rejection, your rejection. I would have believed people, especially you, would never accept me for who I am, a child of God. As a result of this fear, I grew up alone. I grew up with no one to talk to. Eventually, I became distant and aloof, and surprisingly, very, very intelligent. I've always believed the "kids", as so many of us affectionately refer to them, are much smarter than the average Joe, just as a thief is usually a tad bit smarter than his victim. At any given moment, I was at least ten steps ahead of you erasing any essence of my quote unquote, *alternative lifestyle*. So that, by the time you walked by, everything appeared normal. Now, I'm sure there are some of you will who insist you *knew* from the very start. But, I beg to differ. With the exception of my mother, who gave birth to me, and who could sometimes feel my loneliness, because somehow, she was and still is a part of me, and I a part of her, no one knew anything about my life unless I let them know.

But, *(you know there's always a but...)* if anyone reading this has ever donned a mask, you know that keeping your façade from cracking can be quite tedious, and too, meticulous. In my quest to prevent drama, I later learned that all I created was drama. Drama, that caused my life often to be unbearable, and insufferable. I loathed "normal" people because they did not accept me as I was, but rather sought to make me better. And, because of this hatred for you and them, and as a result, hatred of self, I caused my life to be a living hell.

Many times I thought of suicide. Many times I sought counseling. Many times I wondered what was wrong with me. Why had I been born into the world this way? Why was I a curse? Was this some sort of crude trick? Did God, my God, your God, have a sense of humor when he created me, and a million others like me? Believe me when I tell you, I hated my life.

Then, one night, completely fed up with life and its rules, loneliness, unhappiness and my constant pursuit of love, I began to cry. The tears poured out of my eyes, one after another. My sobs grew louder and louder until they were no longer moans of sadness, but rather screams of madness. I screamed to the top of my lungs, *"Why God?! Why?!"* But there was no answer.

My mind raced as I thought of ways to ease the pain. I thought of jumping out the window, maybe that would end the pain. I thought of slicing my wrist, maybe that would end the pain. I thought of taking pills, stabbing myself—you name it I considered it, all to ease the pain. It had reached the point, where I did not care how it ended. I just wanted out of my miserable, useless life. With each scream I knew I had surely gone insane. I knew I was indeed mad. My mind traveled to *Edgar Allen Poe*, and I wondered whether he too had had episodes similar to this. You see, because it has been written that he too was mad.

Frightened, shaking and alone, I whispered three words: *"Help me God..."*

I tell you, no sooner did the words part my lips did I feel the love of God wrap my body like a glove. The sensation began about my feet, then traveled up through my legs, then throughout my entire body until I was fully covered in love—his love. I tell you I had never felt so much peace, so much joy, and so much love in all my life. Instantly, as if on cue, I started to laugh! I started to rejoice! I sang out to the heavens: "Thank you Father; for you have answered my prayer!"

That night, alone in my bed, God saved me. He saved me from a life of misery. He saved me from doing the unthinkable. He helped me breathe again.

From that night forward, I set out on a journey to master love. I wanted to learn everything I could possibly know about this wonderful feeling God had introduced to me. I went deep...uncovering all the lies, all the misconceptions, all the false truths I had ever been told about love. I read. I thought. I asked questions. And when I listened, He answered.

Today, I stand proud of who I am. Today, I stand unashamed of my life and the many mistakes I've made as I traveled this road called Life. Because, each mistake, each wrong turn, has somehow made me into the man I am today. I stand proud today because I know, without a shadow of a doubt, that God loves me, just the way I am! He loves me, because he has always loved me! He loves me, because we are one. Just as you and I are one. We're all connected, and it's all relative.

I encourage you all to go within. I encourage you all to listen to your heart, listen to your soul. Seek the love and peace it desires. Because it is there that God makes his bed. And it is there you will learn: *Ye without sin, cast the first stone...*

God bless you, and keep you, now and always.

Christopher David
www.christopherscypher.com

About the Author

Christopher David, a passionate spirit with much to say, was born to write—but not just write—sing, speak, nurture and motivate. Born and raised in the heart of Bedford Stuyvesant in the borough of Brooklyn, Christopher David is geared up and ready to revolutionize the way the world views him, homosexually and the black experience.

To find out more about Christopher David, his life, and his new book I'm On My Way, please visit him at www.christopherscypher.com.

Printed in the United States
15864LVS00005B/58-684